BBC BEGINNERS' ENGLISH

Judy Garton-Sprenger and Simon Greenall

STAGE ONE
TEACHER'S BOOK

BBC English by Radio and Television
PO Box 76, Bush House
London WC2B 4PH

First published 1986
Reprinted 1987, 1990

ISBN 0 946675 01 5

Printed in Great Britain by Jolly & Barber Ltd, Rugby

Editorial coordination Lucy McCullagh
Design Ian Wileman
Cover design Jim Wire
Cover photograph Jerry Young

Contents

Plan of Stage One

	FUNCTIONS	STRUCTURES	TOPICS
1 MEETING PEOPLE			
	Greeting and meeting people; asking and saying who people are, where they're from	Present simple *to be*; possessive *'s*; personal pronouns	Countries; forms of address; family
2 GETTING TO KNOW PEOPLE			
	Asking and saying what people do, where they live	Present simple *to do, to live*; possessive adjectives	Jobs; nationalities
3 TALKING ABOUT WHERE PEOPLE LIVE			
	Asking and saying how many, what there is, what people have got, how to spell	Quantity, plural—*s*; *have got*; questions with *do* as auxiliary	Rooms of the house, furniture; numbers 1–12, alphabet
4 TALKING ABOUT WHAT YOU LIKE AND WHAT YOU CAN DO			
	Asking and saying what you like, can do; agreeing and disagreeing	*Like* + —*ing*, modal *can*; *So/Nor/Neither do I.*	Sport, leisure activities, town facilities
5 TIMING IT RIGHT			
	Talking about routine activities; asking and saying what people are doing, would like to do, what the time is; making suggestions; inviting, accepting, and refusing invitations	Present simple for habitual actions; present continuous; *want/would like to; Why don't we . . .? Let's . . .*	Numbers to 50; routine activities, time-telling, leisure activities
6 CHECKING WHAT YOU KNOW			
	Revision		
7 GOING TO TOWN			
	Asking and saying where places are, what people want, where you can get things, how much/many, how much things cost	*in, opposite, next to*; countables/uncountables; *a, some, any; How much/many?*	Shops, shopping, food, clothes, colours
8 PLANNING A JOURNEY			
	Asking and saying what the date is, how long journeys take; asking for and giving information	Present simple for time-tables; *How long does it take? on, in, at* for times/dates	Transport; months, days dates, times, ordinal numbers
9 DESCRIBING PLACES – TALKING ABOUT ARRANGEMENTS			
	Asking and saying where places are, what places are like, what people's plans are	Present continuous for future; prepositional phrases of place	Geographical location, features, countries; travel documents; large numbers

FUNCTIONS	STRUCTURES	TOPICS

Introduction

Major Features

BBC BEGINNERS' ENGLISH is a two-stage beginners' course designed to be used in the classroom by adults or by students in the later stages of secondary education. The course takes learners up to a level where they can begin to use and to understand English in a variety of practical and real-life situations.

Major features of this course are:
- its presentation of the varieties of English as a language of international communication;
- its coverage of the language required for simple but effective communication in both social and professional contexts;
- its learner-centred, activity-based approach;
- its authentic oral and written input, in which the tasks rather than the texts are graded to the learner's level;
- its international settings;
- its careful and systematic revision.

An additional feature of the course is that it follows the same syllabus as the weekly radio series for beginners called TAKING OFF, produced by BBC English by Radio and Television. Both the course books and the radio series cover the same functions, structures, vocabulary and other language features required by the learner at this level, and can be used to consolidate and supplement the work of each other. However, they can also function quite independently of each other in order to provide the flexibility of use that local conditions may require. For details about broadcasting times, write to: BBC English by Radio, PO Box 76, Bush House, Strand, London WC2B 4PH, England.

AIMS

The aims of the course can be divided into educational objectives and communicative tasks.

EDUCATIONAL OBJECTIVES

The educational objectives of the course refer to the strategies and skills required to make the learning process as efficient as possible. They are as follows.
- To encourage a positive attitude towards language learning
- To help the learner perform a variety of simple communicative tasks from the very start of the course
- To build up the learner's confidence in communicative situations
- To expose the learner to a broad range of national and regional variations of English and to the features of authentic spoken English
- To encourage and explore the use of English as a medium of international communication
- To establish a core of approximately 2000 lexical items and a variety of structures and functions
- To help the learner recognise the relative importance of fluency and accuracy in communicative situations
- To enable the learner to adapt the newly acquired language competence to his or her own particular needs
- To provide a variety of graded activities for structured work as well as for free and spontaneous practice
- To use realistic communicative tasks as a means of measuring the learner's progress
- To provide a varied and motivating course which will integrate the learner's personal feelings and experience into the learning process
- To encourage the learner to take responsibility for what he/she needs to learn

COMMUNICATIVE TASKS

The communicative tasks which the learner will be able to perform at the end of the course are defined in terms of what he/she should be able to do in a variety of target situations. He/she should be able to do the following.
- Identify and introduce him/herself and others
- Greet people
- Ask for and give personal information concerning age, address, sex, marital status, nationality, occupation, family, etc.
- Understand and complete forms requiring personal information
- Understand and write letters giving personal information
- Describe his/her occupation or intended occupation
- Describe his/her professional and personal abilities
- Talk about other people's professional activities

- Describe types of accommodation: furniture, rooms, houses, etc.
- Understand and write letters requesting information about accommodation.
- Describe geographical features of countries, regions, towns, etc.
- Ask for and give information about services and facilities, etc.
- Understand and write letters and other documents requesting information about countries, regions, towns, etc.
- Ask for and give directions
- Talk about the weather: climate and conditions

- Describe education: subjects and qualifications
- Talk about foreign language skills

- Talk about personal routine and habits
- Talk about past experiences, recent activities and completed actions
- Talk about personal appearance
- Talk about physical and emotional feelings
- Express opinions, praise and criticism
- Talk about personal relationships

- Talk about likes and dislikes
- Talk about leisure activities: intellectual and artistic pursuits, sports and hobbies
- Ask for and give information about leisure activities and related services
- Make, accept and refuse invitations to social activities
- Understand and write letters and other documents concerning leisure activities

- Talk about travel arrangements: means of transport, duration of journey, arrival/departure times, fares etc.
- Ask for and give information about travel arrangements
- Understand written documents concerning travel arrangements
- Talk about future plans
- Take notes
- Use the telephone

- Ask for and give information about food and consumer products
- Order a meal in a restaurant
- Perform simple commercial transactions
- Talk about size, weight and cost

- Describe objects: size, weight, material, etc.
- Describe simple processes
- Understand written and spoken instructions and regulations
- Ask for and give simple instructions
- Ask for and give permission
- Persuade, dissuade, ask and tell people to do things
- Make complaints and apologise about behaviour, actions, etc.

SYLLABUS DESIGN

The course adopts a syllabus design which chooses language items and techniques from the following proto-syllabuses.
- Functions
- Structures
- Notions
- Topics
- Lexis
- Skills
- Phonology
- Learning skills

Functions The functional syllabus concentrates on the *meaning* and *use* of the language being taught, and the approach presents the new items in such a way as to ensure the learner can both see their relevance to his/her needs, and use them in a variety of communicative situations.

Structures The structural syllabus concentrates on the *form* of the language being taught. Despite the importance of a functional approach, some items cannot be presented to and manipulated by the learner without reference to the rule-governed behaviour of language. The structural syllabus provides extra assurance that all necessary items are firmly grasped by the learner.

Notions The notional syllabus concentrates on important concepts such as location, time, direction, dimension. This syllabus is integrated into the course as a whole within the scope of the syllabuses mentioned above.

Topics The topics are the areas of vocabulary presented, and cover a broad range of everyday situations. Students are encouraged to organise their vocabulary building under topic headings.

Lexis The vocabulary has been chosen after careful consultation with such reference works as *The Threshold Level* and *The Cambridge English Lexicon**. The unit by unit guide in the *Teacher's Book* lists all the vocabulary introduced for productive use in each unit.

Skills Reading and Listening are developed by using an extensive range of authentic and semi-authentic material, which exposes the learner to the varieties of language they are likely to encounter in real life. In particular, the recorded listening material involves a number of different speakers with both native and non-native accents. Speaking and Writing are also carefully developed in a number of communicative activities, such as role plays and problem-solving sessions.

Phonology Because a learner will use the full range of sounds in a language right from the start of a course, the phonological syllabus tends to be covered on an *ad hoc* basis. However, guidance in pronunciation, stress and intonation is given for each unit at the back of the *Student's Book*, and covers the most difficult sounds and the most common patterns that the learner is likely to come across in the early stages of learning English.

Learning skills The Learning skills syllabus is included in the *Teacher's Book* at the end of each unit, and is designed to give the learner generative techniques on how to make the learning process more efficient. In this way, he/she is encouraged to take greater responsibility for the success of his/her studies.

The sequence in which the items are introduced is based on a combination of the following criteria.

- Learnability: how easy it is to learn an item based on what has already been acquired by the learner.
- Usefulness: how useful an item is to the learner's particular requirements.
- Relevance: how relevant each item is for the learner's broader communicative purposes.
- Frequency: how often the learner will come across the item in real-life use.
- Coverage: the extent to which the item can be used in more than one situation.
- Generativeness: how the item generates a more intuitive grasp of the language.
- Comprehensibility: the extent to which the item presents conceptual problems.

The language presented in Stage 1 may be described as survival English, in which basic structures and functions are covered, along with approximately 1000 lexical items of everyday use.

In Stage 2 these basic structures and functions are consolidated and expanded, and the topic areas are added to. There is greater emphasis on building up the learner's competence in a broad variety of communicative tasks, and on providing increasing exposure to authentic examples of spoken and written English.

The Threshold Level (Dr J. A. Van Ek *et al.*, Council of Europe, 1976); *The Cambridge English Lexicon* (R. X. Hindmarsh, Cambridge University Press, 1981)

ORGANISATION OF THE COURSE

Each stage has the following components:

Student's Book
Workbook
Teacher's Book
Class Cassette Set, containing the recorded listening material for the lessons
Language Review Cassette Set, containing recorded pronunciation and structure exercises

The *Student's Book* consists of thirty units, each unit taking approximately 3½ – 4 hours to complete. Every sixth unit is a revision unit (called *Checking*

what you know). Apart from Unit 1, all the units have four pages; there is a convenient break between the second and third page of each unit. At the end of the *Student's Book* there is a section with pronunciation exercises and a do-it-yourself Structure Review, with exercises, which are all recorded on the *Language Review Cassette Set*. Teachers are advised to integrate this section into the classroom work at suitable moments. The *Language Review Cassette Set* can be used in both the classroom and the language laboratory.

The *Workbook* provides supplementary written practice material, which gives extra training in using the functions, structures and vocabulary introduced in the unit. It has been designed for use without the help of the teacher, so that the exercises can be done at home.

The *Teacher's Book* provides an overview of the whole course, a unit by unit guide to the language presented and a teaching guide for each unit. It also includes the tapescripts, a series of warm-up activities, and learning skills activities, as well as references to the *Workbook* exercises to be done at the various stages of each unit.

CONTENT

The action of Stage 1 is based in London, New York and Hong Kong and organised around six characters. There is no storyline as such, although the characters appear throughout the book. They are from a variety of different nationalities and races. Further examples of regional and national variation in accent are included in the recorded materials. The intention is to make learners aware that varieties of English are spoken in different settings all over the world, but that the basic language is the same.

METHODOLOGY

Every teacher will have different ideas on how to use the material in *BBC Beginners' English*, and should be encouraged to teach in a way that best suits his/her students' requirements and expectations. However, there are a number of basic techniques used in the course which may need to be explained.

INTRODUCING A NEW ITEM

Each time a language item is introduced, the material is organised into three approximate stages:

Presentation
The teacher/book initially presents the form and conveys the meaning of the new item. Some kind of drilling may be useful at this stage.

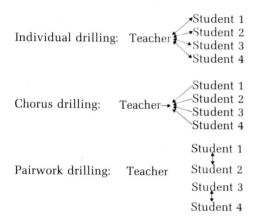

Individual drilling:

Teacher
- Student 1
- Student 2
- Student 3
- Student 4

Chorus drilling:

Teacher →
- Student 1
- Student 2
- Student 3
- Student 4

Pairwork drilling:

Teacher

Student 1 ↕
Student 2

Student 3 ↕
Student 4

It is important to check that learners have understood the meaning and can manipulate the form; accuracy is important at this stage, and teacher correction is more frequent.

Drilling may also be used during the next stage.

Practice
Here the learners are encouraged to use the new item in a controlled situation. At this stage, pairwork is often suggested to provide students with the maximum opportunity for practice.

Free stage
The teacher's role now becomes less directive and more of a stimulus. Role play simulations, games and other activities are used to encourage the learners to consolidate their newly acquired knowledge in conditions of greater creativity and spontaneity. Groupwork is of particular importance here, since it greatly increases the opportunities for both language practice and self-expression.

PAIRWORK AND GROUPWORK

When the students are working in pairs or groups, the teacher should check that they are using correct pronunciation, intonation and stress. Make a note of errors in structure or vocabulary, and when the students have finished one pair or group activity, correct any major errors with the class as a whole. It is not necessary to name the students who made the mistakes! Then ask the students to change roles and/or partners, and to continue the activity.

CORRECTION AND ASSISTANCE

The teacher should be able to judge whether correction and assistance is suitable at a given moment. In general, the teacher has a fairly tight control over the learners' output at the presentation stage, but should take a more secondary role at the practice and free stages. Ideas on techniques for correction and assistance are given in the teaching notes for each unit. It should be remembered however, that communication is the principal aim of the students, and if their inaccuracies do not hinder communication, then they should not be discouraged by too much correction.

AUTHENTIC AND SCRIPTED MATERIAL

The language features to be learnt are presented in the form of either *scripted and graded*, or *authentic and ungraded* listening and reading material. Explain to the learners that a broad variety of this kind of material is included, as it is important for them to be exposed firstly to comprehensible input, which can then be used productively, and secondly to examples of language which are not specially prepared for the learner, but which occur in the realistic context of everyday use. Careful coverage of the receptive skills (reading and listening) will allow the learner to understand the general sense of varieties of English which would otherwise lie beyond his or her immediate level of competence.

Other language skills which develop the learner's independence are also included. For example, where relevant, exercises are supplied which discourage the learner from trying to understand every word. Above all, the skills work is integrated; no skill is practised in isolation.

MULTI-LEVEL CLASSES

Every class will have as many levels as it has students, as, sadly, no teacher ever works in ideal conditions! Pairwork and groupwork can help solve some of the problems created by a class in which some learners are making faster progress than others; weaker students should be paired, wherever practical, with stronger ones. It may also be necessary to vary the pace of each lesson, sometimes working faster and covering extra vocabulary, sometimes working slower and revising more carefully.

REVISION

Systematic revision of everything which has been taught is integrated into the course by the revision units: 6, 12, 18, 24 and 30. In addition, language items are recycled in units and situations other than those in which they are first presented. For example, the language for tourist facilities in Unit 5, which is set in London, is reviewed in Unit 25, which is set in New York. But students should also be allowed time to look back over their work at regular intervals. Some useful tips on organising revision are presented in the Learning Skills section at the end of each unit guide in the *Teacher's Book*.

DICTIONARIES

At a later stage, students are encouraged to use a good monolingual dictionary.

SUPPLEMENTARY READING

You may want to encourage learners to begin reading material outside the coursebook. They should be directed to the guided readers series published by Heinemann Educational Books, Longman and Oxford University Press. You may also decide to organise a class library.

WARM-UP ACTIVITIES

Every lesson should begin with a warm-up activity which revises some aspect of the preceding unit's work or presents the topic of the following unit. Because the warm-up activities in this book are techniques which can be used for different topics and units, they are all described in detail below, rather than in the unit guide. In the teaching guide itself, reference is made to the number of the technique which the teacher should then look for in the list below. There will be some suggestions on how to adapt it to a particular topic or function.

1   The beginning of the course is a suitable time to learn everyone's names and to practise introducing people. Ask students to go round the class saying *Hello, I'm (name)*. They should try and learn the names of as many people as possible. Then form groups of about six or seven, and ask one student to say who he/she is. The student on the right should say who he/she is and then introduce the first student to the others by saying *This is (name)*. The next student should introduce him/herself and the first two students to the others. This should continue until the last student has introduced everybody to the whole group. This game is an amusing way of learning names by repeating them.

2   Trace the outlines of various countries onto pieces of paper. Ask students to form groups of three or four and pass the outlines round each group. They should try and guess the name of each country. This can also be done with outlines of objects.

3   Collect a number of magazine pictures all showing a scene which has something to do with the topic in question. Students should work in groups of four or five. Give a picture to one student in each group. He/she should describe it to the others, and they should then discuss what the topic of the lesson is likely to be. Then ask them to compare their ideas with a neighbouring group by describing (not showing) their pictures. Continue until the groups have decided what the topic is.

4   Revise the names of rooms in a house by collecting a number of magazine pictures showing various rooms. Ask students to form groups of three or four. Give each group a magazine picture and ask them to note down the name of the room. They should pass the picture on and receive the next picture. Continue until they have noted down all the names of the rooms.

5   Collect some postcards of well-known cities. Ask students to form groups of three or four. Give a postcard to one student in each group. He/she has to describe the scene shown on the postcard to the others without showing it to them. They must try and guess the name of the city.

6   Ask students to write down on a piece of paper one thing they like, one thing they dislike, one thing they can do, and one thing they can't do. They should go round the class trying to find other people who like, don't like, can and can't do the same things.

7   Write down the names of different shops on separate cards and collect a large number of pictures showing things you can buy in these shops. Ask students to form groups of three or four. Give each group the name of a shop and pictures of a number of things you can buy in various shops. They must go round the class asking *Have you got a/any . . . ?* trying to think of items they can buy in their shop. The aim of the game is to collect as many item pictures as possible, and to get rid of any items which don't belong to their shop. This game can also be done with words rather than the pictures.

8   Revise vocabulary by asking students to note down two or three topics on cards, and to write down five words, which belong under each topic heading, on other cards. Ask students to form groups of two or three. Collect the topic cards, shuffle them, and give one to each group. Collect the word cards, shuffle, and spread them around the classroom. The groups have to collect all the word cards which belong under their topic heading. When they have finished you can give them another topic card.

9   Ask students to work in pairs. Student A in each pair should be blindfolded. Put a number of chairs in places around the classroom where you would not usually expect to find them. Student B then gives oral directions to Student A and guides him/her across the room avoiding all obstacles. They should change round when they have finished.

10 Ask students to work in pairs. Ask Student A to think of a place in the town where you are at the moment. He/she must give oral directions to Student B without mentioning the name of the place. Student B has to follow the directions in his/her mind and guess the destination. Each pair

scores a point if Student B guesses correctly. Change round when they have finished.

11 Ask the students to work in groups of four. Give the two pairs in each group a picture illustrating the topic which you are about to introduce or have dealt with in the preceding unit. Each pair looks at its picture for thirty seconds. Then they swap pictures; pair A asks questions about pair B's picture, and vice versa.

12 Ask your students to form a circle. Whisper a sentence to the student on your left. He/she must whisper it, once only, to the student on his/her left. This should continue until the sentence reaches the student on your right. He/she should write the sentence on the board or say it aloud. It's very likely that it has changed out of all recognition! You can make the game more interesting by sending a sentence round the circle in the opposite direction at the same time.

13 Collect a number of magazine pictures illustrating the topic which you are about to introduce or have dealt with in a previous unit. Cut the pictures into pieces, the number of pieces totalling the number of students in your class. Give one jigsaw piece to each student. He/she has to go round describing the colours and shapes depicted in the jigsaw piece but without showing it. When a number of students think they have pieces which belong to the same picture, they should show them and try to fit the jigsaw together.

14 Collect a number of pictures showing people, places and action scenes of some kind. Hold them up one by one and ask students to think of a story to link each picture. This is a class activity rather than a group activity; each picture should represent one sentence. Make sure that everyone agrees on the story and can repeat it word for word. When you have finished making up the story, ask students to work in groups of four or five and to write the story down. After two minutes, ask students to pass their version of as much of the story as they have finished to the group on their right; in turn, they will receive the version begun by the group on their left. They should read this new version and carry on with the story where it left off. Give each group another two minutes, then ask them to pass their versions on and to receive new ones. This should continue until each group has finished a complete version of the story.

This game encourages them not only to speak and listen attentively, but also to read carefully and to write.

At various points in the guide to each unit you will see symbols like this:

WB 2.2

This refers to the number of the *Workbook* exercise(s) which can be done at this stage of the unit.

Note:
In the course of certain activities – particularly listening activities – students are asked to tick items, fill in forms, complete charts, and so on. If you prefer the students not to write in their books, we suggest the following alternatives.
a) Ask them to copy the words/forms/charts into their notebooks before they begin the activity.
b) Copy the words/forms/charts on the blackboard; ask students to come up and fill in the answers.
c) Provide sheets of tracing paper or similar thin paper so that students may place the paper over the relevant page and write without marking their books.

1 | Meeting people

UNIT SUMMARY

Note:
When students are working on the Structure Review sections at the back of the *Student's Book*, you can use these summaries to check that they have completed the structure boxes correctly.

Functions	Structures
Greeting people	

Hello, I'm (*name*).

Good	morning. afternoon. evening.

Asking and saying who people are

What's your name?
Who's this?

This is (*name*).

He She	's my (*relation*).

He's She's	. . .'s (*relation*).

Asking and saying where people are from

I'm from (*place*).

Where are you from?

Where's	he she	from?

He She	's from (*place*).

Meeting people for the first time

How do you do?

Asking and saying how you are

How are you?

I'm fine, thanks.
Very well, thank you.

1

Topics

Countries, towns, forms of address, family

Lexical items

- Hello!   meet
- Italy   Jamaica   Japan
- London   New York   Sydney
- Mr   Mrs   Miss   Ms
- boy   brother   child/children   daughter   father   girl   husband   man/men   mother   parent   sister
  son   wife   woman/women

TEACHING GUIDE

This unit introduces the language used when people meet and greet each other. If it is the first time your students have met each other, this language can be presented very meaningfully. However, if your students already know each other, it may be better to give the students a false identity, such as that of a fictional or well-known person. These names can be written on cards which you give the students.

The airline advertisement on page 1 illustrates a familiar formula for greetings.

1   Present the structure *I'm . . . .* by pointing to yourself and saying your name. Then point to students in turn and elicit the structure and their names. When all the students have mastered the structure individually, ask them to go round the room introducing themselves to each other. Explain that *Hello!* is the most common informal way of greeting people.
2   Practise intensive listening by playing the tape; students match the towns or countries with the people.

Tapescript and Answers

KOJI:	Hello, I'm Koji. I'm from Japan.
CARLA:	Hello, I'm Carla. I'm from Italy.
BOB:	Hello, I'm Bob. I'm from Jamaica.
NANCY:	Hello, I'm Nancy. I'm from New York.
DIANA:	Hello, I'm Diana. I'm from London.
RICHARD:	Hello, I'm Richard. I'm from Sydney.

Check that the students recognise the English names for these places. Make sure students understand that the structure refers to where people, are from and not where they live. This will be clearer after the next exercise.

If you have time, you may like to consolidate this structure by showing pictures of well-known people, e.g. the President of the United States of America, the Prime Minister of Great Britain, and various speech bubbles: *I'm from America, I'm from Britain.* Then ask students to match the bubbles with the pictures.

3   Present the structure *I'm from . . . .* by pointing to yourself and saying where you're from.
    Ask students where they're from and elicit the response *I'm from . . . .* Make sure they say where they're from and not where they live.
    Present the structure *Where are you from?* by choral and individual repetition and then by getting students to ask each other where they're from. Write the question and the response on the board, read the sentences aloud with the correct syllable stress, and mark the stress.

> Where are you from? I'm from London.

4   Present *He's/She's from . . . .* by pointing to the characters in the book on page 2 and saying where they're from. Then practise the structure by getting students to point and say where other people are from.
    Present the structure *Where's he/she from?* by choral and individual repetition and then by pair-work. Make sure everyone is aware of the difference between *he* and *she*! If you have already made use of pictures of well-known people, you can use them again to give further practice in this structure.
5   Present the structure *This is . . . .* by pointing to students or pictures and saying who people are. Ask two students to come in front of the class and introduce them to each other: *Carlo, this is Patrice. Patrice, this is Carlo.* Ask students to introduce themselves to another student and then to take it in turns to introduce each other to the rest of the class.

WB 1.1

6   Practise extensive listening. Each of the characters who were presented in 2 are connected in some way and meet each other at the airport. Explain that it is not necessary to understand every word of the dialogues, merely to find out who meets whom. The listening passage is an advertisement for an airline.

Tapescript

SUSIE:	Hello, I'm Susie. Fly Air Hampton. Your attention please. We're landing in a few minutes. Please fasten your seatbelts . . .
ANNOUNCER:	Fly Air Hampton and meet people.
DIANA:	Excuse me – are you Koji Yamashita?
KOJI:	Yes?
DIANA:	Good afternoon – I'm Diana Pye. How do you do?
KOJI:	Ah, how do you do?
ANNOUNCER:	Fly Air Hampton and say hello to your friends.
NANCY:	Bob! Bob! Hello.
BOB:	Hello, Nancy! How are you?
NANCY:	I'm very well, thanks. How are you?
BOB:	Fine, thanks.
NANCY:	Did you have a good flight?
ANNOUNCER:	Fly Air Hampton, the family airline . . .
RICHARD:	Carla!
CARLA:	Richard!
RICHARD:	Darling!
ANNOUNCER:	. . . the family airline that brings people together.

Answers

Diana meets Koji.
Nancy meets Bob.
Richard meets Carla.

7 Present *Mr/Mrs/Miss/Ms* and *How do you do?*. Explain that these forms of address are used when you meet someone for the first time in a formal situation. Practise these forms of address by asking students to go round introducing themselves to each other in groups of three in a formal way; make sure they have understood the difference between *Mrs* and *Miss*, and explain that *Ms* is pronounced *Mizz*, and is used quite often in both Britain and the United States for a woman whose marital status is unknown or irrelevant. Then practise the form of address for people who meet informally; in this circumstance, first names are often used.

8 Practise recognising responses by playing the tape and asking the students to tick the box corresponding to the reply they hear.

Tapescript and Answers

BOB:	Hello, Nancy! How are you?
NANCY:	I'm very well, thanks. How are you?
BOB:	Fine, thanks.

Explain that *all* the answers shown in the *Student's Book* are correct answers to the question. However, you may like to suggest that students choose and use *one* of the five forms. Ask students to practise the question and response with others in the class.

9 Practise writing by asking students to complete the dialogue with the missing words. Then write the dialogue on the board, and ask students to come up and fill in the blanks with their answers. When you play the dialogue, ask one student to underline any mistakes in the version on the board.

Tapescript and Answers

BOB:	Hello, Nancy! How are you?
NANCY:	I'm very well, thanks. How are you?
BOB:	Fine, thanks.
NANCY:	Bob, this is Carol Robinson. She's from Canada.
BOB:	Hello, Miss Robinson. How do you do?
CAROL:	How do you do? Where are you from?
BOB:	I'm from Jamaica.

WB 1.2, 1.3

10 Present *Good morning, Good afternoon, Good evening* by asking students to match the words with the pictures.

Answers

1 B, 2 C, 3 A
4 Good evening. 5 Good afternoon.
6 Good morning.

Explain that *Good morning* is used until midday, *Good afternoon* is used until 5 or 6 p.m., and that *Good evening* is used after 6 p.m. *Good night* is only used as a farewell.

You may like to practise these greetings further by using a 24-hour clock, changing the time and asking the students to respond with a suitable greeting.

WB 1.4

11 Practise the structure *This is . . .* by pointing to the people in the photograph and saying who they are. Ask students to read the two short passages about Carla's family. Make sure everyone has understood the meaning of the vocabulary for members of the family. If you like, you can ask students to work in pairs. Student A looks at the passage on the left and Student B looks at the passage on the right. Then they should exchange information about the family.

12 Present the possessive *'s* by eliciting the answers to the questions. Revise *He's/She's*. Check that everyone understands the difference between *'s* in

contractions (e.g. *who's = who is, he's = he is*), and *'s* for possession (e.g. *Carla's husband = the husband of Carla*).

Answers

Who's Richard?	He's Carla's husband.
Who's Nina?	She's Carla's daughter.
Who's Joe?	He's Carla's son.
Who's Joe?	He's Nina's brother.
Who's Nina?	She's Joe's sister.
Who's Richard?	He's Joe's and Nina's father.

13 Practise the possessive *'s* and *my* by asking students to write the names of their family on a piece of paper and, working in pairs, to ask and say what relation each member of the family is to the student. Students use this information to built up their partner's family tree.

WB 1.5, 1.6

WB 1.7

Note:
Explain that *he is* is the full form of *he's* (contraction). Tell students that full forms are generally used in written English, while contractions are used in spoken English.

LEARNING SKILLS

Point out that there are many 'international' words like *television, radio, football, tennis, spaghetti, pizza, Coca Cola* which sound almost the same in many languages.

Say the English names of various countries and towns from all over the world. Ask students to raise their hand if they recognise the places. In many cases, they will sound the same in English as they do in the student's own language. If you have a map of the world with English names, ask students to note down six countries whose names look like the names in their own language.

Your students may have begun to make notes about what they've learnt so far. If you have a monolingual group and speak their language, ask individual students about the kind of points they've noted down while doing Unit 1. Has everyone noted down the same kind of things? Explain that you'll be giving them some more ideas on how to organise their notes as the course proceeds.

PRONUNCIATION TAPESCRIPT

Note:
These tapescripts also serve as answer keys to the exercises because the stress and intonation patterns are marked, when this is what the student has to do.

In some of the pronunciation exercises, the student is asked to do some work based on the *Student's Book*, before or after listening to the tape. These additional instructions are not part of the tapescript and do not appear here.

1.1 Listen and repeat.

Carla	mother
Koji	father
Nancy	sister
Richard	brother

1.2 Listen and repeat.

Very well	Italy
Thank you	Sydney
Good morning	London
Good afternoon	Japan

1.3 Listen and repeat.

a) This is Koji. He's from Japan.

b) This is Diana. She's from London.

c) This is Nancy. She's from New York.

d) This is Bob. He's from Jamaica.

e) This is Carla. She's from Italy.

f) This is Richard. He's from Sydney.

STRUCTURE REVIEW TAPESCRIPT

Note:
These tapescripts also serve as answer keys to the exercises, and the sentence given in italics is what the student has to say.

1.1 Say who these people are, like this:

Pascal.
This is Pascal.

Now you.

a) Pascal.
This is Pascal.
b) Lee.
This is Lee.
c) Kelly.
This is Kelly.
d) Federico.
This is Federico.
e) Heidi.
This is Heidi.
f) Luigia.
This is Luigia.

Note:
As they say the names, students should point at the appropriate picture.

4

1.2 Say where the people are from, like this:

Where's Heidi from?
She's from Germany.

Now you.

a) Where's Heidi from?
   She's from Germany.
b) Where's Kelly from?
   She's from London.
c) Where's Federico from?
   He's from Spain.
d) Where's Luigia from?
   She's from Italy.
e) Where's Pascal from?
   He's from Paris.
f) Where's Lee from?
   He's from Hong Kong.
g) Where are you from?
   ....

1.3 Meet people for the first time, or say how you are and ask others how they are, like this:

How do you do?
How do you do?

Hi, how are you?
I'm fine, thanks. How are you?
Very well, thank you.

Now you.

How do you do?
How do you do?

Hi, how are you?
I'm fine, thanks. How are you?
Very well, thank you.

1.4 Look at the family tree and say who the people in Carla's family are, like this:

Who's Anna?
She's Carla's mother.

Now you.

a) Who's Anna?
   She's Carla's mother.
b) Who's Paolo?
   He's Carla's brother.
c) Who's Nina?
   She's Carla's daughter.
d) Who's Richard?
   He's Carla's husband.
e) Who's Joe?
   He's Carla's son.
f) Who's Bruno?
   He's Carla's father.

2 Getting to know people

UNIT SUMMARY

Functions	Structures

Asking and saying which country people are from

Where	are	you they	from?
	is	he she	

I'm You're He's She's We're They're	from (*place*).

Asking and saying what nationality people are

Are	you they	
Is	he she	(*nationality*)?

Yes,	I am. he is. she is. we are. they are.	No,	I'm not. he isn't. she isn't. we aren't they aren't.

Asking and saying what people do

What	do	you they	do?
	does	he she	

I'm He's She's	a an	(*job*).

Asking and saying where people live

Where	do	you they	live?
	does	he she	

Functions

I You We They	live	in (*place*).
He She	lives	

Talking about possession

Personal pronouns	Possessive adjectives
I you he she we they	my your his her our their

Topics

Jobs, countries, nationalities, family

Lexical items

- country   Australia   Great Britain   United States of America
- American   Australian   British   Italian   Jamaican   Japanese
- live   surname   first name   married
- computer company   job   actor   businessman   doctor   engineer   housewife   journalist
  marketing manager   musician   secretary   singer   student   teacher   unemployed

TEACHING GUIDE

This unit introduces a number of countries, nationalities and occupations. However, it is particularly important that students know their own countries, nationalities and occupations, so you should be ready to supply further items where necessary.

WARM-UP

Suggested warm-up activity: 1. If all the students know each other well, use fictitious names.

1   Revise *This is* . . . . by asking students to point at the map and say the names of the countries. If possible, this activity should be performed using a large map of the world; but if this isn't available, hold the book up and point at the countries, saying their names. Explain that Great Britain and the United States of America are often referred to as Britain and America/the States/the USA.
2   Revise *Where's . . . from? He's/She's from* . . . . by asking students to say where the six characters

introduced in Unit 1 are from. Give two or three examples of the model sentence, then ask students to practise in pairs. Check on pronunciation, stress and intonation.

3   Present various nationalities by playing the tape and asking students to listen and match the nationalities with the pictures. Write the numbers 1 to 6 on the board and ask students to write them in their notebooks. Tell them to note down the letter which corresponds to the nationality of each character as they listen.

Tapescript

VOICE:	Koji's from Japan.
KOJI:	I'm Japanese.
VOICE:	Nancy's from the United States of America.
NANCY:	I'm American.
VOICE:	Carla's from Italy.
CARLA:	I'm Italian.
VOICE:	Diana's from Great Britain.

DIANA:	I'm British.
VOICE:	Bob's from Jamaica.
BOB:	I'm Jamaican.
VOICE:	Richard's from Australia.
RICHARD:	I'm Australian.

Answers

1 F, 2 E, 3 C, 4 D, 5 B, 6 A

Get students to check their answers by asking one student to write the answers on the board.

Point to yourself and say what nationality you are, using *I'm* . . . . Then point to each student in turn and say what nationality he/she is. Ask each student to say what nationality he/she is, using *I'm* . . . . Practise nationalities by asking students to say what nationality other students are. Use magazine photographs of famous people and ask students to say what nationality the people are.

4 Practise writing nationalities by asking students to complete the sentences. Make sure everyone realises that both country and nationality take a capital letter.

Answers

1 Kōji's from Japān. He's Japanēse.
2 Nāncy's from Amērica. She's Amērican.
3 Cārla's from Ītaly. She's Itālian.
4 Diāna's from Brītain. She's Brītish.
5 Bob's from Jamāica. He's Jamāican.
6 Rīchard's from Austrālia. He's Austrālian.

Mark the stress as shown above on one or two of the sentences on the board. Then practise stress and intonation by asking students to read the sentences aloud.

WB 2.1

5 Present *Is he/she . . . ? Yes, he/she is. No, he/she isn't.* by getting students to ask and answer questions about people's nationalities. You may wish to give further practice by using the magazine pictures of famous people.

6 Present the various occupations illustrated in the *Student's Book* by reading the words aloud for recognition. Check that students understand all the words, then practise listening for specific information by playing the tape and asking students to complete the chart. Explain that it isn't necessary to understand every word in the conversation, merely to find out each person's occupation.

Tapescript

OFFICIAL:	Now, Mr Yamashita – just one or two questions. You're from Japan?
KOJI:	Yes, that's right.
OFFICIAL:	Are you in London for a holiday?
KOJI:	No, no, I'm a businessman. I'm here to visit a computer company . . .
OFFICIAL:	I see – and how long . . .
INTERVIEWER:	Er, Miss Goldberg – I need some information. What's your first name?
NANCY:	Nancy.
INTERVIEWER:	Are you American?
NANCY:	Yes, I am.
INTERVIEWER:	And what do you do?
NANCY:	I'm a student.
INTERVIEWER:	(*writing*) Occupation . . . student.
WOMAN:	John, this is Carla King, and her husband Richard.
MAN:	How do you do?
WOMAN:	Carla's a journalist – she works for a newspaper in Hong Kong.
MAN:	Oh, how interesting! And what do you do, Mr King?
RICHARD:	Me – oh, I'm an engineer.
WOMAN:	Hello . . . don't I know you?
BOB:	Er, no – I don't think so.
WOMAN:	Wait a minute – are you a singer?
BOB:	No, I'm not. In fact, I'm an actor.
WOMAN:	Oh, of course! You're Bob Armstrong!
BOB:	Yes, that's right.

WB 2.2

Answers

Name	Occupation
Koji Yamashita	businessman
Nancy Goldberg	student
Carla King	journalist
Richard King	engineer
Bob Armstrong	actor

You may like to ask students to act out the dialogue in pairs.

7 Present *What does he/she do? He's/She's a(n)* . . . . by asking students to check their answers to 6 orally. Give two or three model sentences and elicit the correct responses. Then ask students to practise in pairs. Insist on the weak form of *does* /dəz/. Make sure everyone includes the indefinite article (*an* in front of vowels).

8 Present *What do you do? I'm a(n) . . . .* and *Are you a(n) . . . ? Yes, I am. No, I'm not.* by giving one or two model sentences and eliciting suitable replies. Give the students the English words for their jobs. If possible, bring pictures to illustrate any other jobs which may be useful. Get the students to go round the class asking and saying what they do. If necessary, teach *I haven't got a job. I'm unemployed. I'm still at school.*

WB 2.3

9 Present *Where does he/she live? He/She lives in . . . . Where do they live? They live in . . . .* by getting students to look at the addresses, and asking and saying where people live. Give one or two model questions and elicit suitable responses. Then ask students to work in pairs and practise the structures. Point out that the third person singular takes *–s* (which is pronounced /z/ in *lives*). You may like to extend this activity by bringing pictures of famous people and asking where they live.

10 Present *Where do you live? I live in . . . .* by asking students where they live and eliciting a suitable response. Ask students to go round the class asking and saying where they live.

WB 2.4

11 Ask students to say where the six characters live and are from, and practise *He's/She's from . . . .* and *He/She lives in . . . .* Explain the difference between *and* and *but.* Begin by giving a model sentence and then ask individual students to make similar sentences about the other characters.

12 Practise listening for specific information by playing the tape and asking students to complete the form. Explain that they will hear a conversation between Carla and a man doing a survey at the airport. Remind students that it isn't necessary to understand every word; in fact, they already have all the information they need to perform the task. When they have finished, elicit the question forms which relate to each item on the form; e.g. SURNAME: *What's your surname?*, OCCUPATION: *What do you do?* Play the tape again so that students can concentrate on the question forms.

Tapescript

MAN:	Excuse me, madam. I'm doing a passenger survey. Can I ask you some questions?
CARLA:	Yes, all right.
MAN:	Thank you very much. First, what's your name?
CARLA:	King . . . Carla King.

MAN:	Uh huh . . . are you married?
CARLA:	Yes, this is my husband.
MAN:	Oh, good afternoon, sir.
RICHARD:	Good afternoon.
MAN:	So it's *Mrs King* . . . and you're married. What do you do?
CARLA:	I'm a journalist.
MAN:	Oh, how interesting. And, er, where do you live?
CARLA:	In Hong Kong.
MAN:	Hong Kong . . . OK. Where do you come from? You aren't English, are you?
CARLA:	No, I'm Italian.
MAN:	Nationality . . . Italian.
RICHARD:	Ahem, are there a lot more questions?
MAN:	No, sir, no. Just one or two . . . now which flight . . .

Answers

423/8921/KT	
Airport passenger survey	
SURNAME: KING	FIRST NAME: CARLA
MARRIED/~~SINGLE~~	~~Mr~~/Mrs/~~Miss~~/~~Ms~~
TOWN/CITY: HONG KONG	NATIONALITY: ITALIAN
OCCUPATION: JOURNALIST	

13 Practise the language for exchanging personal information by asking students to complete the form for another student. Make sure everyone is using the correct question forms. Give some more practice in pronunciation, stress and intonation if you have time.

WB 2.5, 2.6

14 Practise reading for specific information by asking students to work in pairs and to follow the instructions in their books. Make sure they don't look at each other's passage. They have to complete the family tree with names taken from the passage. Encourage them to guess the meaning of *his/her/their.*

Answers

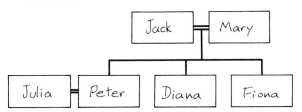

9

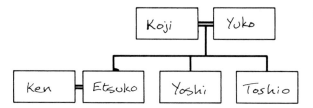

Students should then ask and answer questions about each other's family tree. Make sure they are using the correct question forms. You may want to help them by giving a model exchange. Go round and check on pronunciation, stress and intonation.

You may wish to extend this exercise by asking students to write a similar passage about their own families. They can use the family trees they composed in Unit 1. Alternatively, they can choose a well-known person and describe his/her family in a similar way.

LEARNING SKILLS

By now, students will have come across a mixture of content and structure words. Explain that content words are words like *engineer, husband, say*; structure words are words like *he, she, from, in, the*. Ask students to look through Units 1 and 2, and note down six content words and six structure items. Then ask how many of the structure words they have found have only one syllable. Ask students if they think these 'little' words are important in English, and if they have many 'little' words in their own language.

In some languages, there aren't many 'little' structure words, and speakers of these languages learning English sometimes overlook these important words.

PRONUNCIATION TAPESCRIPT

2.1 Listen and repeat.

/θ/

this	mother
that	father
then	brother

2.2 Listen and repeat.

the answer	They live in Hong Kong.
the people	their father and mother
that man	that's right

2.3 Listen and repeat.

a) What's her name?   d) What does he do?

b) Where's he from?   e) Where's she from?

c) Where do you live?   f) What do you do?

2.4 Listen and repeat.

a) Where do they live?   d) What does she do?

b) What's his name?   e) Where does he live?

c) Where are you from?   f) What's your name?

STRUCTURE REVIEW TAPESCRIPT

2.1 Ask where these people are from, like this:

Henri.
Where's Henri from?
He's from France.

Now you.

a) Henri.
Where's Henri from?
He's from France.
b) João.
Where's João from?
He's from Brazil.
c) Toni and Rosella.
Where are Toni and Rosella from?
They're from Italy.
d) Mitzi.
Where's Mitzi from?
She's from Canada.
e) Sarah and Tom.
Where are Sarah and Tom from?
They're from America.
f) Kevin.
Where's Kevin from?
He's from Ireland.

Note:
As they listen, students should note down each person's country.

2.2 Now say where these people are from, like this:

Where's Henri from?
He's from France.

Now you.

a) Where's Henri from?
He's from France.
b) Where's João from?
He's from Brazil.
c) Where are Toni and Rosella from?
They're from Italy.
d) Where's Mitzi from?
She's from Canada.
e) Where are Sarah and Tom from?
They're from America.
f) Where's Kevin from?
He's from Ireland.
g) Where are you from?
....

2.3 Look at the chart of nationalities and answer yes or no, like this:

Is Henri French?   Is João Spanish?
Yes, he is.   *No, he isn't.*

Now you.

a) Is Henri French?
   Yes, he is.
b) Is João Spanish?
   No, he isn't.
c) Are Toni and Rosella German?
   No, they aren't.
d) Is Mitzi Canadian?
   Yes, she is.
e) Are Sarah and Tom American?
   Yes, they are.
f) Is Kevin Italian?
   No, he isn't.
g) Are you English?
   ....

2.4 Say where the people live, like this:

Where does Henri live?
He lives in Paris.

Now you.

a) Where does Henri live?
   He lives in Paris.
b) Where does João live?
   He lives in Rio de Janeiro.
c) Where do Toni and Rosella live?
   They live in London.
d) Where does Mitzi live?
   She lives in Brussels.
e) Where do Sarah and Tom live?
   They live in Chicago.
f) Where does Kevin live?
   He lives in Ireland.
g) Where do you live?
   ....

Note:
Some of these characters are from one place and live in another; this is intentional.

2.5 Ask these people what they do, like this:

Henri.
What do you do, Henri?
I'm a journalist.

Now you.

a) Henri.
   What do you do, Henri?
   I'm a journalist.
b) João.
   What do you do, João?
   I'm an engineer.
c) Toni.
   What do you do, Toni?
   I'm a singer.
d) Mitzi.
   What do you do, Mitzi?
   I'm a secretary.
e) Sarah.
   What do you do, Sarah?
   I'm a doctor.
f) Kevin.
   What do you do, Kevin?
   I'm a teacher.

Note:
As they listen, students should note down each person's job.

2.6 Now say what the people do, like this:

What does Henri do?
He's a journalist.

Now you.

a) What does Henri do?
   He's a journalist.
b) What does João do?
   He's an engineer.
c) What does Toni do?
   He's a singer.
d) What does Mitzi do?
   She's a secretary.
e) What does Sarah do?
   She's a doctor.
f) What does Kevin do?
   He's a teacher.

2.7 Look at the list, and say the first names of the people, like this:

Mr Royat.
His name is Henri.

Now you.

a) Mr Royat.
   His name is Henri.
b) Mr Franca.
   His name is João.
c) Mr and Mrs Maffi.
   Their names are Toni and Rosella.
d) Ms Walker.
   Her name is Mitzi.
e) Mr and Mrs Calder.
   Their names are Sarah and Tom.
f) Mr Fogarty.
   His name is Kevin.

3 Talking about where people live

UNIT SUMMARY

Functions	Structures

Functions

Asking and saying what the rooms in a flat/house are

Structures

What's this room?

It's the (*name of room*).

Has it got a (*room*)?

Yes, it has.	No, it hasn't.

Asking and saying how many

How many rooms has it got?

It's got (*number*).

Asking and saying where people live

Do	you they	live in (*place*)?
Does	he she	

Yes,	I we they	do.	No,	I we they	don't.
	he she	does.		he she	doesn't.

Asking and saying what people have got

I've You've He's She's It's We've They've	got	a table.
		some chairs.

12

Functions

Structures

I You We They	haven't	got	a table.
He She It	hasn't		any chairs.

Asking and saying how you spell words

How do you spell (*word*)?

Topics

Rooms of the house, types of housing, furniture, numbers, alphabet

Lexical items

- bathroom bedroom dining room garden kitchen room sitting room toilet
- upstairs downstairs apartment flat house
- one two three four five six seven eight nine ten eleven twelve
- armchair bath double bed single bed chair cooker fridge shower sink sofa table TV/television toilet washbasin small large

TEACHING GUIDE

This unit presents the language used when talking about your home. Encourage the students to talk about their homes as much as possible; it is always more interesting for them if you allow them time to talk about themselves and their own experiences. You may also like to bring a plan of your own home which you can use to illustrate some of the structures and vocabulary.

WARM-UP

Suggested warm-up activity: 2.

1   Present the vocabulary of the various rooms in Nancy's flat and make sure that everyone can pronounce the words. Give the model sentence *What's room one?* and present the numbers *one* to *six* by asking about the other rooms. The main point at this stage is for the students to recognise and say the names of the rooms. Explain that the definite article (*the*) is used before nouns of which there is only one. There is only one kitchen in Nancy's flat, so we say *It's the kitchen*. Give further practice by using magazine pictures of various rooms of the house and asking *What's this room?*

It may well be necessary to give further practice in pronouncing and recognising numbers *one* to *six* and extending them to *ten*. Write the following chart of numbers on the board:

STUDENT **A**		STUDENT **B**	
HEAR	SAY	HEAR	SAY
345	679	134	357
298	134	679	567
357	523	523	345
254	286	174	254
567	174	286	298

Ask the students to work in pairs: A and B. When each student hears a set of numbers they should say the numbers opposite. To start the game, simply say in a loud voice 5 – 2 – 3. Student B should then reply 3 – 4 – 5.

2   Practise listening for specific information by playing the conversation between Bob and Nancy in the taxi. Explain that background noise is very common when you listen and can often make it more difficult to understand. Explain also that they do not need to understand every word in the dialogue. They should simply listen to distinguish the different rooms of the house and how many there are of them.

Tapescript

NANCY:	Bob, tell me about your apartment – oh, you don't say apartment in Britain, do you? You say flat.
BOB:	That's right. But it isn't.
NANCY:	It isn't what?
BOB:	It isn't a flat. It's a house.
NANCY:	A house?

BOB:	Uh huh.
NANCY:	How big is it? I mean, how many rooms has it got?
BOB:	Well, downstairs there's a large kitchen, a beautiful dining room, and two sitting rooms.
NANCY:	Two sitting rooms! And upstairs?
BOB:	Upstairs it's got two large bedrooms and two small bedrooms . . .
NANCY:	That's four bedrooms!
BOB:	Mm . . . and there are two bathrooms, and a toilet. Oh yes, and it's got a toilet downstairs too.
NANCY:	Hey! You've got a very big house!

Answers

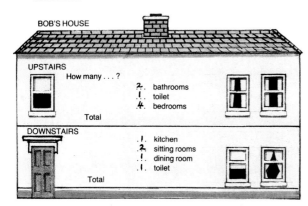

As you correct this exercise, explain that the plural of nouns is formed by adding –s or –es; make sure students are pronouncing the /s/ or /z/ sounds as required. Point out that American English uses *apartment*, and British English uses *flat*. However, both words are usually understood by people from either country.

3 Present the structure *How many . . . has it got?* by chorus and individual drilling. Then ask students to work in pairs to practise the structure by asking and answering questions about Bob's house.

You can give further practice in numbers and recognising the structure by pointing to things in the classroom, such as light switches, power points, chairs and table, window, etc. and asking *How many . . . ?* There is no need at this stage to teach the actual vocabulary for these items.

4 Practise *How many . . . has it got?* and revise *This is the . . . .* Remind students that *This is . . . .* can be used to introduce people to each other.

5 Practise the structures which have been presented so far by writing the dialogue which appears in the *Student's Book* on the board. When students have completed it, ask one or two of them to come to the board and write the correct answers in the blanks.

Then students listen to the dialogue on tape to check their answers. Use the dialogue in the *Student's Book* to practise stress and intonation. Mark the stress on the words in the dialogue and ask students to practise in pairs. Go round each pair and check that they are using the correct stress and intonation patterns. This dialogue will be used as a model for 6.

Tapescript

BOB:	Where do you live, Nancy?
NANCY:	In New York.
BOB:	Nancy, I know that! But which part?
NANCY:	Oh, I see. I live in Brooklyn.
BOB:	Uh huh. Do you live in an apartment?
NANCY:	Yes, I do.
BOB:	How many rooms has it got?
NANCY:	Six. The rooms are small, but it's a nice apartment.
BOB:	Has it got a garden?
NANCY:	A garden? In Brooklyn! No, it hasn't! Have you got a garden?
BOB:	Yes, I have.
NANCY:	Oh, you're lucky.

Answers

BOB:	Where do you live?
NANCY:	In New York.
BOB:	Do you live in an apartment?
NANCY:	Yes, I do.
BOB:	How many rooms has it got?
NANCY:	Six.
BOB:	Has it got a garden?
NANCY:	No, it hasn't.

6 Practise the structures by asking students to go round the class asking four students about their homes. Ask them to use the dialogue they have practised in 5 in the *Student's Book* as a model for this exercise.

7 Practise the structures by asking students to work in pairs and to discuss the answers to their questionnaires in 6. Make sure they are using short answers: *Yes, he/she does/dʌz/, No, he/she doesn't/dʌznt/.*

8 Practise writing short paragraphs about students' homes like the description of Nancy's home. Correct their versions in class by marking any mistakes with a cross in the margin; each mistake is given one cross. Then ask students either to work out what their mistake is, or to ask other students for help.

9 Practise listening for specific information. Explain that it isn't necessary to understand every word in this dialogue. Copy the words labelled on the picture on the board and ask students in turn to come up and tick the items that Bob's got.

Tapescript

BOB:	Yes, I've got a big house. But I need some furniture.
NANCY:	Haven't you got any furniture?
BOB:	Well, there's a sofa and a TV in one of the sitting rooms . . . but I haven't got any armchairs.
NANCY:	What about the dining room?
BOB:	Oh, yes . . . I've got some chairs. In fact, there are twelve chairs in the dining room.
NANCY:	And a table?
BOB:	No, I haven't got a table.
NANCY:	No table! Where do you eat?
BOB:	Well, I usually go to a restaurant.
NANCY:	Oh, Bob!
BOB:	But you should see the kitchen – it's lovely. I've got a cooker, and a fridge – and a brand new sink!
NANCY:	Have you got a bath?
BOB:	What! In the kitchen?
NANCY:	No, in the bathroom!
BOB:	No, I haven't. But there's a shower in the large bathroom. And a washbasin. The toilet is next door.
NANCY:	And where do you sleep? On the floor?
BOB:	Oh, no. I've got a bed. I'm not stupid!

Answers

table   armchair   fridge √ TV √ toilet √ chair √ sofa √ cooker √ shower √ washbasin √ sink √ bed √ bath

WB 3.1

Note:
Explain the word *letters* by contrasting it with *numbers*.

WB 3.2

Note:
Students are not expected to understand everything in the advertisements, but simply to work out what the abbreviations mean.

WB 3.3, 3.4

10 Present *some* and *any* by talking about Bob's house. Give a few model sentences and then practise the words with individual, chorus and pairwork drilling, if necessary. Insist on the weak form of *some* /səm/, and make sure that students use *any* with plural nouns in negative sentences. When students start the pairwork, they should look at the pictures of Nancy's apartment on page 10.

You can also give further practice in the vocabulary and structures with magazine pictures of different rooms.

11 Present *any* with questions by asking students what furniture they have in their homes. Practise short answers *Yes, I have, No, I haven't.* Make sure that their intonation of the question forms is correct.

WB 3.5, 3.6, 3.7

WB 3.8

Note:
Check that students understand that they can look up words in the dictionary.

12 Present the letters of the alphabet by playing the tape and asking the students to repeat. You may wish to do this two or three times. Then write up the chart shown in the *Student's Book* on the board. Ask students to come and complete it by placing the letters which sound the same in one column. Wipe the chart off the board, then ask students to do the exercise again using their books as a guide. Finally, play the tape again so they can check their answers.

Tapescript

ABC	DEF	GHI	JKL	MNO
PQR	STU	VW	XYZ	

AHJK
BCDEGPTV
FLMNSXZ

Answers

/eɪ/	/i:/	/e/	/aɪ/	/əʊ/	/ju:/	/a:/
A	B	F	I	O	Q	R
H	C	L	Y		U	
					W	
J	D	M				
K	E	N				
	G	S				
	P	X				
	T	Z				
	V					

13 Present the structure *How do you spell . . .?* by getting students to answer the questions, and then to practise in pairs asking and saying how you spell words. Students can continue practising the structure in groups; each student should ask someone in the group to spell a word. If the latter spells the word correctly he/she asks someone else to spell another word. The most common words we have to spell are our names, so make sure students can do this successfully.

14 Practise reading for general sense by matching the pictures with the descriptions. Clearly, students will not understand every word, so explain to them that this is not necessary for this exercise. Point out that the passages are authentic and if they manage to do the exercise successfully, emphasise how much they've understood rather than how little.

Answers   1 B, 2 C, 3 A

15 This activity practises numbers, and the vocabulary for rooms of the house and furniture. Students work in groups to plan their ideal home and then write a description of it. Encourage them to use their imagination! If possible, put the plans and descriptions up on the classroom wall.

LEARNING SKILLS

If your students' native language uses a Roman alphabet, ask them to form groups of three or four; give each group a page taken from an English magazine or newspaper. Ask them to find words which look like words in their own language, including proper nouns. If their native language doesn't use a Roman alphabet, read a short passage aloud to them, such as a newspaper article. Ask students to make a note or put their hand up when they hear any words which sound like words in their own language. The aim of this exercise is to encourage students to recognise English words that have cognates in their native language.

PRONUNCIATION TAPESCRIPT

3.1 Listen and repeat.

apartment	(3)	hall	(1)
kitchen	(2)	bedroom	(2)
eleven	(3)	flat	(1)

Now listen again. How many syllables are there in each word?

3.2 Listen and repeat. Mark the stressed syllables.

c͞ooker	(2)	sh͞ower	(2)
c͞ity	(2)	wa͞shbasin	(3)
ga͞rden	(2)	a͞rmchair	(2)

3.3 Listen and repeat.

/ə/

shower	kitchen
cooker	seven
sofa	table

STRUCTURE REVIEW TAPESCRIPT

3.1 Look at page 10 and talk about Bob's house, like this:

How many rooms has it got?
It's got twelve rooms.

Now you.

a) How many rooms has it got?
It's got twelve rooms.
b) How many bedrooms has it got?
It's got four bedrooms.
c) How many sitting rooms has it got?
It's got two sitting rooms.
d) How many bathrooms has it got?
It's got two bathrooms.
e) How many toilets has it got?
It's got two toilets.
f) How many dining rooms has it got?
It's got one dining room.

3.2 Ask about Diana's flat, like this:

Ask how many rooms it's got.
How many rooms has it got?

Now you.

a) Ask how many rooms it's got.
How many rooms has it got?
b) Ask how many bedrooms it's got.
How many bedrooms has it got?
c) Ask how many sitting rooms it's got.
How many sitting rooms has it got?
d) Ask how many bathrooms it's got.
How many bathrooms has it got?
e) Ask how many toilets it's got.
How many toilets has it got?

3.3 Look at page 10 and talk about Nancy's apartment, like this:

Has it got a kitchen?
Yes, it has.

Has it got a garden?
No, it hasn't.

Now you.

a) Has it got a kitchen?
Yes, it has.
b) Has it got a bathroom?
Yes, it has.
c) Has it got a garden?
No, it hasn't.
d) Has it got a sitting room?
Yes, it has.
e) Has it got a study?
No, it hasn't.

3.4 Talk about where people live, like this:

Does Nancy live in an apartment?
Yes, she does.

Does Bob live in Paris?
No, he doesn't.

Now you.

a) Does Nancy live in an apartment?
Yes, she does.
b) Does Bob live in Paris?
No, he doesn't.
c) Does Koji live in Tokyo?
Yes, he does.
d) Do Richard and Carla live in Rome?
No, they don't.
e) Does Diana live in a flat?
Yes, she does.
f) Do Joe and Nina live in Hong Kong?
Yes, they do.
g) Do you live in London?
....

3.5 Talk about people's furniture, like this:

Has Bob got any chairs?
Yes, he's got some chairs.

Has Diana got any armchairs?
No, she hasn't got any armchairs.

Now you.

a) Has Bob got any chairs?
Yes, he's got some chairs.
b) Has Diana got any armchairs?
No, she hasn't got any armchairs.
c) Has Nancy got any tables?
Yes, she's got some tables.
d) Have Carla and Richard got any beds?
Yes, they've got some beds.
e) Has Koji got any chairs?
No, he hasn't got any chairs.

4 Talking about what you like and what you can do

UNIT SUMMARY

Functions

Asking and saying what you like

Asking and saying what you like doing

I We They	like	flying.
He She	likes	football.

Do	you they	like	flying?
Does	he she		football?

I We They	don't	like	flying.
He She	doesn't		football.

Agreeing and disagreeing

I	like love	dancing.

So do I.

I don't like museums.

Nor Neither	do I.

I	like love	football.

Do you? I don't.

I don't like flying.

Don't you? I do.

Asking and saying what you can do

I You He She We They	can swim.

I You He She We They	can't dance.

18

Structures

Can	you he she they	swim?

	I	
Yes,	we he	can.
No,	she they	can't.

Topics

Sport and leisure activities, town facilities, languages

Lexical items

- film (horror films) food football guitar hamburger jazz piano motorbike music (rock/classical) tennis
- all right
- cook (-ing) dance (dancing) drive (driving) eat (-ing) fly (-ing) go (-ing) learn (-ing) play (-ing) read (-ing) run (running) shop (shopping) sightsee (-ing) speak (-ing) sunbathe (sunbathing) swim (swimming) travel (travelling) type (typing) use (using) visit (-ing) watch (-ing)
- cathedral concert gallery market museum restaurant river shop (n) theatre
- English French German Spanish

TEACHING GUIDE

This unit presents some of the vocabulary used to talk about likes and dislikes. However, it is possible that not all the words to describe the likes and dislikes of your students will be covered, so you may have to supply further vocabulary to meet your students' personal requirements. Once again, encourage students to talk about themselves as much as possible; the language in the course is presented to be useful to the students and not to suit the characters of the book!

Before the lesson, ask students to bring to the class some brochures or other materials which describe their home towns; these should be in English if possible, but can be in the students' native language if necessary.

WARM-UP

Suggested warm-up activity: 4.

1 Revise the structure *Yes, I do/No, I don't* by asking students if they like the objects or activities illustrated in their books. Make sure they understand the meaning of *It's/They're all right*; this is a non-committal response meaning one doesn't mind. Check that their pronunciation is correct with chorus and individual drilling.

Present the structure *Do you like . . . ?* by asking students what they like and then practise by getting them to ask each other what they like. Check everyone's pronunciation, stress and intonation.

2 Present *Do you like —ing?* by asking students if

they like doing the activities listed in their books. Make sure everyone understands the new vocabulary. You can mime the activities; then get students to ask their partners if they like doing the activity in your mime. Check on pronunciation of —ing/iŋ/. Revise *Yes, I do./No, I don't*. Make sure no one is saying *Yes, I like./No, I don't like*.

3 Present *I like . . . ./I don't like . . . .* by pointing to two of the objects or activities in 1 and 2 and saying which you like and don't like. Then students can practise using the structure in pairs: ask them to tell each other about three things they like and three things they don't like. Present *So do I*, and *Do you? I don't*, by asking two students to say what they like and give the model responses. Then ask two students to say what they don't like and do the same with *Nor/Neither do I.* and *Don't you? I do*. Explain that these structures can be used to agree and to disagree with people. Practise the structures by asking students to go round the class asking and saying what they like, and agreeing or disagreeing with people.

WB 4.1

4 Practise writing by asking students to complete the chart, and then to work in pairs to discuss the results, using the structures *What does (name) like/like doing?* and *He/She likes/doesn't like . . . .* Check that everyone is using the correct word order for *Wh-* questions. Lead a class discussion about what people like/like doing and use *How many . . . ?* from Unit 3. Check on their pronunciation of plural /s/ or /z/.

5 Practise writing by using the results of the questionnaire in 4. Present *everybody* and *nobody* at a suitable moment. When students have finished writing their reports, go round and correct them by marking a cross in the margin of any line in which a mistake occurs; ask students to try and decide what the mistake is.

6 Practise listening for specific information to find out what Koji likes and doesn't like doing. Draw attention to the difference in strength of *love* and *like*. Remind students once again that they don't have to understand every word of the dialogue.

Tapescript

KOJI:	Miss Pye! Miss Pye!
DIANA:	Ah, Mr Yamashita. I hope your room is all right.
KOJI:	Oh, yes, it's fine. It's on the twenty-first floor – I can see all of London!
DIANA:	Do you like London?
KOJI:	Yes, I love it. There's so much to do here.
DIANA:	Tell me, what do you like doing?
KOJI:	Well, I love visiting the museums . . . especially the British Museum.
DIANA:	Yes, there are some wonderful museums. Do you like sightseeing?
KOJI:	Oh, yes, I do. There are so many places to see in London . . . and I like going to concerts.
DIANA:	So do I. What kind of music do you like?
KOJI:	Classical music, and jazz.
DIANA:	Ah . . . do you like going to the theatre?
KOJI:	No, not very much . . . you see, my English isn't very good.
DIANA:	Oh, come on, you speak very well.
KOJI:	But I can't understand everything.
DIANA:	Anything else you don't like?
KOJI:	I don't like shopping in London.
DIANA:	Why not?
KOJI:	I spend too much money.
DIANA:	What about restaurants?
KOJI:	I love eating in restaurants in London. You can eat food from all over the world.
DIANA:	Well, there's a very good Italian restaurant near the hotel. Do you like Italian food?
KOJI:	Oh, yes, I love it. Let's go!

Answers

Koji loves visiting museums, eating in restaurants.
Koji likes sightseeing, going to concerts.
Koji doesn't like going to the theatre, shopping in London.

Ask students to say if they agree or disagree with Koji. You may also get students to work in pairs and to act out a similar dialogue using Diana and Koji's conversation as a model.

7 Practise the structures *likes/doesn't like/loves* by asking students to complete the sentences. When they have finished, correct them quickly and then practise pronunciation, stress and intonation with the completed sentences. If necessary, mark the stresses and the intonation on the sentences.

Answers

Koji likes sightseeing in London, but he doesn't like shopping.

He loves visiting museums and eating in restaurants.

He likes going to concerts, but he doesn't like going to the theatre.

8 Practise reading for general sense by asking students to match the headings with the paragraphs. Remind the students that they do not have to understand every word of the tourist information. If necessary, you may like to give them some information about the places mentioned.

Big Ben is the bell in the clock tower by the Houses of Parliament, although the clock tower itself is usually called by this name.
The *Houses of Parliament* are the two debating chambers, the House of Commons and the House of Lords, where Members of Parliament and peers meet to discuss and vote on new laws and government policy.
The *Tower of London* is the old Norman castle by Tower Bridge. It contains, among many other items of interest, the Crown Jewels.
St Paul's Cathedral is the second largest church in the world (the first is St Peter's in Rome). It was built by Sir Christopher Wren and has a large dome.
The *British Museum* is the largest museum in Britain.
Oxford Street is one of the best-known shopping streets in London.
Knightsbridge is a district south of Hyde Park famous for its luxury shops and houses.
Soho is a district with many night clubs just south of Oxford Street.
Covent Garden is the site of the former fruit and vegetable market, which has now been turned into a shopping centre. The Royal Opera House is also in Covent Garden.

Charlotte Street has a large number of very good restaurants.

The *River Thames* is the name of the river running through London.

The *National Theatre* is on the south bank of the River Thames and is the home of the National Theatre Company which puts on many new or classical plays.

The *Royal Festival Hall* is a concert hall next to the National Theatre.

The *Royal Albert Hall* is a concert hall in Kensington, built in memory of Queen Victoria's husband, Prince Albert.

Trafalgar Square is a large square in Charing Cross with the famous statue of Nelson, the sailor, in the middle.

The *National Gallery* has a huge collection of paintings from all over the world.

The *Tate Gallery* contains a collection of British paintings as well as modern art. It's especially famous for its collection of paintings by Turner.

Westminster Abbey is the church next to the Houses of Parliament where the kings and queens of the United Kingdom are crowned.

Portobello Road is a market for antiques and second-hand clothes in Notting Hill.

Answers

Paragraph 1: Sightseeing
Paragraph 2: Museums and galleries
Paragraph 3: Shopping
Paragraph 4: Theatre
Paragraph 5: Music
Paragraph 6: Restaurants

When students have done this exercise they should practise further reading for general sense by completing the information sheet.

Answers

9 Practise the language used to describe likes and dislikes by asking students to prepare an information sheet for their own towns. If they have brought suitable brochures about these towns, they can use them to give them some extra ideas. If students come from different towns, they should write about a town which they know well.

10 Use the role cards to role play a dialogue between a person who knows a lot about a town and someone who knows nothing at all. As students perform their role plays, you should go round and listen, noting down any mistakes you hear. When everyone has finished, you can draw attention to the various mistakes without mentioning the names of the people who made them. Then ask students to change partners and roles, and to perform the role play again.

11 Present the structure *Can she . . . ? Yes, she can/ No, she can't.* by playing the recording and asking students to complete the chart.

Answers

Can Diana . . .	✓ = YES ✗ = NO
sing?	✗
type?	✓
play the guitar?	✗
swim?	✓
drive?	✓
play the piano?	✓
speak French?	✓
speak Japanese?	✗

12 Practise the structures in 11 by asking students what Diana can do and eliciting replies. Then ask them to practise the question and short answer form in pairs. Go round and listen to each pair,

What to do	Where to go
Sightseeing	Big Ben, Houses of Parliament, Tower of London, St Paul's Cathedral
Museums and Galleries	British Museum, National Gallery, Tate Gallery
Shopping	Oxford St, Knightsbridge, Covent Garden, Portobello Road
Theatre	National Theatre
Music	Royal Albert Hall, Royal Festival Hall, Ronnie Scott's
Restaurants	Soho, Charlotte St

correcting them if necessary. Pay special attention to pronunciation of *can*/kæn/and *can't*/ka:nt/.

13 Practise *Can you . . . ? Yes, I can/No, I can't.* by asking students to choose one activity each and to question the other students for a class survey. Then ask each student to tell the class how many people can swim/drive/type, etc., each student giving a sentence in turn. Insist on the weak form /kən/ in sentences like *Five people can swim.*

WB 4.5, 4.6, 4.7, 4.8

14 Give further practice in listening by asking students to complete the interview forms and then to decide which of the applicants is the right person for the job.

Tapescript

DIANA:	Ah, Miss Susan Hayne, isn't it. How do you do? Please sit down.
SUSAN:	How do you do? Thank you.
DIANA:	Now tell me, what do you do?
SUSAN:	I'm a secretary for a computer company in Croydon.
DIANA:	So you can use a computer – and you can type?
SUSAN:	Yes, I can.
DIANA:	What about foreign languages?
SUSAN:	Um, I can speak Spanish.
DIANA:	Spanish – can you speak French?
SUSAN:	Not really – no.
DIANA:	Not to worry – oh, can you drive?
SUSAN:	Yes, I can.
DIANA:	Good . . . and what are your interests?
SUSAN:	Well, I like cooking and sport . . . and music and films.
DIANA:	Cooking . . . sport . . . music . . . films . . . and why do you . . .
DIANA:	Could you spell your name, Mr Morton?
MICHAEL:	Er, M-O-R-T-O-N. My first name is Michael.
DIANA:	And you're a teacher, I see.
MICHAEL:	Yes, that's right. But I like travelling, so I'm looking for a new job.
DIANA:	I see. Can you use a computer?
MICHAEL:	Yes, I can.
DIANA:	And can you type?
MICHAEL:	Well, no – I can't type. But I can speak a lot of foreign languages – French, Spanish, Italian and Japanese.
DIANA:	Languages . . . French . . . Spanish . . . Italian . . . and Japanese . . .
MICHAEL:	And I can drive.
DIANA:	Oh, that's good. And what about your interests, apart from travelling?

MICHAEL:	I like swimming – and tennis and football.
DIANA:	Miss Jean Wallace?
JEAN:	Yes. You spell it I-S at the end, not A-C-E.
DIANA:	Oh, thank you. My mistake. So that's W-A-double L-I-S?
JEAN:	That's right.
DIANA:	Well now, I see that you can type and use a computer. What do you do?
JEAN:	Er, I haven't got a job. I'm unemployed.
DIANA:	Can you drive?
JEAN:	Yes, I can.
DIANA:	Good – and can you speak any languages?
JEAN:	Yes – German and French.
DIANA:	Excellent – now you say that you like the cinema and the theatre . . .
JEAN:	Yes, and I like travelling – and meeting people.

Answers

SURNAME *HAYNE* FIRST NAME *Susan*
OCCUPATION *Secretary*
SKILLS *Can – use a computer*
– type
– drive
LANGUAGES *Spanish*

INTERESTS
Cooking, sport, music, films

SURNAME *MORTON* FIRST NAME *Michael*
OCCUPATION *Teacher*
SKILLS *Can – use a computer*
– drive
LANGUAGES *French, Spanish, Italian, Japanese*

INTERESTS
Travelling, swimming, tennis, football

SURNAME *WALLIS* FIRST NAME *Jean*
OCCUPATION *—*
SKILLS *Can – type*
– use a computer
– drive
LANGUAGES *German, French*

INTERESTS *Travelling, cinema, theatre, meeting people*

Jean Wallis is the right person for the job.

LEARNING SKILLS

By now, your students will have noted down a number of content words. Explain that they need to revise everything they learn at regular intervals. Ask them to look back over the first four units and to note down six words which they think are most useful to them. Then ask them to check that they understand the meaning, and to think of a way of learning these meanings. For example, the sound of the word may conjure up some image or perhaps a colour or an emotion in their minds. Ask them to try and link the word and its meaning to some kind of code. They should then say what each word makes them think of. Note down two or three examples from each student and test them on these words during the next lesson. See if they can remember the meaning using the code. Then ask them if they think this way of learning vocabulary might be useful.

PRONUNCIATION TAPESCRIPT

4.1 Listen and repeat.

/s/	/z/
likes	sings
speaks	lives
types	loves
shops	theatres
flats	girls
motorbikes	chairs

4.2 Listen and repeat.

students	sinks
plays	maps
houses	tables

4.3 Listen and repeat.

a) Is he married?

b) Does she live in a flat?

c) Can you swim?

d) Are they brothers?

e) Has he got a garden?

f) Do you like cooking?

4.4 Listen and repeat.

a) Can she type?

b) Does he like sightseeing?

c) Do they live in Italy?

d) Are you married?

e) Is there a sitting room?

f) Have they got any children?

STRUCTURE REVIEW TAPESCRIPT

4.1 Say what you like doing, like this:

Do you like reading?
Yes, I do. or *No, I don't.*

Now you.

a) Do you like reading?
....
b) Do you like football?
....
c) Do you like dancing?
....
d) Do you like tennis?
....
e) Do you like swimming?
....
f) Do you like learning English?
....

4.2 Ask if people like doing things, like this:

Ask if Bob likes dancing?
Does Bob like dancing?

Now you.

a) Ask if Bob likes dancing.
Does Bob like dancing?
b) Ask if Diana likes reading.
Does Diana like reading?
c) Ask if Richard and Carla like driving.
Do Richard and Carla like driving?
d) Ask if Koji likes eating in restaurants.
Does Koji like eating in restaurants?
e) Ask if Nancy likes going to the theatre.
Does Nancy like going to the theatre?
f) Ask if Nina and Joe like swimming.
Do Nina and Joe like swimming?

4.3 Agree with these people, like this:

I like reading.
So do I.

I don't like rock music.
Nor do I.

Now you.

a) I like reading.
So do I.
b) I don't like rock music.
Nor do I.
c) I love dancing.
So do I.
d) I like football.
So do I.

e) I don't like tennis.
   Nor do I.
f) I love hamburgers.
   So do I.

4.4 Disagree with these people, like this:

I like sightseeing.
Do you? I don't.

I don't like visiting museums.
Don't you? I do.

Now you.

a) I like sightseeing.
   Do you? I don't.
b) I don't like visiting museums.
   Don't you? I do.
c) I love going to the theatre.
   Do you? I don't.
d) I don't like eating in restaurants.
   Don't you? I do.
e) I love swimming.
   Do you? I don't.

4.5 Look at the chart, and say what these people can do, like this:

Can Bob swim?
Yes, he can.

Can he type?
No, he can't.

Now you.

a) Can Bob swim?
   Yes, he can.
   Can he type?
   No, he can't.
b) Can Nancy cook?
   No, she can't.
   Can she dance?
   Yes, she can.

c) Can Diana cook?
   Yes, she can.
   Can she sing?
   No, she can't.
d) Can Koji dance?
   No, he can't.
   Can he type?
   Yes, he can.

4.6 Now talk about these people, like this:

Bob
Bob can swim, but he can't type.

Now you.

a) Bob
   Bob can swim, but he can't type.
b) Nancy
   Nancy can dance, but she can't cook.
c) Diana
   Diana can cook, but she can't sing.
d) Koji
   Koji can type, but he can't dance.

4.7 Now say if you can do the same things, like this:

Can you swim?
Yes, I can. or No, I can't.

Now you.

a) Can you swim?
   ....
b) Can you dance?
   ....
c) Can you type?
   ....
d) Can you cook?
   ....
e) Can you sing?
   ....

5 | Timing it right

UNIT SUMMARY

Functions

Saying what people do every day

Asking and saying what time things happen

Asking and saying what people are doing now

Structures

Present simple tense

I We They	get up have breakfast go to bed	
He She	gets up has breakfast goes to bed	at (*time*).

What time When	do	you they	got up? have breakfast? start work? go to bed?
	does	he she	

What time When	is the programme on?

At half past ten. From 10.30 to 11.30.

What's on TV?

There's (*name of programme*) at (*time*).

What	are	you they	doing?
	is	he she	

I'm He's She's We're They're	getting up. having breakfast. going to bed.

25

Functions	Structures

Functions

Structures

Are	you they	getting up? having breakfast? going to bed?
Is	he she	

Asking and saying what people would like to do

What would	you they he she	like to do?

What	do	you they	want to do?
	does	he she	

I'd We'd They'd He'd She'd	like to	go swimming. watch TV.

I We They	want to	go swimming. watch TV.
He She	wants to	

Inviting

Would you like to (*do something*)?

Accepting and refusing invitations

Yes, I'd love to.

I'm sorry, I can't. I'm busy.

Asking and saying what the time is

What's the time?

It's (*time*).

Making suggestions

Why don't we . . .?

Accepting and refusing suggestions

Good idea! Let's do that.

No, I don't want to.
No, I'm afraid I don't like . . .

Topics

Numbers, routine activities, time-telling, leisure activities

Lexical items

- bring home   come home   cook dinner   do the washing up   finish   get up   go to bed   go running
  go shopping   go to sleep   have a bath   have breakfast/lunch   phone (v)   start   take   work
- at night   in the afternoon   in the evening   in the morning
- cinema   disco   school
- *Numbers* 0–50   o'clock   a quarter (past/to)   at (*time*)   on (What's on?)

TEACHING GUIDE

This unit presents, among other structures, the present simple for habitual actions, and the present continuous in its present rather than future sense.

WARM-UP

Suggested warm-up activity: 6.

1 Present *What time is it?/What's the time?* and *It's (time).* by asking students to look at the map in the book and to say what time it is in the different places when it's 12 o'clock GMT (Greenwich Mean Time) in London. Present the hours first of all; students learnt numbers 1 to 12 in Unit 3. Get them to practise the question form in pairs. Ask them to say what time it is in their countries when it's midday Greenwich Mean Time.

2 Present time-telling by asking students to match the times with the clocks, and then to ask and say what time it is. Students should be able to deduce the meanings of *a quarter to, half past, twenty,* and *twenty-five,* but be prepared to help them if they have problems. Ask and say what time it is now; students need constant practice in time-telling, so ask them what the time is every so often. Explain, if necessary, that the twenty-four hour clock is used in English-speaking countries, but mostly for timetables, etc.

WB 5.2

3 Present the use of the present simple for habitual actions by asking students to put the pictures in order according to the clock times. Ask students to say what they do at these times of day. Ask them if there are any other habitual actions that they perform at regular times of the day.

Answer   D F E C A B

Present *What time does he/she . . .? When does he/she . . .?* and *At (time)* by asking students to ask and answer questions about Carla's day. Write the

cue sentence on the board and ask students to listen and complete the stress and intonation pattern.

What time When	does she have breakfast?

4 Practise *What time does she   ?* by asking students to guess when Carla is likely to do the activities described in the *Student's Book.* Explain any items of vocabulary if necessary. Ask students to say when they do the actions mentioned in this exercise. Play the recording and ask students to check; they should then complete the chart for Carla. Check their pronunciation of the third person singular of different verbs, e.g. gets /s/, comes /z/, watches /iz/.

Tapescript

CARLA: Well . . . on a typical day, we get up at half past seven. We have breakfast at a quarter past eight, and Richard takes the children to school at twenty to nine. Then I start work . . . at a quarter to ten. At half past twelve, I go running for half an hour. After that, I have lunch, at about one o'clock. Then I finish my work, and phone the newspaper office at about half past two. At three o'clock I go shopping to buy food for dinner, and I collect the children from school at a quarter to four. I start cooking dinner when Richard comes home, at about half past six, and we all have dinner together at half past seven. The children go to bed after dinner . . . . I do the washing up, and then I sit down with a cup of coffee to watch the news on TV at half past nine. I have a bath at eleven, and I go to bed at half past eleven . . . . I like reading in bed, but I usually go to sleep by midnight.

	CARLA'S DAY
7.30	We get up.
8.15	We have breakfast.
8.40	R. takes children to school.
9.45	I start work.
12.30	I go running.
1.00	I have lunch.
2.30	I phone the office.
3.00	I go shopping.
3.45	I collect the children from school.
6.30	I cook dinner.
7.30	We have dinner.
9.30	I watch TV.
11.00	I have a bath.
11.30	I go to bed.
12.00	I go to sleep.

WB 5.3

5 Present *What time/When do you . . .?* and practise *At (time).* by asking students questions about their habitual actions. Get them to practise the question form in pairs. Practise writing by asking them to write a few sentences about their day. Go round and correct their versions individually.

WB 5.4

6 Present the present continuous by telling the students that it is a quarter past eight and asking them to imagine what Carla is doing *now*. Make sure they understand that the present continuous is used to describe actions which are happening at the moment. Practise the question form by getting the students to ask and say what Carla is doing, in pairs. Use the other pictures to give further practice.

7 Practise the present continuous and present *I think . . ..* by asking students to say what people are doing at the moment in other parts of the world. Use the map on page 18 to remind you what time it is in different parts of the world.

8 Present *Are you + —ing?* and *Yes, I am. No, I'm not.* by asking a student to think of an action and to mime it. You should then guess what he/she's

doing by asking at least four or five questions. He/she can only answer *Yes* or *No.* Then ask another student to mime something, and get the other students to ask what he/she's doing. Write the example sentences on the board and mark in the intonation.

> Are you playing the piano? No, I'm not.
>
> Are you typing? Yes, I am.

Then ask students to work in pairs and to mime different actions. You may want to suggest that they mime some of the actions in 4.

WB 5.5

9 Present the alternative way of telling the time (seven twenty-five, seven thirty, etc.) by playing the recording and then asking the students to ask and answer questions about the programmes. They can refer to the number chart where necessary.

Tapescript

ANNOUNCER: And now let's look at the line-up of programmes for this Saturday evening on English ATV.

In a few moments, we have *Police Report* at seven twenty-five, followed by *Newsline* at seven thirty. Then at eight o'clock there's *News at Eight* – with a round-up of the world news for this week. At eight thirty we bring you a programme on *Entertainment This Week,* followed by the *News in Brief* at nine thirty.

Then there's another exciting assignment for Bodie and Doyle in *The Professionals* at nine thirty-five. At ten thirty-five, there's an hour with *Sky Trax* cable TV, followed by the *Late News* at eleven thirty-five. Our final programme for the evening is our *Saturday Night Feature* film which starts at eleven forty-five. Our film tonight is *Forget Me Not,* starring Benjamino Gigli, Joan Gardner and Ivan Brandt.

And now it's time for *Police Report.*

10 Practise asking and saying what the time is by asking the students to work in pairs and to follow the instructions in the *Student's Book.* This exercise uses the clocks in 2, but requires students to use the alternative time-telling system. If necessary, draw some clock faces on the board and give further practice by asking students to say what the time is.

11 Practise listening for specific information by playing the tape and asking students to note down the programmes that Richard and Carla want to watch. Explain that they don't need to understand every word of the conversation; they should simply listen out for the information that is stressed.

Tapescript

CARLA:	Richard – have you got a paper? Let's see what's on TV this afternoon.
RICHARD:	Hmm – oh there's *Buster Keaton Comedy*. I'd like to watch that.
CARLA:	And there's *Shakespeare Theatre* – I'd like to watch that!
RICHARD:	But they start at the same time . . . the children like Buster Keaton too . . .
CARLA:	Oh, all right, you can watch Buster Keaton. What about this evening? What's on later?
RICHARD:	Well, there's *Police Report* . . . There's the news . . .
CARLA:	Oh! There's *Vampire* at 9.35! I'd like to see that!
RICHARD:	Oh, no. I don't like horror films. I want to watch *The Professionals* . . .
CARLA:	Look, you can watch Buster Keaton, and I can watch *Vampire*. . .. And then I'd like to watch the *Japanese Movie Selection* at 11.45 . . .
RICHARD:	But I want to watch the other film – *Forget Me Not!*
CARLA:	Oh, have it your own way. I'll go to bed early . . . with a good book!

Present *in the morning, in the afternoon, in the evening, at night* by asking students when the programmes that Richard and Carla want to see are on. Present *What does he/she want to see?/What would he/she like to see?* by checking the answers to the listening comprehension passage. Explain that *want to* and *would like to* mean more or less the same thing in this context.

Answers

	NAME OF PROGRAMME	FROM	TO
Carla	Shakespeare Theatre	3	6
	Vampire	9.35	11.30
	Japanese Movie Selection	11.45	1.30
Richard	Buster Keaton Comedy	3	5.15
	The Professionals	9.35	10.35
	Forget Me Not	11.45	1.10

Practise *What does he/she want to . . .? What would he/she like to . . .?* by asking students to work in pairs and to ask and answer questions about the programmes that Carla and Richard want to see.

WB 5.1

12 Practise *What time/When does . . . start/finish?* and practise *At (time)* by getting students to ask and answer questions about the programme times. Make sure that everyone is using the question form correctly.

13 Practise asking and answering questions about what's on television and when the programmes start/finish by bringing copies of your local TV guide to class and by getting students to use them in a conversation about the day's TV. It doesn't matter if the programme guide is not in English. Teach *There's (name of programme) at (time).* as a set phrase. When they have finished, students should change partners.

14 Revise talking about likes and dislikes by asking students to ask each other about their interests and to complete the chart with five different names. Check that they understand the difference between *like doing* (general feeling) and *would like to do* (specific wish meaning *want to do*).

15 Present *Would you like to . . .? I'm sorry, I can't. I'm busy./Yes, I'd love to!* by inviting students to go out to one of the places mentioned in the chart in 14. Get them to work in pairs and to invite each other out. Make sure they understand that *I'm sorry, I can't. I'm busy.* is a polite way of refusing an invitation.

16 Present *Why don't we . . .? Good idea! Let's do that! No, I don't want to . . ..* and *No, I'm afraid I don't like . . ..* by getting students to plan an evening out with one of the people chosen in 15. Use the local entertainments guide to help them make suggestions on where to go.

WB 5.6

LEARNING SKILLS

Write the following list of words on the board: *doctor, flat, family, scrump, unemployed, tangle, town, room, student, kitchen, famished, bath.* Give them about thirty seconds to learn the list, and then wipe it off the board.

Ask students to think of as many international words to do with leisure activities as possible. Remind them of words like *television, radio, football, rugby,* etc.

Now ask students to try and remember the list of words they learnt before the last activity. How many can they remember?

Which words are easier to remember? If students couldn't remember words such as *scrump, tangle, famished,* explain that it is always easier to recall words which are meaningful and which can be fitted into some kind of mental framework than words which, at least for the time being, don't mean anything. Point out that they will come across a great deal of vocabulary during the course, but they will not always be expected to learn every word. The words that they do learn should be meaningful and belong to some kind of mental framework.

PRONUNCIATION TAPESCRIPT

5.1 Listen and repeat.

/æ/	/e/
man	men
can	Ken
bad	bed
tan	ten

Now listen and tick the words you hear.

men   Ken   bad   tan

5.2 Listen and write the words in the correct column.

any twelve map flat breakfast tennis married actor

Answers

/æ/	/e/
map	any
flat	twelve
married	breakfast
actor	tennis

5.3 Listen and repeat.

a) What's the time?

b) What time do you get up?

c) What's she doing?

d) What's on at the cinema?

e) What would you like to watch?

f) When do you want to leave?

STRUCTURE REVIEW TAPESCRIPT

5.1 Look at the chart. Say what time Bob and Nancy do things, like this:

What time does Bob get up?
He gets up at half past seven.

Now you.

a) What time does Bob get up?
He gets up at half past seven.
What time does Nancy get up?
She gets up at a quarter past seven.

b) What time does Bob have breakfast?
He has breakfast at half past eight.
What time does Nancy have breakfast?
She has breakfast at half past seven.

c) What time does Bob start work?
He starts work at half past nine.
What time does Nancy start work?
She starts work at a quarter to nine.

d) What time does Bob have dinner?
He has dinner at eight o'clock.
What time does Nancy have dinner?
She has dinner at half past seven.

e) What time does Bob go to bed?
He goes to bed at eleven o'clock.
What time does Nancy go to bed?
She goes to bed at half past ten.

5.2 Ask what time people do things, like this:

Ask when Koji gets up.
When does Koji get up?

Now you.

a) Ask when Koji gets up.
When does Koji get up?

b) Ask when Richard and Carla have breakfast.
When do Richard and Carla have breakfast?

c) Ask when Koji starts work.
When does Koji start work?

d) Ask when Diana has lunch.
When does Diana have lunch?

e) Ask when Nina and Joe have dinner.
When do Nina and Joe have dinner?

f) Ask when Diana goes to bed.
When does Diana go to bed?

5.3 Say what these people are doing, like this:

What's Bob doing?
He's cooking breakfast.

Now you.

a) What's Bob doing?
He's cooking breakfast.

b) What's Diana doing?
She's playing the piano.

c) What's Koji doing?
He's going for a walk.

d) What are Richard and Carla doing?
They're visiting a museum.

e) What's Nancy doing?
She's running.

5.4 Ask what these people are doing, like this:

Ask if Bob is getting up.
Is Bob getting up?

Now you.

a) Ask if Bob is getting up.
Is Bob getting up?

b) Ask if Nancy is working.
Is Nancy working?

c) Ask if Richard and Carla are visiting friends.
Are Richard and Carla visiting friends?
d) Ask if Diana is playing tennis.
Is Diana playing tennis?
e) Ask if Koji is phoning his wife.
Is Koji phoning his wife?

5.5 Say what these people would like to do, like this:

What does Ben want to do?
He wants to go swimming.

What would Emma like to do?
She'd like to visit a museum.

Now you.

a) What does Ben want to do?
He wants to go swimming.
b) What would Emma like to do?
She'd like to visit a museum.
c) What does Laura want to do?
She wants to play tennis.
d) What would Tom like to do?
He'd like to watch TV.
e) What would Pat and Karen like to do?
They'd like to go for a walk.
f) What does David want to do?
He wants to write a letter.

5.6 Accept or refuse invitations, like this:

Would you like to come to the theatre with me?
Yes, I'd love to.

Would you like to have lunch tomorrow?
I'm sorry, I can't. I'm busy.

Now you.

a) Would you like to come to the theatre with me?
Yes, I'd love to.
b) Would you like to have lunch tomorrow?
I'm sorry, I can't. I'm busy.
c) Would you like to go to a football match?
Yes, I'd love to.
d) Would you like to have dinner with me?
I'm sorry, I can't. I'm busy.
e) Would you like to go for a walk?
I'm sorry, I can't. I'm busy.
f) Would you like to go to the cinema this evening?
Yes, I'd love to.

6 Checking what you know

SUMMARY

Functions

In Units 1 to 5, students learnt how to:

Greet people
Introduce themselves and others
Talk about where they're from
Talk about what they do
Talk about where they live
Ask and say how to spell words
Count up to 50
Talk about what they like and like doing
Talk about what they can do

Ask and say what the time is
Talk about habitual actions in the present
Talk about what they are doing at the moment
Talk about what they would like to do
Invite people to do things
Accept and refuse invitations
Make suggestions
Accept and refuse suggestions

Topics

The topics covered have been:

Names of countries, towns, forms of address, family, jobs, nationalities, rooms of the house, types of housing, furniture, numbers, the alphabet, sport, leisure activities, town facilities, languages, routine activities, time-telling.

TEACHING GUIDE

WARM-UP

Suggested warm-up activities: 1, 2 (using objects), 3 or 6.

WB

Students should be able to do the *Workbook* exercises at any stage of this revision unit.

WB 6.1

Note:
Make sure that students understand what capital letters are. Remind students that sentences begin with capital letters, and so do names of people, towns, countries, nationalities and languages (in English). Check that students understand that *he's* is the *contraction* of *he is*.

WB 6.2

Note:
Check that students understand that e.g. *book* is singular (one) and *books* is plural (more than one).

1   Practise reading for general sense by asking students to read the newspaper article about Bob and to put the headings with the right paragraphs.

When they have finished, ask students to check their answers in pairs.

Answers

LIKES
I like meeting people, and I love talking to children. . . .

A TYPICAL DAY
I get up at 7.30 and I go running. . . .

DISLIKES
I don't like hamburgers; . . .

FAMILY
My parents live in Kingston, Jamaica. . . .

HOME
I live in a house in North Kensington, London, . . .

2   Revise the question forms of the present simple using the auxiliary *do* by getting students to work in pairs and to ask and answer questions about Bob. Make sure that the stress and intonation

pattern of the question form is being used correctly. Check that everyone is using suitable prepositions in their replies to the questions: *in*, *at*; and structures *He's a. . . .* , *He's got. . . .* , *He likes/doesn't like. . . .*

3 Revise the second person question form and replies by asking students to write the questions which the journalist of the newspaper article would actually ask Bob during the interview.

Answers

Where do you live?
What does your mother/father do?
How many brothers and sisters have you got?
What time/When do you get up/go to work, etc.?
What do you like doing?
What do you dislike (doing)?
What kind of sport/music, etc. do you like?

Students should work in pairs and interview each other using these or similar questions. When they have finished they should use their notes to write a profile of their partner, using the headings in the article. Go round and check their versions individually and then draw the class's attention to any common mistakes.

4 Practise reading for specific information by asking students to look at the newspaper listing for cinemas and find out where they can see the films in the chart. Teach *How do you pronounce L-O-E-W-S?* /loʊz/ and encourage students to ask about the pronunciation of other unfamiliar words.

Answers

Film	A Cinema	B Telephone	C Times
The Purple Rose of Cairo ✓	Cinema Studio 2	877 4040	2.15, 4.25, 6.40, 8.55
Pale Rider	Loews 3	877 3600	
Dangerous Moves	Paris	688 2013	
A Passage to India	Festival	757 2715	
Amadeus ✓	Lincoln Plaza 3	757 2280	1.30, 4.25, 7.20, 10.15

5 Practise listening for specific information by asking students to listen to the conversation and to tick the films that Nancy and Bob want to see. Remind students that they don't need to understand every word they hear. Bob and Nancy are consulting the movie listings in *The New Yorker*. Point out that American English uses *movie* and *movie house*, where British English uses *film* and *cinema*.

Tapescript

BOB:	Why don't we go and see a film tonight?
NANCY:	A movie? Hey, that's a good idea. What would you like to see?
BOB:	Well, there's *Pale Rider* with Clint Eastwood . . .
NANCY:	No, I don't like Clint Eastwood.
BOB:	Then there's *A Passage to India*, directed by David Lean.
NANCY:	No, I saw that last month. It's very good, but I don't want to see it again.
BOB:	All right – then there's a Woody Allen film – *The Purple Rose of Cairo*.
NANCY:	Yes, I want to see that – I like Woody Allen.
BOB:	So do I. Anything else you'd like to see?
NANCY:	I'd like to see *Amadeus* – they say the music is wonderful.
BOB:	Yes, I want to see that too.
NANCY:	And there's *Dangerous Moves* with Michel Piccoli – that's in French.
BOB:	No, I don't want to see that. Let's find out what time the Woody Allen film and *Amadeus* are showing.
NANCY:	OK, I'll just find the phone numbers of the movie houses . . .
BOB:	Fine.

Answers   See 4

6 Practise listening for specific information by asking students to complete the boxes in the chart with the programme times. Play the tape at least twice. If your students find it difficult to understand the numbers, you can give them the information in random order on the board, and ask them to put it in the right boxes.

Tapescript

This is Cinema Studio One and Two. The two movies showing today are: Theatre 1, *The Home and the World*, with separate programmes at 1.10, 3.30, 6.00 and 8.30; and Theatre 2, *The Purple Rose of Cairo*, with programmes at 2.15, 4.25, 6.40 and 8.55.

This is the Lincoln Plaza. Our programmes today are as follows: Theatre 1: *A Flash of Green*, starting at 1.10, 3.30, 6.50 and 9.10. Theatre 2 is showing Martin Bell's documentary, *Streetwise*, at 1.20, 3.35, 5.50 and 7.05. In Theatre 3 we have *Amadeus*, a movie about the life of Mozart, showing at 1.30, 4.25, 7.20 and 10.15.

Answers See 4

7 Practise listening for recognition of letters and
📼 numbers by playing the tape of three people booking cinema seats. Students should note down the letters and numbers of the seats which are booked, and the names of the people.

Tapescript and Answers

1	CLERK:	Cinema Studio, can I help you?
	CUSTOMER:	Hello, could I book seats for the Woody Allen movie tonight at five to nine?
	CLERK:	How many seats do you want?
	CUSTOMER:	Three, at the front if possible.
	CLERK:	OK – that's seats C3, C4 and C5. What's your name please?
	CUSTOMER:	Barnes – B-A-R-N-E-S.
	CLERK:	Thank you.
2	CLERK:	Cinema Studio, can I help you?
	CUSTOMER:	Hello, I'd like to book ten seats for *The Purple Rose of Cairo* tonight at five to nine?
	CLERK:	Hold the line, please . . . I can give you ten seats, but not all together.
	CUSTOMER:	That's OK.
	CLERK:	That will be seats M1, M2, and M3. Then seats P16, P17 and P18 – and finally G21, 22, 23 and 24. Could I have your name, please?
	CUSTOMER:	Sanders – S-A-N-D-E-R-S.
	CLERK:	Thank you.
3	CLERK:	Cinema Studio – can I help you?
	BOB:	Hello, I'd like to book two seats for the Woody Allen film this evening.
	CLERK:	For six forty or eight fifty-five?
	BOB:	Eight fifty-five.
	CLERK:	That's seats F7 and F8. Could I have your name please?
	BOB:	Armstrong – A-R-M-S-T-R-O-N-G.
	CLERK:	Thank you.

8 Revise various vocabulary items by asking students to put the words under suitable headings. When they have finished, they should work in pairs and check, then find two more words to put in each column.

Answers See table on page 35

9 Present the vocabulary items by asking students to match the words with the pictures. They can use a dictionary if they like. Then they should ask and say what other words mean, using *What's this in English?* Practise the structure by getting students to ask you what certain items in and around the classroom are.

10 Revise the present continuous by asking students to read the sentences on the left and to match them with the actions on the right.

Answers

1 Bob's cooking.
2 Diana's playing the piano.
3 Richard and Carla are having dinner.
4 Koji's getting up.
5 Nancy's having a shower.

11 This activity revises *can/can't* and other structures and vocabulary items from Units 1 to 6. Ask students to write a few sentences saying what they have in common with their partners.

12 This activity revises numbers, letters and the vocabulary for rooms of the house and furniture. Students decide where to position the rooms and furniture on their ground plans, and then have to guess where other students have placed theirs. Make sure pairs take it in turns to call out letters and numbers.

LEARNING SKILLS

Your students will have noted down a number of content and structure words while working on the first six units of the book. Explain that this may be a suitable moment to organise these words into some kind of system which will allow them to revise what they have learnt more easily. The words can be organised by topic such as *jobs, houses,* by function such as *talking about likes and dislikes, saying what you can or can't do,* or by situation such as *in class, at a job interview.*

  Ask students to look back over their notes and begin to organise them under headings. You may help them decide on suitable headings by looking at the topics and functions mentioned in the Unit Summaries of each unit in the *Teacher's Book.*

  Now ask them to look back at Units 1 to 5 and to note down four words from each unit which they think are likely to be most useful to them. Encourage students to begin thinking about their personal needs in learning English.

actor	son	swimming	kitchen	teacher	Italian
toilet	father	Italy	bathroom	Australian	tennis
British	America	secretary	daughter	football	mother
bedroom	Japan	engineer	running	Japanese	Australia

FAMILY	NATIONALITIES	COUNTRIES	JOBS	ROOMS	SPORTS
Son	British	America	secretary	toilet	Swimming
father	Australian	Japan	actor	bedroom	running
daughter	Japanese	Italy	engineer	Kitchen	Football
mother	Italian	Australia	teacher	bathroom	tennis

7 Going to town

UNIT SUMMARY

Functions	Structures

Functions

Structures

Asking and saying where places are

Where's the	bank? post office? chemist's?

It's	in the High Street. opposite the supermarket. next to the bookshop.

Saying what people need/want

I We They	need want	some stamps. an airletter.
He She	needs wants	

Asking and saying where people can get things

Where can	I we they he she	get	some stamps? an airletter?

At a post office.

There's a post office near here.

Asking and saying what things people have got

I We They	've	got some	eggs. cheese.
He She	's		

I We They	haven't got	any	eggs. cheese.
He She	hasn't got		

Functions

Asking and saying how much things cost

Structures

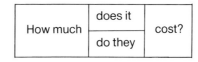

| How much | does it | cost? |
| | do they | |

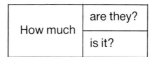

| How much | are they? |
| | is it? |

Asking and saying how much or how many

| How much butter | do | I
we
they | buy? |
| How many eggs | does | he
she | |

Topics

Shops and services, shopping items, food, clothes, colours

Lexical items

- bank   bookshop   chemist's   newsagent's   post office   supermarket
- airletter   aspirin   dictionary   map   magazine   money   newspaper   razor   traveller's cheques toothbrush
- apple   biscuit   bread   butter   coffee   cheese   egg   fruit   meat   milk   orange orange juice   steak   sugar   tea   tomato   vegetable   water
- dozen   half   kilo   pence   pound
- Numbers 60–100
- boot   jacket   pullover   shirt   shoe   skirt   sock   suit   tie   tights   trousers   T-shirt   wear
- colour   black   blue   green   red   white   yellow

TEACHING GUIDE

This unit presents the language used in shopping situations.

WARM-UP

Suggested warm-up activity: 3.

1   Present names of shops by asking students to listen to the tape and to match the names of the shops with the pictures. Before you play the tape, explain the meaning of *opposite* and *next to* by showing the position of the theatre and the restaurant in relation to the cinema.

Tapescript

DIANA: Come in – oh, good morning, Mr Yamashita. How are you?
KOJI: I'm very well, thank you. How are you?
DIANA: I'm fine, thanks.

KOJI: Miss Pye, can you help me? I want to change some money – where's the bank?
DIANA: Oh, it's very near the office. It's just off the High Street, in Turnbull Road . . . next to the Chinese restaurant.
KOJI: Oh, yes, I know. And I want to get some aspirin.
DIANA: You'll get those at the chemist's in the High Street. It's opposite the Chinese restaurant . . . next to the theatre.
KOJI: Oh, fine – and what about some stamps? I want to post some letters.
DIANA: You can get stamps at the post office – it's opposite the bank in Turnbull Road. Oh – while you're there, can you get me a newspaper? The newsagent's is on the corner, next to the post office.
KOJI: Yes, of course. That reminds me – where can I get a map of Britain?
DIANA: Well, the best place for that is the

37

bookshop – next to the newsagent's in the
High Street.

KOJI: And is there a supermarket near here?

DIANA: Oh, yes – there's a big supermarket in the
High Street. It's opposite the bookshop.

KOJI: Oh, that's wonderful. Everything's very
close. . . .

Answers

1 chemist's   2 supermarket   3 newsagent's
4 bookshop   5 bank   6 post office

Present *Excuse me, where's the post office? It's
in Turnbull Road, opposite/next to . . . .* by
role playing the exchange with two or three
students. Then ask students to practise in pairs.
Make sure they are all using the correct stress and
intonation pattern.

2   Present shopping items by asking students to say
where you can get the items listed in the *Student's
Book.* You can illustrate the words with actual
objects or pictures. Alternatively, ask students to
work in pairs and look up new words in the
dictionary. Then present the model sentence
Where can I get some/a . . .? by individual and
chorus drilling. Then ask students to practise the
exchanges in pairs. Get them to go round the room
asking and saying where you can get things. Make
sure they understand that *a/an* is used for single
countable nouns, *some* for uncountable or plural
countable nouns. Insist on the weak form /səm/.

Present *I need/I want . . .* in a similar way.
Explain that you can reply to a statement such as *I
want an airletter.* with another statement such as
There's a post office near here. Remind students
that they learnt *There's . . . .* in Unit 5.

3   Practise asking and saying where places are, where
you can get things and what people need or want
by asking students to act out the roles presented in
the *Student's Book.* When they have completed
one role play, they should change partners and
roles.

WB 7.1

4   Present vocabulary items for food by asking
students to look at the first picture in their books
and to memorise the names of the items. After two
minutes tell them to cover the first picture and
then look at the second; they should try and name
the items illustrated. When they have finished
they should check with another student.

Answers

1 orange juice   2 cheese   3 biscuits   4 fruit
5 bread   6 water   7 butter   8 vegetables   9 eggs
10 meat.

5   Practise listening for specific information and
present *They've got some. . . . They haven't got
any. . . .* by asking students to listen to the tape.
They should put a tick by the items Diana and
Fiona need for the weekend, and a cross by those
they don't need.

Tapescript

FIONA: What do you want from the supermarket?
I'll make a shopping list.

DIANA: Well, let me see – we haven't got any
eggs . . .

FIONA: So we need some eggs . . .

DIANA: . . . and some butter . . .

FIONA: . . . butter . . . what about milk?

DIANA: No, there's some milk in the fridge, and
we've got some cheese . . .

FIONA: So we don't need any cheese. Have we got
any bread?

DIANA: No, we need some bread. And can you get
some cheese biscuits too?

FIONA: Bread, and cheese biscuits. OK. Anything
else?

DIANA: Oh, we haven't got any coffee. And there
isn't any sugar.

FIONA: So, coffee . . . sugar . . . tea?

DIANA: No, there's lots of tea – I never drink it.

FIONA: All right, here's the list . . . eggs, butter,
bread . . .

DIANA: Wait a minute, there's some meat in the
fridge, but we haven't got any vegetables
to eat with it. And I want some fruit . . .

FIONA: OK, so this is what we need . . . eggs,
butter, bread, biscuits, coffee, sugar
vegetables, and fruit – is that all?

DIANA: Is that *all*? It's too much.

FIONA: Too much? What do you mean?

DIANA: You can't carry all that – let's go shopping
together!

Answers

SHOPPING LIST

✓ COFFEE   ✓ BREAD

✗ TEA   ✓ BISCUITS

✓ SUGAR   ✓ FRUIT

✗ MILK   ✓ VEGETABLES

✓ EGGS   ✗ MEAT

✓ BUTTER

✗ CHEESE

Check their answers by giving the model sentences *They've got some . . . . They haven't got any . . . .* for two or three items, then elicit similar sentences about the other items. Explain that *some* is used for affirmative statements about uncountable nouns and plural countable nouns, *any* is used for negative statements about uncountable and plural countable nouns. Ask students to practise the structures in pairs.

Practise *They need some. . . . They don't need any. . . .* using the same shopping list.

WB 7.2

6 Present numbers *60, 70, 80, 90, and 100* and the words *pence, pound, a dozen.* Practise reading for specific information by asking students to read the newspaper report and to ask each other about prices of food. Present the model sentence *How much is . . .? How much does . . . cost?* for two or three items; then present *How much are . . .? How much do . . . cost?* Elicit a suitable reply and present *kilo* and *pence.* Then ask students to practise the structures in pairs, changing partners every two or three questions. They will want to look up some of the words in a dictionary; it may be better to suggest that they choose three words to look up and then ask other students for the meanings of any other unfamiliar words.

WB 7.3

7 Practise listening for specific information by playing the recording and asking students to write down how much/many Diana and Fiona buy of each item.

Tapescript

FIONA:	Now, let's have a look at the list – butter . . . eggs – ah, here's the butter. How much do we need, Di?
DIANA:	Oh, half a kilo, I think. And the eggs are over here – how many do we want? Twelve?
FIONA:	Yes, let's get a dozen, of size three. OK, now bread . . .
DIANA:	Ah, we want some fruit and vegetables . . . six oranges . . . and a kilo of apples. Do you like tomatoes?
FIONA:	Oh, yes, but aren't they expensive at the moment?
DIANA:	Let's see . . . no, that's cheap. We'll have half a kilo of tomatoes . . . and a cucumber.
FIONA:	What about some new potatoes?
DIANA:	Ah, yes . . . we'll take two kilos. Right – what else do we need?
FIONA:	Em . . . bread, biscuits, coffee, and sugar. Oh, here's the coffee.

DIANA:	Uh huh – half a kilo of coffee and a kilo of sugar.
FIONA:	I'm looking for the bread.
DIANA:	It's over the other side, next to the biscuits – here we are. Do you like brown bread?
FIONA:	Yes, I love it.
DIANA:	OK, so we'll get a large loaf – and all we want now is a packet of biscuits.
FIONA:	These are only eighteen pence.
DIANA:	Then let's get two packets – that's the lot!

Answers

butter:	half a kilo
eggs:	twelve/a dozen
fruit:	six oranges, kilo of apples
vegetables:	half a kilo of tomatoes, a cucumber, two kilos of new potatoes
coffee:	half a kilo
sugar:	kilo
bread:	one large loaf
biscuits:	two packets

It may be necessary to pre-teach the following items: *packet, loaf, a dozen* and remind students of the meaning of *half.*

Explain also that in Britain and the USA, weights are often measured in pounds and ounces (1 kilo = 2.2 pounds approximately).

Then get students to practise using the structures by getting them to ask and say what Fiona and Diana buy and how much/many.

WB 7.4

8 Practise reading for specific information and using numbers/weights by asking students to work out the total cost of Diana and Fiona's shopping trip.

Answers

½ kilo butter @ 96p/half kilo	=	96p
12 eggs @ 70p/dozen	=	70p
6 oranges @ 10p each	=	60p
1 kilo apples @ 65p/kilo	=	65p
½ kilo of tomatoes @ 80p/kilo	=	40p
1 cucumber @ 35p each	=	35p
2 kilos of potatoes @ 50p/kilo	=	£1.00p
½ kilo of coffee @ £4.50/kilo	=	£2.25p
1 kilo of sugar @ 68p/kilo	=	68p
1 large loaf @ 65p each	=	65p
2 packets of biscuits @ 18p each	=	36p
TOTAL	=	£8.60p

9 Present items of clothing by asking students to match the descriptions with the pictures. Pre-teach some of the items by pointing to clothes which people are wearing. Then practise *He/she's*

wearing . . . by eliciting suitable replies from the students using the pictures as a prompt. Practise *What's he/she wearing?* by getting students to practise in pairs. Present the colours by pointing to people's clothes and saying what colour they are. Practise *It's (colour)/They're (colour).* by asking students what colour other students' clothes are. Then practise *How much is it/are they? How much does it/do they cost?* by asking students to refer to the picture in their books again. Students should then practise all the structures in pairs.

Answers

1 Mark   2 Carol   3 Tessa

WB   7.5, 7.6

10 Give further practice in using the structures presented in this unit by asking students to write down descriptions of what other students are wearing, and to give their descriptions to you. You should read out the descriptions to the whole class and they should say who is being described.

WB   7.7

11 Practise listening for specific information by playing the dialogues and asking students to complete them:

Tapescript and Answers

1	ASSISTANT:	Good morning, can I help you?
	CUSTOMER:	Yes, please. I want a toothbrush.
	ASSISTANT:	Here you are. That's eighty-five pence, please.
	CUSTOMER:	Thanks very much. Goodbye.
2	ASSISTANT:	Good afternoon, can I help you?
	CUSTOMER:	Yes, please. I'd like half a kilo of apples.
	ASSISTANT:	Here you are. That's seventy pence, please.
	CUSTOMER:	Thank you. Goodbye.
3	ASSISTANT:	Good evening, can I help you?
	CUSTOMER:	Yes, please. I'm looking for a black jacket.
	ASSISTANT:	I'm sorry, we haven't got any jackets.
	CUSTOMER:	Never mind. Thank you. Goodbye.

Practise the dialogues by asking students to work in pairs and to act out the exchanges between customer and shop assistant. Then ask students to role play similar dialogues with the customer asking for other items.

LEARNING SKILLS

Write the following on the board:

WHAT TO DO WITH DIFFICULT VOCABULARY

Try to guess the meaning
Ask each other
Look in dictionary
Ask teacher
Ignore it and read on

Then ask students to decide which strategy they would adopt for dealing with difficult vocabulary. Explain that there is no right answer, but that each strategy can be useful according to the situation.

Teach *What does . . . mean?* and revise *I don't know.* Ask students to look at one of the units 1–7 and to choose two or three words which they don't understand. Get them to ask each other what the word means. They should ask the question as many times as is necessary to get a suitable answer.

PRONUNCIATION TAPESCRIPT

7.1   Listen and repeat.

/æ/	/ɑ:/
am	arm
cat	cart
pack	park
hat	heart

Now listen and tick the words you hear.

arm   cat   pack   heart

7.2   Listen and write the words in the correct column.

afternoon /ɑ:/   bank /æ/   bath /ɑ:/   can /æ/ can't /ɑ:/   garden /ɑ:/   manager /æ/ stamp /æ/

7.3   Listen and tick the numbers you hear.

forty   sixteen   nineteen   thirty   seventeen fifty   eighty

STRUCTURE REVIEW TAPESCRIPT

7.1   Say where these places are, like this:

Where's the bank?
It's opposite the post office.

Now you.

a) Where's the bank?
   It's opposite the post office.
b) Where's the bookshop?
   It's next to the newsagent's.
c) Where's the post office?
   It's in Turnbull Road.

d) Where's the theatre?
   It's next to the chemist's.
e) Where's the supermarket?
   It's opposite the bookshop.
f) Where's the chemist's?
   It's next to the theatre.

7.2 Ask where you can get things, like this:

You want some stamps.
Where can I get some stamps?
At a post office.

You want a map.
Where can I get a map?
At a bookshop.

Now you.

a) You want some stamps.
   Where can I get some stamps?
   At a post office.
b) You want a map.
   Where can I get a map?
   At a bookshop.
c) You want a newspaper.
   Where can I get a newspaper?
   At a newsagent's.
d) You want a razor.
   Where can I get a razor?
   At a chemist's.
e) You want some tea.
   Where can I get some tea?
   At a supermarket.
f) You want a toothbrush.
   Where can I get a toothbrush?
   At a chemist's.

7.3 Look at the shopping list, and say what they've got or haven't got, like this:

Eggs.
They've got some eggs.

Cheese.
They haven't got any cheese.

Now you.

a) Eggs.
   They've got some eggs.
b) Cheese.
   They haven't got any cheese.

c) Butter.
   They've got some butter.
d) Fruit.
   They've got some fruit.
e) Tea.
   They haven't got any tea.
f) Biscuits.
   They haven't got any biscuits.

7.4 Ask how much things cost, like this:

You want to know how much the vegetables cost.
How much do they cost?

You want to know how much the tea is.
How much is it?

Now you.

a) You want to know how much the vegetables cost.
   How much do they cost?
b) You want to know how much the tea is.
   How much is it?
c) You want to know how much the butter costs.
   How much does it cost?
d) You want to know how much the meat is.
   How much is it?
e) You want to know how much the eggs are.
   How much are they?
f) You want to know how much the biscuits cost.
   How much do they cost?

7.5 Ask how much or how many they buy, like this:

Eggs.
How many eggs do they buy?

Tea.
How much tea do they buy?

Now you.

a) Eggs.
   How many eggs do they buy?
b) Tea.
   How much tea do they buy?
c) Meat.
   How much meat do they buy?
d) Vegetables.
   How many vegetables do they buy?
e) Stamps.
   How many stamps do they buy?
f) Milk.
   How much milk do they buy?

8 Planning a journey

UNIT SUMMARY

Functions	Structures

Functions

Asking and saying what the date is

Structures

What's the date today?

(It's) the twenty-first of July.

Talking about journeys and timetables

What time		train		Dallas?
When	does the	plane	leave	London?
		coach		

At three fifteen in the afternoon.

At ten o'clock at night.

Asking and saying how long journeys take

How long does it take (to get from London to Dallas)?

About twelve and three-quarter hours.

Asking for and giving information

I'd like some information on . . . , please.

I want to go by coach/plane/train/plane.

Topics

Means of transport, ordinal numbers, months of the year, days of the week, dates, times, journeys

Lexical items

- boat bus car coach plane train tube underground
- airport arrive birthday calendar date day flight hotel hour leave journey minute month station timetable tour transport week
- first second third fourth fifth sixth eleventh twelfth thirteenth twentieth twenty-first twenty-second thirtieth
- January February March April May June July August September October November December
- Monday Tuesday Wednesday Thursday Friday Saturday Sunday
- a.m. p.m.

TEACHING GUIDE

The students are already familiar with most of the structures in this unit (see Unit 5); here the present simple is treated in the context of talking about timetables and schedules.

WARM-UP

Suggested warm-up activity: 7.

1 Present vocabulary items to do with means of transport by pointing to the pictures and asking students to say what they are. They should then point to the various tickets and say what type of transport you can use them on. If possible, bring to the class a number of tickets for types of transport in the town where you are now. Hold them up in turn and get students to say on which type of transport you can use each one.

Answers

1 train   2 coach   3 tube   4 bus   5 plane

2 Present dates by reading the various dates aloud and then asking students to repeat. Ask them to say today's date as well. Point out that the year is divided into two parts: *nineteen* and *eighty-four*, and not pronounced as one figure: one thousand nineteen hundred and eighty four, etc. You may need to spend some time on revising the various numbers needed for saying what year it is. Check also that everyone has understood that *first*, *second*, *third*, etc. are used for dates rather than *one*, *two*, *three*, etc. Present the months of the year by asking students simply to repeat them after you. Then ask questions using ordinal numbers: *What's the third/seventh/twelfth month of the year?*

WB 8.1

3 Practise saying what the date is by asking students to work in pairs and to say the dates shown in their books. Explain that in English 12/6/67 is the twelfth of June and *not* the sixth of December. Point out that there are two ways of saying the date.
4 Practise recognising the date by playing the tape and asking students to note down the dates they hear. Remember that it is much more difficult to understand spoken dates than written ones, so you may need to play the tape two or three times.

Tapescript

1	Good morning. I want to travel to Exeter on Tuesday the fifth of June.
2	Could you tell me if I can get to Madrid by the twenty-seventh of June?

---

3 Here's your ticket. Your outward journey is for tomorrow, the second of February, nineteen eighty-four. You must use the return ticket by the first of April.
4 Can you change the date on this cheque? It's the twelfth of October, not the eleventh.
5 I'd like to go on May the first, nineteen eighty-five and come back on May the fifth.
6 I'm planning a trip to China and Japan in August nineteen eighty-seven. Can you give me some details please?

Answers

1 5th June
2 27th June
3 2nd February, 1984; 1st April
4 12th October; 11th October
5 May 1st, 1985; May 5th
6 August 1987

5 Practise asking and saying what the date is by getting students to work in pairs and to talk about the dates of the occasions shown in their books. Go round each pair and check that there are no serious errors. You may like to ask students to go round the class asking and saying what dates the various occasions are, changing partners each time.

WB 8.2

6 Present the days of the week by asking students to match the words with the abbreviations. Explain that these abbreviations are the ones most commonly used in timetables.
7 Practise listening for specific information by playing the tape and asking students to complete the columns A–C as they listen. There will be some vocabulary in the dialogues which may be unfamiliar to them, but explain that they don't need to understand every word in order to do the exercise.

Tapescript

1	ASSISTANT:	Good morning. Can I help you?
	CUSTOMER:	Yes, I'd like some information on flights from London to Hong Kong.
	ASSISTANT:	Yes – when do you want to travel?
	CUSTOMER:	I'd like to go next Wednesday.
	ASSISTANT:	Next Wednesday. That's the twentieth of June. Just a moment.
2	CUSTOMER:	Can you tell me if there's a plane from London to Geneva in the evening?

43

ASSISTANT: Yes, there is. When would you like to go?
CUSTOMER: Well, next Saturday, if possible.
ASSISTANT: Right. That's June the twenty-third. Hold on, please.

3 CUSTOMER: I'd like some information on flights from London to Dallas in Texas.
ASSISTANT: When would you like to travel?
CUSTOMER: Thursday the twenty-first of June, if there are any seats.
ASSISTANT: I'll have a look.

Answers

	A	B	C	D	E
	To	Day of Travel	Date	Leaves	Arrives
1	Hong Kong	Wednesday	20th June	10 am.	10.10 am.
2	Geneva	Saturday	23rd June	5.25 p.m.	7.55 p.m.
3	Dallas	Thursday	21st June	3.15 p.m.	10 p.m.

8 Practise asking about and saying times by getting the students to look at the timetable and to complete columns D and E in the chart. They should then ask and say what time the flights leave and arrive. The structure *What time does . . .?* was introduced in Unit 4 but students may need to be reminded of how it is used. In this exercise, students are asked to reply using the 12-hour clock; explain that the 24-hour clock is used in written timetables, but the 12-hour clock is used when talking about the times. Make sure everyone understands the abbreviations *a.m.* and *p.m.*; point out that 10 p.m. can either be said *ten pee-em*, or *ten (o'clock) at night/in the evening.* Remind students that, as a rough guide, morning lasts until midday; afternoon goes on until about six o'clock; evening is used until about nine or ten p.m. (see p.20 in the *Student's Book*).

Answers   See 7

WB 8.3

9 Present *How long does it take to get from . . . to . . .?* by asking students how long it takes to get from London to Paris by coach (9½ hours). Point out that they need to subtract one hour for the journey time from Britain to France or Spain.
  Then practise the structures used in this unit so far by getting students to ask for and give travel information using the coach and train timetables. Write a model sentence on the board and ask students to come up and mark in the stress and intonation pattern. Insist on the weak form of *does* /dəz/.

What time does the eighteen oh five train from London arrive in Swindon?

What time does the coach arrive in Cordoba?

How long does it take?

WB 8.4

10 Practise structures used for asking for information by getting students to complete the dialogues with the right phrases. They have already practised *I'd like (to) . . . .* and *I want (to) . . . .* in Units 5 and 7.

Play the tape and ask students to correct their versions. Practise the dialogues by asking students to work in pairs and to act out the exchanges between the customer and the assistant.

Tapescript and Answers

1 CUSTOMER: Good morning. I'd like some information on trains to Bath from Reading.
ASSISTANT: Yes, certainly. When do you want to travel?
CUSTOMER: On Wednesday the twentieth of June, in the evening.
ASSISTANT: I'll just get the train timetables. Yes, there's a train at six thirty in the evening.
CUSTOMER: How long does it take?
ASSISTANT: About fifty-five minutes.
CUSTOMER: Thank you.

2 CUSTOMER: I want to go by coach to Paris from London.
ASSISTANT: When would you like to travel?
CUSTOMER: Well, I'd like to go on Monday the twenty-fifth or Tuesday the twenty-sixth, and I want to be there by Tuesday evening.
ASSISTANT: I'll have a look at the timetable. Yes, there's a coach on Monday.
CUSTOMER: What time does it leave London?
ASSISTANT: At nine o'clock in the morning.
CUSTOMER: And what time does it arrive?
ASSISTANT: At half past seven in the evening.

11 Practise the structures presented in this unit by asking students to work in pairs and to role play dialogues between customer and travel agent.

WB 8.5

12 Practise reading for general sense by asking students to read the paragraphs from the tour brochure and to decide which day each paragraph refers to. Remind them that Koji is staying in London at the moment.

Answers

LONDON–YORK: Day 1
YORK–EDINBURGH: Day 2
EDINBURGH–LAKE DISTRICT: Day 3
LAKE DISTRICT–CHESTER: Day 4
CHESTER–LONDON: Day 5

There will be some words which the students may not understand in the passages. The exercise can nevertheless be done without understanding every word. You may want to give your students an opportunity to find out more about the places mentioned in the tour.

13 Practise reading for specific information by asking students to look back at the paragraphs and to complete the schedule with as much information as possible.

Answers

NORTH OF ENGLAND AND SCOTLAND TOUR SCHEDULE Departure: London Date: 20 June Time: 9 a.m.				
	Place	Arrive	Leave	Hotel
DAY 1	Cambridge	12 noon	3 p.m.	—
	York	7 p.m.	—	DALES
DAY 2	York	—	9.30 a.m.	—
	Edinburgh	1 p.m.	—	CARNEGIE
DAY 3	Edinburgh	—	9 a.m.	—
	Lake District	4 p.m.	—	LAKEVIEW
DAY 4	Lake District	—	2 p.m.	—
	Chester	4.30 p.m.	—	CHESHIRE
DAY 5	Chester	—	10 a.m.	—
	Stratford	12.15 p.m.	3.15 p.m.	—
	London	6.30 p.m.	—	—

14 Practise listening for specific information by playing the tape and asking students to complete the schedule with information from Koji's conversation with the travel agent's assistant.

Tapescript

KOJI:	I'd like some information about the coach tour of the north of England and Scotland.
ASSISTANT:	Yes, of course. When do you want to go?
KOJI:	June the twentieth if possible.
ASSISTANT:	Yes, there are still some places left.
KOJI:	What time does the coach leave London?
ASSISTANT:	At nine o'clock in the morning. It drives to Cambridge.
KOJI:	What time does it arrive?
ASSISTANT:	At twelve o'clock. You have three hours there and then the coach goes to York, arriving at seven o'clock in the evening.
KOJI:	And on the second day, what time do we arrive in Edinburgh?
ASSISTANT:	At one o'clock in the afternoon.
KOJI:	And what about the next day?
ASSISTANT:	On day three, you leave Edinburgh at nine o'clock and go to Gretna Green, where you have lunch. And then you drive to the Lake District. And on day four, you leave the Lake District at two o'clock in the afternoon for Chester . . .
KOJI:	I see.
ASSISTANT:	And on the fifth day, you leave Chester at ten o'clock in the morning and arrive in Stratford at twelve fifteen in the afternoon. You have about three hours there. Then you drive back to London.
KOJI:	So we leave at ten, get to Stratford at twelve fifteen . . .
ASSISTANT:	Yes.
KOJI:	. . . leave at three fifteen and arrive back in London at six thirty in the evening.
ASSISTANT:	That's right.
KOJI:	Thanks very much.

Answers   See 13

LEARNING SKILLS

Play a recording of the radio news or a listening comprehension passage at advanced level. Ask students to put their hand up when they recognise a word; stop the tape and ask the student to repeat the word he/she heard. Encourage them to put their hands up for proper names as well. Point out how much they understand rather than how little.

PRONUNCIATION TAPESCRIPT

8.1 Listen and repeat.

/θ/ and /ð/

the	third	they
think	this	that
thing	thirteen	thanks

8.2 Listen and repeat.

/θ/	/ð/
birthday	other
thirty	sunbathing
three	then
Thursday	there

8.3 Listen and mark the stressed syllables in each of these sentences.

a) When's your birthday?

b) What time does the train leave?

c) How long does it take?

d) How much is it?

e) When does the bus arrive?

f) Where can I get some information?

STRUCTURE REVIEW TAPESCRIPT

8.1 Say what the date is, like this:

What's the date today?
It's the fifteenth of August.

Now you.

a) What's the date today?
It's the fifteenth of August.
b) What's the date today?
It's the twenty-second of December.
c) What's the date today?
It's the third of March.
d) What's the date today?
It's the thirty-first of January.
e) What's the date today?
It's the eleventh of October.
f) What's the date today?
It's the seventh of May.

8.2 Say what time the train leaves or arrives, like this:

What time does the train leave London?
At seven thirty in the morning.

Now you.

a) What time does the train leave London?
At seven thirty in the morning.
b) What time does the train arrive in Bristol?
At nine o'clock in the morning.

c) What time does the train leave Edinburgh?
At one thirty in the afternoon.
d) What time does the train leave London?
At six o'clock in the evening.
e) What time does the train leave Exeter?
At nine thirty in the evening.
f) What time does the train arrive in London?
At two o'clock in the morning.

8.3 Ask what time things happen, like this:

You want to know when the museum opens.
When does the museum open?

You want to know what time the plane leaves.
What time does the plane leave?

Now you.

a) You want to know when the museum opens.
When does the museum open?
b) You want to know what time the plane leaves.
What time does the plane leave?
c) You want to know what time the film starts.
What time does the film start?
d) You want to know when the train arrives.
When does the train arrive?
e) You want to know when the bank closes.
When does the bank close?
f) You want to know what time the play finishes.
What time does the play finish?

8.4 Ask how long journeys take, like this:

You want to know how long it takes to get from Bristol to London.
How long does it take to get from Bristol to London?

Now you.

a) You want to know how long it takes to get from Bristol to London.
How long does it take to get from Bristol to London?
b) You want to know how long it takes to get from Exeter to Edinburgh.
How long does it take to get from Exeter to Edinburgh?
c) You want to know how long it takes to get from Paris to Marseille.
How long does it take to get from Paris to Marseille?
d) You want to know how long it takes to get from New York to Los Angeles.
How long does it take to get from New York to Los Angeles?
e) You want to know how long it takes to get from Hong Kong to London.
How long does it take to get from Hong Kong to London?
f) You want to know how long it takes to get from Tokyo to Osaka.
How long does it take to get from Tokyo to Osaka?

Describing places – talking about arrangements

UNIT SUMMARY

Functions

Structures

Asking and saying where places are

Where's Montego Bay?

It's	on the	north south east west	coast	
	in the	middle centre north south east west		of (*place*).

Asking and saying what places are like

What's Cadaqués like?

It's a	(very)	large small	old modern	town/city. village. port.

It's	an industrial centre. a commercial centre. a tourist centre.

Asking and saying what people's plans are

Where	are	you they	going for	your their	holidays?
	is	he she		his her	

I	'm	
We They	're	going to America.
He She	's	

When	are	you they	going away?
	is	he she	

Structures

What	are	you they	doing on Tuesday morning?
	is	he she	

Topics

Geographical location, geographical features and description, continents, countries, oceans, seas, large numbers, travel documents

Lexical items

- north south east west north-east north-west south-east south-west
- beach between capital city coast holidays island mountain near ocean population port sea tourist town village year
- beautiful commercial industrial interesting modern old pretty ugly
- identity card passport visa
- thousand million

TEACHING GUIDE

This unit focuses on describing places using the present simple, and introduces the present continuous with future reference for talking about arrangements.

WARM-UP

Suggested warm-up activity: 13.

1 Present vocabulary items for describing geographical features by asking students to read the passage and to match the place names with the black dots on the map. The students should be able to mark the places on the map very easily; all they have to do is find the black dot in the appropriate square (D-2, B-2, etc.)

Answers See map below

Then ask students to re-read the passage and to note down any words which they don't understand. Ask them to try and work out the meaning of each word from the context. Get them to check their answers with another student. Write all the difficult words on the board and explain their meanings.

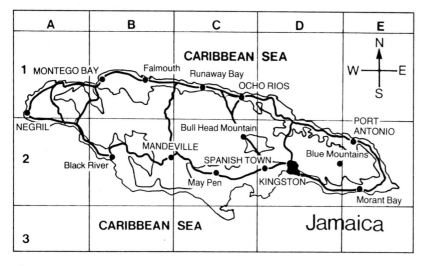

48

2 Present *north, south, east, west*, etc. by showing students the compass points and asking them where places in Jamaica are. Then get them to practise the vocabulary of geographical location in pairs.

3 Practise listening for specific information by playing the tape and asking students to match the place names with the red dots on the map. If necessary, remind them that they will not understand all the words in the passage, but they will know enough to do the exercise. Tell them to concentrate on words for direction (west, north, etc.). Explain that the conversation takes place in a tourist information bureau.

Tapescript

RECEPTIONIST:	Good morning, can I help you?
GUEST:	Er, yes, please. I'd like to drive round Jamaica – can you give me some information?
RECEPTIONIST:	Yes, of course. Let's look at the map . . . Right, so we're here in Kingston. If you take the road west from Kingston, you come to Spanish Town . . . It's very interesting. Then you continue west through May Pen – here – to Mandeville.
GUEST:	What's Mandeville like?
RECEPTIONIST:	Oh, it's a lovely town in the mountains. The main road west from Mandeville joins the coast at Black River, here, and runs from there to Negril. You can stop for a swim there – there's a beautiful long beach.
GUEST:	Good idea. And then can I drive north to Montego Bay?
RECEPTIONIST:	Yes, you can . . . it takes about two hours to get from Negril to Montego Bay. And about thirty kilometres east of Montego Bay is Falmouth . . . it's a charming small town . . .
GUEST:	Ah, yes, I see.
RECEPTIONIST:	. . . Then drive east along the north coast to Runaway Bay . . . Columbus made his first landing near here.
GUEST:	Oh, really?
RECEPTIONIST:	Yes. And then you come to the beautiful beaches of Ocho Rios . . .
GUEST:	Ah, yes.
RECEPTIONIST:	Now, you can drive back to Kingston from Ocho Rios, this way, south past Bull Head Mountain to Spanish Town. But if you have time, take the coast road east from Ocho Rios to Port Antonio, over here.
GUEST:	How long does it take?
RECEPTIONIST:	From Ocho Rios to Port Antonio?
GUEST:	Yes.
RECEPTIONIST:	About two and a half hours.
GUEST:	Oh, that's OK.
RECEPTIONIST:	Port Antonio is lovely – it lies at the foot of the Blue Mountains. And then from Port Antonio you go round the east coast, through Morant Bay, here, and back to Kingston.
GUEST:	Oh, that's wonderful . . . thank you.
RECEPTIONIST:	Not at all. Have a nice trip!

Answers See map on page 48

Practise *Where's . . .? It's in the centre of . . . ./on . . ./near. . ./between. . . .* by getting students to ask and say where the places are in order to check their answers to the listening activity. If necessary, explain the meaning of *in the centre of . . .*

WB 9.1

4 Practise the structures used for describing the location of places by getting students to work in pairs and to ask and say where various places are. After they have completed the list in their books, ask them to think of other places and ask their partners to say where they are. Use the map of the world on page 35 for this activity.

5 Practise using the vocabulary of geographical description by asking students to complete the puzzle in their books.

Answers

1	Hong Kong	5	Dallas
2	Oporto	6	Amsterdam
3	Lyon	7	York
4	Italy	8	Santiago

This kind of puzzle is very easy to make. Ask students to work in pairs and to make one of their own, based on the vertical words SUNSHINE or TOURISM.

6 Present *What's the capital of . . .?* and names of countries and capital cities by asking students to match the cities with the countries.

Answers

Canada:	Ottowa	Nigeria:	Lagos
Fiji:	Suva	Peru:	Lima
Greece:	Athens	Sri Lanka:	Colombo
Hungary:	Budapest	USSR:	Moscow
Iceland:	Reykjavik	Zambia:	Lusaka

Present large numbers by asking students to say what the populations of these countries and towns are. Write the numbers and the words for 1,000 (*a thousand*) and 1,000,000 (*a million*) on the board and say them. Then change the numbers to 2,000 and 2,000,000; say them and get students to repeat.

Make sure they do not use a plural -s ending. Ask students to work in pairs and to practise the numbers; then ask them to say what the population of their countries is, followed by the capital city and its population.

WB 9.2

7 Present vocabulary items for geographical description by getting students to match the pictures with the descriptions. At first they may only be able to guess the answers to this exercise, but you may like to illustrate the meaning of key words such as *modern*, *old* and *port*, etc. in each description and then ask them to check their answers. When they have completed the exercise you should give further explanation of any unfamiliar vocabulary items, with reference to places in the student's own countries.

Answers 1 B, 2 D, 3 A, 4 C

Present *What's . . . like?* by asking students to use the information in the descriptions in full sentences. Give two or three model questions and answers, and then get students to ask and say what the places are like in pairs. You may like to give a further example of the language used for describing what places are like by giving a description of the town where you are now. You should add any necessary vocabulary items to the list in the *Student's Book*.

8 Practise the language of saying what places are like by getting students to ask and say what the places in Jamaica are like. Give further practice by asking them to talk about what places in their own countries are like. Be prepared to supply students with extra vocabulary so that they can describe their own countries.

9 Practise writing descriptions of places by getting students to use the model paragraph to write a brief description of two places in their countries. When they have finished, ask students to exchange and correct each other's versions.

WB 9.3, 9.4, 9.5, 9.6, 9.7

10 Present *He/She's going to . . . in . . . .* by asking students to read the clues and decide where the six characters are going on holiday and when. If students have difficulty in getting started, point out that there is a lot of information in the fifth clue (about Diana).

Answers See 11

▭ Practise listening by playing the tape of two people talking about the problem. Their conversation should help any students who are stuck.

Tapescript

WOMAN:	. . . now – Diana's going to the *north* of Italy . . .
MAN:	. . . so she's going to Venice . . .
WOMAN:	. . . and she's going away one month before Koji.
MAN:	. . . Well, there are only two months together – September and October . . . so that means Diana's going away in *September* to Venice . . .
WOMAN:	. . . and Koji's going away in *October*. And he isn't going to Italy or Spain . . .
MAN:	. . . and he isn't going to Mexico, because he's going in October and someone's going to Mexico in *May*. So that leaves Hong Kong. Koji's going to Hong Kong in October!

11 Get students to write their answers by completing the sentences.

Answers

1 Bob is going to Spain in July.
2 Carla and Richard are going to Rome in December.
3 Diana is going to Venice in September.
4 Koji is going to Hong Kong in October.
5 Nancy is going to Mexico in May.

12 Practise the structure by getting students to ask and say where they're going on holiday and when. Give two or three model exchanges and then ask them to work in pairs. Make sure they're using all the structures used in this unit.

WB 9.8

13 Practise reading for specific information by asking students to look through the information on passport control for visitors to Britain and to find out which documents they will need. Remind students that they don't need to understand every word; in fact, it would be unusual to read this document all the way through.

Answers

Koji needs a passport and a visa; Nancy only needs a passport.

LEARNING SKILLS

Write the following list of words on the board:

office, breakfast, question, watch, newspaper, fruit, read, tour, centre, sentence

Give students about thirty seconds to learn the list, and then wipe it off the board.

Remind students that it is necessary to revise everything they learn at regular intervals. Ask them to go through Units 1 to 9 and to note down any more words which they consider to be especially relevant to their particular needs.

Now ask students to try and remember the list of words they learnt before the last activity? How many can they remember? How many words are in the right order? Which words are easier to remember? It is probable that some students will not be able to recall words like *question, watch, read, centre, sentence* because it is less easy to link these words with an image. Explain that some words, particularly those which are less concrete, need more effort to learn.

PRONUNCIATION TAPESCRIPT

9.1 Listen and repeat.

/ɜ:/	/ɔ:/
work	walk
first	forced
firm	form
bird	board

Now listen and tick the words you hear.

work   forced   form   bird

9.2 Listen and write the words in the correct column.

four /ɔ:/   girl /ɜ:/   learn /ɜ:/   morning /ɔ:/
north /ɔ:/   nurse /ɜ:/   port /ɔ:/   shirt /ɜ:/

9.3 Listen and mark the stressed words.

a) It's a small modern town.
b) It's a large tourist centre.
c) It's a pretty Italian village.
d) It's a beautiful old town.
e) It's an ugly industrial port.
f) It's a very large commercial centre.

STRUCTURE REVIEW TAPESCRIPT

9.1 Say where the places are, like this:

Where's Brighton?
It's on the south coast of England.

Now you.

a) Where's Brighton?
   It's on the south coast of England.
b) Where's Paris?
   It's in the north of France.
c) Where's New York?
   It's on the east coast of the United States.
d) Where's Madrid?
   It's in the centre of Spain.

e) Where's Los Angeles?
   It's on the west coast of the United States.
f) Where's Nairobi?
   It's in the south of Kenya.

9.2 Say where people are going for their holidays, like this:

Where's Bob going for his holidays?
He's going to Spain.

Now you.

a) Where's Bob going for his holidays?
   He's going to Spain.
b) Where's Nancy going for her holidays?
   She's going to Mexico.
c) Where are Koji and his wife going for their holidays?
   They're going to Hong Kong.
d) Where's Diana going for her holidays?
   She's going to Venice.
e) Where are Richard and Carla going for their holidays?
   They're going to Rome.
f) Where are you going for your holidays?
   ....

9.3 Ask when people are going away, like this:

Bob.
When's he going away?

Nancy.
When's she going away?

Now you.

a) Bob.
   When's he going away?
b) Nancy.
   When's she going away?
c) Koji and his wife.
   When are they going away?
d) Diana.
   When's she going away?
e) Richard and Carla.
   When are they going away?

9.4 Say what people are doing in the future, like this:

What's Phil doing next Tuesday?
He's flying to Paris.

Now you.

a) What's Phil doing next Tuesday?
   He's flying to Paris.
b) What's Jill doing next Wednesday?
   She's going to the theatre.
c) What are Henry and Joan doing next Sunday?
   They're having lunch with friends.
d) What's Sheila doing on Monday?
   She's meeting someone at the airport.
e) What are Geoff and Margaret doing on Saturday?
   They're staying at home.
f) What's Pete doing on Tuesday?
   He's watching football on TV.

10 Taking a break

UNIT SUMMARY

Functions

Talking about hotel facilities

Making requests
Agreeing to and refusing requests

Asking for and giving directions

Structures

Is there a . . . ?
Has it got a . . . ?
Do the rooms have . . . ?

Can you	tell help show	me (etc.)?

Yes,	of course. certainly.

No, I'm	afraid not. sorry.

Can I	borrow your pen? have a single room? help you?

(Excuse me), how do	I we you	get to (*place*)?

(Excuse me), can you tell	me us	the way to (*place*)?

Go	straight ahead. along the High Street.

Turn	left right	(into *street*).

It's	opposite next to	(*place*).

Topics

Hotel facilities, hotel formalities, street directions, tourist facilities and sights

Lexical items

- accept address along bar bill book (n and v) borrow call (n and v) car park central heating change (v) credit card coffee shop college double room full left library lift (n) pay private make (a phone call) pub ready reception receptionist reserve right sign (v) single room straight ahead swimming pool telephone telephone number turn (left/right) with without

TEACHING GUIDE

This unit presents some of the vocabulary most commonly used in the context of hotels and sightseeing. Most of the structures have already been presented in earlier units; here, *can* is practised in the context of making polite requests, and the imperative is used for giving simple directions.

WARM-UP

Suggested warm-up activity: 5.

1 Present the vocabulary for talking about hotel facilities by asking students to read the passage describing the Randolph Hotel and to complete the chart. The new vocabulary items are explained by the symbols in the chart itself. All the vocabulary in this passage should be learnt for productive use. Point out that *Is there a . . .?* is the question form of *There's a . . . .* (Unit 7); *have got* was presented in Unit 3.

Answers

♀	bar	✔
🛁 🚿	rooms with private bath/shower	109
Ⓟ	car park	✔
▥	central heating in rooms	✔
☕	coffee shop	✔
Ⓥ	credit cards accepted	✔
②	double rooms	66
Ⓛ	lift	✔
¶Ⓞ¶	restaurant(s)	2
①	single rooms	43
🎾	sports facilities	✗
🏊	swimming pool	✗
☎	telephone in rooms	✔
📺	TV in rooms	✔

Students may want to read the passage, complete the chart and then ask and answer

questions about its facilities, or complete the chart at the same time as they ask and answer the questions. Check that everyone is using a suitable stress and intonation pattern.

2 Practise the vocabulary and structures used for talking about hotel facilities by getting students to look at the symbols describing the Westgate Hotel and to ask and answer questions about its facilities. There are fewer facilities than at the Randolph Hotel, so students will be using the negative form of the reply more often.

3 Practise writing by asking students to write a description of the Westgate Hotel. Tell them to use the description of the Randolph Hotel as a model. Make sure they don't include any negative features of the hotel (unless you want them to write an 'objective guide' rather than an advertising-type brochure). Correct any mistakes individually.

WB 10.1

4 Practise listening for specific information by playing the tape and getting students to complete the reservation form.

Tapescript

RECEPTIONIST:	Hello, Westgate Hotel. Can I help you?
MAN:	Oh, yes, please. Have you got any rooms for this weekend?
RECEPTIONIST:	Is that for one night or two?
MAN:	Erm, two nights – Friday and Saturday.
RECEPTIONIST:	That's Friday the twenty-fourth and Saturday the twenty-fifth. Yes – do you want a single or double room?
MAN:	Oh, double, please.
RECEPTIONIST:	With or without bath?
MAN:	With bath, please.
RECEPTIONIST:	So that's a double room with bath for Friday the twenty-fourth and Saturday the twenty-fifth of June.
MAN:	Yes, that's right.
RECEPTIONIST:	Can you tell me your name?

MAN:	It's Morris. Jim Morris.
RECEPTIONIST:	How do you spell it?
MAN:	M-O-double R-I-S.
RECEPTIONIST:	Is that M for mother or N for number?
MAN:	M for mother.
RECEPTIONIST:	I see . . . Mr Morris. And can I have your address?
MAN:	Yes – 22B, Lofton Road, that's L-O-F-T-O-N Road, London SW4.
RECEPTIONIST:	And your telephone number?
MAN:	O-one seven-two-O six-three-double eight.
RECEPTIONIST:	Thank you, Mr Morris. We'll see you on Friday evening, then.
MAN:	Yes. Thank you very much. Goodbye.
RECEPTIONIST:	Goodbye.

Answer

The Westgate Hotel 1 Botley Road, Oxford. (Near railway station).   Tel: Oxford 726721

ACCOMMODATION RESERVED

No. of nights ___2___

Date(s) ___June 24th and 25th___

~~Single~~/Double room _____

With/~~without~~ private bathroom _____

Name ___MORRIS   Jim___

Address ___22B   Lofton Road___

___London   SW4___

Tel. ___01 720 6388___

5   Practise asking for and giving information by getting students to ask each other for their names, addresses and phone numbers. When they have done this once they should change partners and roles. Make sure everyone is pronouncing the letters of the alphabet correctly.

6   Practise the language used when asking for and giving information by getting students to complete the dialogue. You may like to ask them to do this without looking at the list of suggested responses. When they have tried to complete it on their own, they should then look at the list to check their answers.

Tapescript and Answers

RECEPTIONIST:	Good evening. Can I help you?
KOJI:	Yes, please. Have you got any rooms for tonight?
RECEPTIONIST:	Yes – do you want a single or a double room?
KOJI:	A single room please.
RECEPTIONIST:	With or without a bathroom?
KOJI:	With a bath, please.

RECEPTIONIST:	Hm. We've got a single room with a shower, but no bath. Is that all right?
KOJI:	Yes, that's fine.
RECEPTIONIST:	Good. Well, that's Room 104. Can you sign the book, please?
KOJI:	Can I borrow your pen?
RECEPTIONIST:	Yes, of course.

▭ Practise listening by playing the tape and getting the students to check their answers.

7   Practise the language used for asking for and giving information by getting the students to role play the situations shown in their books.

WB   10.2, 10.3

8   Present the structures for making requests and agreeing to or refusing requests by getting students to match the statements with the correct responses. Point out that questions can sometimes be answered with another question.

Answers

A3 No, B5 No, C1 Yes, D6 Yes, E2 Yes, F4 No

▭ Practise listening for specific information by playing the tape and asking students to check their answers.

Tapescript

A	Can you change traveller's cheques?
3	I'm afraid not. There's a bank opposite the hotel.
B	Can I pay by American Express?
5	No, I'm sorry. We don't accept credit cards.
C	Can I make a phone call?
1	Yes, of course. Can you give me the number?
D	Can you call me at 7.30?
6	Certainly, sir. Would you like breakfast in your room?
E	Can we have dinner here?
2	Yes, of course. The restaurant is open till 10.30.
F	Can you give me my bill?
4	No, I'm sorry. It's not ready yet.

9   Practise making, agreeing to and refusing requests by getting students to work in pairs and to make the requests in 8 and give the full responses. Point out that I'm afraid not is an apologetic way of saying No, and that Certainly is a way of saying

Yes that shows willingness. Explain that *Yes, of course.* and *Certainly.* can be used interchangeably during this activity. Equally, *No, I'm sorry.* and *I'm afraid not.* are interchangeable negative responses.

WB 10.4, 10.5

10 Practise listening for specific information by playing the tape and asking students to follow the route described by the tourist information officer, and to number the six places which are listed in the orange box, on the map. Make sure they have understood where the tour begins and which places they are being asked to identify. Point out that they won't be able to understand every word of the conversation, but that they will know enough to be able to perform the task. The language used in the conversation is very common in this kind of tourist/guide context. Before you begin, make sure they have also understood the difference between *left* and *right*, and the meaning of *straight ahead.*

Tapescript

TOURIST:	Excuse me.
ASSISTANT:	Yes sir. Can I help you?
TOURIST:	Yes, we'd like to look round Oxford. Can you tell us what there is to see?
ASSISTANT:	Certainly sir. Have you got a map of the town?
TOURIST:	No. No, we haven't.
ASSISTANT:	Here you are. Now, we're here, in St Aldates, next to Carfax, the centre of the town.
TOURIST:	Ah yes, I see. Right.
ASSISTANT:	Now, go along St Aldates to Christ Church College. It's on the left here. Then, go into Christ Church College and opposite you can see the Cathedral. It's very beautiful. Then go through the college and into Christ Church Meadow. On your right there's the River Thames.
TOURIST:	Er, can you wait a minute? . . . Cathedral . . . Christ Church Meadow . . . River Thames, ah, yes.
ASSISTANT:	When you leave the Meadow, turn right into Merton Street. There's lots to see there. Go along Merton Street to the High Street and turn right. Magdalen College is opposite.
TOURIST:	Magdalen College?
ASSISTANT:	Yes, next to Magdalen Bridge. It's spelt M-A-G-D-A-L-E-N, but you say Magdalen. All right?
TOURIST:	Oh, I see. It's on the road to London.
ASSISTANT:	That's right. Why don't you visit the college? It's very beautiful. Then go along the High Street towards Carfax. Turn right into Queen's Lane.

	Queen's Lane goes into New College Lane. It's a very pretty little road.
TOURIST:	And can we visit New College?
ASSISTANT:	Certainly. Then turn right into Catte Street and then left . . .
TOURIST:	Catte Street? C-A-double T-E?
ASSISTANT:	That's right. And then turn left into Broad Street. On the left you can see the Bodleian Library. It's a very old building. All right? Then go along Broad Street and turn left into Turl Street. On the right is Jesus College.
TOURIST:	Ah yes, I see.
ASSISTANT:	Go along Turl Street and turn right into the High Street. Then go straight ahead. There you are, Carfax. That's where we are now.
TOURIST:	Fine. How long does the tour take?
ASSISTANT:	Oh, about three hours.
TOURIST:	Good. Is there a museum?
ASSISTANT:	Yes, the Ashmolean Museum.
TOURIST:	How do you get there?
ASSISTANT:	Well, start at Carfax. Go along Cornmarket and turn left into Beaumont Street. It's opposite the Randolph Hotel.
TOURIST:	Right. And is there a theatre?
ASSISTANT:	Yes, there are two. The Playhouse Theatre is next to the Randolph Hotel. And the Apollo Theatre is very near, in George Street.
TOURIST:	Fine. Oh, and can you tell me the way to the railway station?
ASSISTANT:	Start at Carfax. Go along Queen Street, then along New Road, and into Park End Street, and Botley Road. Go straight ahead. The station is there.
TOURIST:	Thank you very much.
ASSISTANT:	You're welcome. 'Bye.

Answers

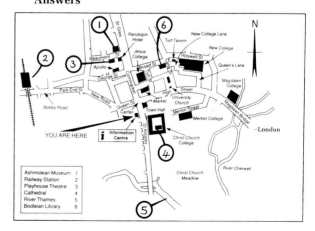

11 Practise asking for and giving directions by getting students to role play the situation presented in 10.

Get them to work in pairs and to decide which is the tourist and which is the tourist information officer. Explain that *Excuse me* is a polite way of attracting someone's attention before you ask them a question. Make sure everyone realises that the role play conversation takes place in the Tourist Information Centre.

12 Practise asking for and giving directions by getting students to draw a simple map of their home towns, or a town they know well, but which their partners do not. Get them to ask for and give directions to places in each others' town.

WB 10.6

13 Practise asking for and giving directions and revise talking about likes and dislikes by asking students to work in pairs and read their role cards. Play the tape and ask them to note down information concerning the things which they want to do.

Tapescript

How about spending a day in Oxford? With the colleges and museum, theatres and shops, there's lots to see and do there. Let's start with the colleges. There's the tour which starts at the Information Centre in St Aldates. It takes about three hours and you can visit Christ Church, Magdalen and New College, and the small colleges like Jesus, as well as the Cathedral and the Bodleian Library. There's a large museum in Beaumont Street with paintings and old furniture. It's called the Ashmolean Museum. It takes about two hours to go round, but remember, it closes at four o'clock. How about some lunch? There are plenty of pubs with very good food between twelve and two o'clock. Try the Turf Tavern, near New College. And tea? You can have tea in the Randolph Hotel where famous people stay when they come to Oxford, people like kings, queens, film stars and rock singers. The best time to go is at four o'clock. In the evening there are lots of films, plays and concerts. Go to the Playhouse Theatre to see a play, or to the Apollo Theatre to see a rock concert. For classical music there are plenty of concerts in the colleges or in the Town Hall. They usually begin at eight o'clock. Try to have dinner in one of the excellent restaurants. Many close at ten thirty, but there are some which are open until midnight. Have a nice day in Oxford!

Then they should role play the conversation in which they decide how to spend their day in Oxford.

LEARNING SKILLS

Ask students to think of as many international words to do with public facilities and signs as they can. Remind them of words like *stop*, *information*, *hotel*, *restaurant*.

Show students another way of making vocabulary lists. Tell them to write down an adjective. Around the adjective they should write nouns with which you could use the adjective. Then around these nouns, they should try and think of other words they could put with the nouns. Ask them to do this with *large*, *small*, *cheap*, *expensive*.

Example:

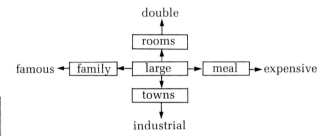

PRONUNCIATION TAPESCRIPT

10.1 Listen and mark the stressed syllable on each of these words.

cápital Decémber compúter cústomer
potáto télephone muséum mánager
cómfortable commércial umbrélla hóliday

10.2 Listen and repeat.

cár park cóffee shop crédit card
swímming pool phóne call ráilway station
shópping list póst office sítting room

10.3 Listen and repeat.

a) Is there a bar in the hotel?

b) Can you tell me the way?

c) What's your telephone number?

d) Can I pay by cheque?

e) How do you get to the cinema?

f) How many rooms are there?

STRUCTURE REVIEW TAPESCRIPT

10.1 Reply to these requests, like this:

Can I pay by cheque?
Yes, of course.

Can you change £20?
No, I'm sorry.

Now you.

a) Can I pay by cheque?
Yes, of course.
b) Can you change £20?
No, I'm sorry.
c) Can you call me a taxi?
Yes, of course.
d) Can I have dinner in my room?
No, I'm sorry.
e) Can I leave my car here?
No, I'm sorry.
f) Can you give me the bill?
Yes, of course.

10.2 Ask how you get to places, like this:

You want to get to the cinema.
Excuse me, how do you get to the cinema?

Now you.

a) You want to get to the cinema.
Excuse me, how do you get to the cinema?
b) You want to get to the theatre.
Excuse me, how do you get to the theatre?
c) You want to get to the post office.
Excuse me, how do you get to the post office?
d) You want to get to the hotel.
Excuse me, how do you get to the hotel?
e) You want to get to the market.
Excuse me, how do you get to the market?
f) You want to get to the High Street.
Excuse me, how do you get to the High Street?

10.3 Say how to get to places, like this:

Can you tell me the way to the town hall?
Turn left, and it's next to the bank.

Now you.

a) Can you tell me the way to the town hall?
Turn left, and it's next to the bank.
b) Can you tell me the way to the market?
Turn right, and it's opposite the town hall.
c) Can you tell me the way to the hospital?
Turn left, and it's next to the market.
d) Can you tell me the way to the cathedral?
Go straight ahead, and it's opposite the hotel.
e) Can you tell me the way to the station?
Go along the High Street, and it's next to the post office.
f) Can you tell me the way to the car park?
Go straight ahead, and it's opposite the cinema.

11 | Getting what you want

UNIT SUMMARY

Functions

Asking what words mean

Offering

Ordering a meal

Making requests

Saying what you must or mustn't do

Structures

| What does (*word*) mean? |

| Would you like (something to eat/drink)? |

| What would you like to eat/drink? |

| I'd like / I'll have | (something to eat/drink). |

| Could I have (something to eat/drink)? |

| Could / Can | you | tell bring show | me | (*something*)? |

| You must stop. |

| You mustn't park here. |

Topics

Food, restaurants, British and American English, instructions, hotels

Lexical items

- bacon   baked (potato)   banana split   beer   cake   coke   drink (v)   French fries   fruit salad   grilled (steak)   ice cream   meal   menu   mixed (vegetables)   omelet   onion   pie   pizza   salad   soup   waiter
- front desk clerk   lock (v)   safe (n)   stranger   valuable things

GB	US
bill	check
chemist	drugstore
chips	French fries
cinema	movie house
flat	apartment
lift	elevator
railway	railroad
trousers	pants
underground/tube	subway

58

TEACHING GUIDE

This unit introduces the language to be used by an English-speaking visitor in situations requiring more than the simple fomulaic constructions presented so far. It also shows some of the differences in vocabulary between British and American English.

WARM-UP

Suggested warm-up activity: 9 or 10.

1 Present the vocabulary for various prepared foods by asking students to match the names of the dishes with their pictures. Remind students, if necessary, that they learnt a number of items for food in Unit 7.

Answers

A 2, B 11, C 18, D 3, E 8, F 4, G 10, H 17, I 15, J 6, K 9, L 1, M 14, N 13, O 7, P 12, Q 5, R 16

2 Present *What's . . .? What are . . .?* by getting students to ask you or each other about words they don't understand. Make sure they use the plural form where necessary. You may like to give further practice of this simple structure by encouraging students to ask about other English words which they don't understand.

WB 11.1

3 Practise listening for specific information by playing the tape and asking students to write down the numbers of the dishes Nancy and Bob order. Point out that Nancy says *tomato* to rhyme with *potato*. /təmeɪdoʊ/ is American English; /təmɑ:təʊ/ is British English.

Tapescript

WAITER:	Are you ready to order now?
NANCY:	Yes, I think we are.
WAITER:	What would you like to start with, ma'am?
NANCY:	I'd like onion soup, please.
WAITER:	And what would you like to follow?
NANCY:	Could I have a cheese and tomato pizza?
WAITER:	Certainly, ma'am. Do you want any vegetables, or a salad?
NANCY:	Yes, please. I'll have mixed salad with a baked potato.
WAITER:	Thank you, ma'am. And for you, sir?
BOB:	Could I have tomato juice to start with?
WAITER:	Tomato juice – and what would you like to follow?
BOB:	I'll have grilled steak, please, with chips.

WAITER:	Grilled steak and French fries – do you want any vegetables, sir?
BOB:	Yes, please. I'd like mixed vegetables.
WAITER:	Mixed vegetables – and would you like something to drink?
BOB:	What do you want, Nancy?
NANCY:	Oh, I'll have a Coke, please.
BOB:	So that's a Coke, and a beer for me, please.
WAITER:	Coming right up, sir – thank you.

Answers

Nancy: 4, 7, 10, 12 (+ Coke)
Bob: 1, 5, 13, 11 (+ beer)

4 Practise writing the vocabulary for food by asking students to complete the dialogues in their books.

Answers   See tapescript for 3

Practise listening for specific information by playing the tape again and asking students to check their answers.

5 Present the structures for ordering a meal by asking students to act out the dialogue between the waiter and Bob. Choose one student and act out a model dialogue with you playing Bob's role. Then ask students to practise the dialogue in pairs. Make sure everyone is using the structures correctly.

6 Practise ordering a meal by getting the students to work in groups of three and to act out the dialogue in Danny's Restaurant. Point out that the waiter may want to ask people what they would like using *Would you like something to drink/eat?*

WB 11.2, 11.3

7 Present *Could you . . .?* by asking students to match the requests with the responses.

Answers 1C, 2A, 3B

Explain that requests can be made with both *Could you . . .?* and *Can you . . .?* (see Unit 10). *Could you . . .?* is sometimes considered more polite, but in reality everything depends on intonation: even *please* can sound rude!

Practise listening for specific information by playing the tape and asking students to listen and check their answers. Point out that the passage is quite long, and also highlights some differences between British and American English. Ask students if they can remember some of these words. Then play the tape again, and ask them to note down the four pairs of words as they hear them.

Tapescript

NANCY:	So what are you doing this afternoon, Bob?
BOB:	I'm going to the Empire State Building – I must do that while I'm in New York.
NANCY:	Yes, there's a great view of the city from the top.
BOB:	Can I walk up?
NANCY:	Well, there are 1860 steps . . . I think it's better to take the elevator! What do you call that in England?
BOB:	Elevator? We say lift. Yes, you're right. I'll take the lift!
NANCY:	Oh, wait a minute, Bob – you can't go like that!
BOB:	What do you mean?
NANCY:	You mustn't wear jeans – you must wear pants!
BOB:	Pants! Oh, you mean I must wear trousers!
NANCY:	That's right. You can't go to the Empire State Building in jeans.
BOB:	Oh, well – I can go tomorrow.
NANCY:	Could you tell me the time?
BOB:	It's nearly half past two.
NANCY:	Is it? Oh, I didn't think it was so late – I must get back to work.
BOB:	Er, excuse me . . .
WAITER:	Yes, sir?
BOB:	Could you bring us the bill, please?
WAITER:	The check, sir? Certainly.
BOB:	Thank you.
NANCY:	Thank you, Bob – that was a very nice lunch. Will you excuse me – I must go now.
BOB:	Yes, of course – oh, Nancy, could you tell me the way to the underground station?
NANCY:	You mean the subway!
BOB:	Could you tell me the way to the subway!
NANCY:	That's better – you go out of here and turn left, and it's on the left. Have a nice day!

8 Present some items of British and American vocabulary by asking students to match the two types of words. By now they have come across all the listed words except *railroad* and *drugstore*. Explain that the major differences between British and American English concern the vocabulary and the pronunciation. However, it is essential to point out that there are far more similarities than differences.

Answers

flat	apartment
chemist's	drugstore
bill	check
cinema	movie house
trousers	pants
underground/tube	subway
film	movie
chips	French fries
lift	elevator
railway	railroad

9 Practise American and British English vocabulary and making requests by asking students to work in pairs and ask each other the questions shown in their books. They should use rising intonation.

Answers

STUDENT **A**

Can/Could	you bring me some French fries, please?
	you tell me the way to the railroad station?
	you come to my apartment?
	you get me something from the drug-store, please?

STUDENT **B**

Can/Could	you bring me the check, please?
	you tell me the way to the subway, please?
	you call the movie house, please?
	you carry my case to the elevator, please?

WB 11.4, 11.5

10 Present *You must* . . . . and *You mustn't* . . . . by playing Bob and Nancy's conversation again. Ask students to raise their hands when they hear the two structures.

Practise the structures by asking students to read the notice on Bob's hotel room door and to say what you must or mustn't do. You may need to pre-teach some of the vocabulary items. Unlike many reading activities in *BBC Beginners' English*, it may be better to explain all the unfamiliar words in this passage.

WB 11.6

11 Practise reading for specific information by asking students to read the passage about the American way of life and to find the answers to the questions. It is important that they realise it isn't necessary to understand every word; however, you should explain that they do know enough English to be able to perform the reading task without too much difficulty. Remind them that this is a fairly common type of reading task for low level learners in which they use the small amount of language they have acquired to extract information from a passage of authentic language.

Answers

1. You can buy medicines, birthday cards, cosmetics and clocks in a drugstore – in fact, almost anything (paragraph 2).
2. In restaurants, department stores, hotels, museums and railroad stations (paragraph 5).
3. Ham and eggs, followed by toast and marmalade (paragraph 1).
4. They carry food home with them in a 'doggie' bag (paragraph 6).
5. No, the national sport is American football, which is different from soccer (paragraph 4).
6. There isn't one (paragraph 3).

12. Practise talking about cultural differences between countries by asking students to discuss what aspects of life and customs in their own countries may surprise visitors. Ask them to make notes and then to discuss their ideas with the rest of the class. It is likely that you'll be asked for a number of words to describe aspects of life; get them to use the structure *What's (word) in English?* It may be better if they don't make a note of all the new vocabulary items.

LEARNING SKILLS

Revise expressions such as:

What does . . . mean?
What's the word for . . .?
How do you pronounce . . .?
How do you spell . . .?

Then ask students to think of two or three words to ask questions about, and to go round the class using the various expressions.

PRONUNCIATION TAPESCRIPT

11.1 Listen and write these words in the correct column.

would /ʊ/, fruit /uː/, two /uː/, book /ʊ/, good /ʊ/, could /ʊ/, food /uː/, soup /uː/

11.2 Listen and repeat.

a) I'll have pizza, salad and chips.

b) I need to buy a map, some stamps and a toothbrush.

c) He's wearing blue trousers, a white shirt and a red tie.

d) She's going to France, Spain and Portugal.

e) You can get there by coach, train or plane.

f) I like swimming, tennis and football.

11.3 Listen and mark the intonation with arrows.

a) It's got two bedrooms, a kitchen, a bathroom and a sitting room.

b) The children are called Robert, Sarah and David.

c) I'm going to the bank, the supermarket and the post office.

d) The bus leaves at seven thirty, one o'clock and four fifteen.

e) You can have coffee, tea or milk.

f) It's open on Mondays, Wednesdays and Fridays.

STRUCTURE REVIEW TAPESCRIPT

11.1 Say what you'd like to eat and drink, like this:

What will you have to eat?
I'll have pizza, please.

What would you like to drink?
I'd like coffee, please.

Now you.

a) What will you have to eat?
I'll have pizza, please.
b) What would you like to drink?
I'd like coffee, please.
c) What will you have to drink?
I'll have orange juice, please.
d) What would you like to eat?
I'd like steak, please.
e) What will you have to eat?
I'll have ice cream, please.
f) What would you like to eat?
I'd like apple pie, please.

11.2 Make requests, like this:

You want someone to tell you the time.
Could you tell me the time, please?

Now you.

a) You want someone to tell you the time.
Could you tell me the time, please?

b) You want someone to bring you the bill.
   Could you bring me the bill, please?
c) You want someone to lend you some money.
   Could you lend me some money, please?
d) You want someone to take you home.
   Could you take me home, please?
e) You want someone to show you the way.
   Could you show me the way, please?
f) You want someone to call you a taxi.
   Could you call me a taxi, please?

11.3 Say what you must or mustn't do, like this:

Park here.
You mustn't park here.

Lock the door.
You must lock the door.

Now you.

a) Park here.
   You mustn't park here.
b) Lock the door.
   You must lock the door.
c) Wear jeans.
   You mustn't wear jeans.
d) Drive over 30 miles per hour.
   You mustn't drive over 30 miles per hour.
e) Leave your key with reception.
   You must leave your key with reception.
f) Learn five new English words a day.
   You must learn five new English words a day.

12 | Checking what you know

SUMMARY

Functions

In Units 7 to 11, students learnt how to:

Ask and say where places are
Ask and say where you can get things
Ask and say what things people have got
Ask and say what things people want/need
Ask and say how much things cost
Ask and say how much or how many
Ask and say what people are wearing
Ask and say what the date is
Talk about journeys and timetables
Ask and say how long journeys take

Ask for and give information about travel
Ask and say what places are like
Ask and say what people's plans are
Talk about hotel facilities
Make requests
Agree to and refuse requests
Ask for and give directions
Ask what words mean
Offer
Order a meal
Say what you must and mustn't do

Topics

The topics covered have been:

Shops and services, shopping, clothes, colours, means of transport, ordinal numbers, months of the year, days of the week, dates, times, journeys, geographical location, geographical features and description, continents, countries, oceans, seas, numbers over 50, travel documents, hotel facilities, hotel formalities, street directions, tourist facilities and sights, food, restaurants, British and American English, instructions.

TEACHING GUIDE

WARM-UP

Suggested warm-up activities: 3, 5, 7, 8, 9, 10 or 13.

WB

Students should be able to do the *Workbook* exercises at any stage of this revision unit.

1 Practise reading for general sense by asking students to look at the tourist information about Hong Kong and to match the headings with paragraphs. Draw their attention to the inset map of the territory on the opposite page. The structures and much of the vocabulary have already been presented in Units 7 to 11. However, there may be some words which the students don't understand at first. Encourage them to do the exercise before you answer any vocabulary queries. This will help them become accustomed to reading for general sense rather than stopping at every unfamiliar word. If there are any vocabulary problems, ask students to choose five or six words and to try and work out the meaning from the context. Get them to write down an approximate meaning for each of the unfamiliar words. When

they are ready, they should discuss the meaning of any unfamiliar words with another student. Limiting the number of words to work on and to explain makes them think very carefully about which are the most important words in a passage; it also ensures that they do not have many words to learn and to revise at the end of the lesson.

Answers

Paragraph 1: *POSITION AND AREA*
Paragraph 2: *POPULATION AND LANGUAGE*
Paragraph 3: *SHOPPING HOURS*
Paragraph 4: *OFFICE AND BANKING HOURS*
Paragraph 5: *TRANSPORT*

2 Revise asking for and giving information and talking about journeys and timetables by asking students to role play the situation shown in their books. As usual, go round and listen to each pair in turn, and note down any serious errors. Draw everyone's attention to any common mistakes,

then ask them to change partners and roles, and to choose another topic. The language in this exercise is particularly useful if the students ever need to use English as tourists. Remind them that this may well happen in countries where English is not the native language.

3 Revise asking for and giving directions by playing the tape and asking students to follow the directions and to note down the names of the places. Remind students that the directions are given starting from the Information Centre.

Tapescript

1 Go along Salisbury Road and turn left into Nathan Road. It's on the left, opposite the Holiday Inn.
2 Go along Salisbury Road and turn left into Chatham Road. Then turn right into Mody Road. It's on the right, opposite the Royal Garden Hotel.
3 Go along Salisbury Road and turn left into Nathan Road. Then turn right into Middle Road. It's on the left, opposite the car park.
4 Go out of here and turn left into Canton Road. Go straight ahead, and it's on the left, opposite Kowloon Park.
5 Go along Salisbury Road and turn left into Nathan Road. Then turn right into Cameron Road. It's on the left, next to the Park Hotel.
6 Go along Salisbury Road and turn left into Science Museum Road. Then turn left into Mody Road. It's on the right, opposite the Holiday Inn.

Answers

1 Hyatt Hotel
2 Tsim Sha Tsui Centre
3 Post Office
4 Prince Hotel
5 International Hotel
6 South Sea Centre

4 Revise asking for and giving directions by getting students to ask and say where the six places in 3 are. They should work in pairs for this activity, changing partners now and then until they have corrected their answers.
5 Practise asking for and giving information and asking for and giving directions by getting students to act out the situations in their books. When they have finished, you may like to give further practice by asking students to ask for and give directions from and to other places on the map.
6 Revise talking about hotel facilities by asking students to work in pairs and act out the role play. Make sure they don't look at each other's information. Check that they are using the structures *Has it got . . .?* and *Is there a . . .?*, and suitable vocabulary. If necessary they should remind themselves of the lexical items used in this situation by looking back at Unit 10. As in 2, this

activity involves language which the students are very likely to use as tourists.
7 Revise asking and saying what people's plans are by asking students to work in groups of three and to solve the problem. The technique of jigsaw reading as shown in this exercise is particularly useful as it creates a genuine information gap, and makes the students share their knowledge in a realistic way. Use the baggage labels to practise letters of the alphabet and numbers. Colour vocabulary was taught in Unit 7 but you may need to teach *brown*, *grey*, *orange* and *pink*. Then ask students to perform the activity. Point out that each name begins with a different letter of the alphabet (for easy reference if students make notes).

Answers

Mrs Adams – 217 – white
Dr Backhouse – 5 – orange – Hong Kong
Miss Capra – 188 – pink – Africa
Mr Donat – 20 – white
Professor Eckstein – 801 – brown
Mr Fernandes – 110 – grey
Ms Guo – 201 – brown
Dr Harris – 1 – yellow
Mr Imberto – 114 – green
Mrs Jackson – 982 – red
Miss Klinger – 72 – yellow
Dr Lam – 2 – red

LEARNING SKILLS

Write on the board the following lists of words:

It's a large modern city in the north of France	and	small south of it's village a in Spain the old

Make sure they're in lists, not in sentences. Give them about thirty seconds to learn the lists, and then wipe them off the board.

Choose a topic covered in Units 7 to 12 (see page 63). Students have two minutes to write down as many words connected with the topic as possible. Then each pair calls out their words, and the highest number of appropriate words wins.

Now ask students to try and remember the lists you asked them to learn before the last activity. How many words can they remember? How many are in the right order? Which list is easier to recall? Why? Explain that vocabulary is easier to learn if it's noted down in the context of a sentence. This obviously takes more time but is ultimately more efficient.

13 | Talking about the past (1)

UNIT SUMMARY

Functions

Asking and saying what happened in the past

Structures

Did	I we you they he she	leave at nine o'clock?

Yes,	I we you they he she	did.	No,	I we you they he she	didn't.

Where did	you they he she	go?	I We They He She	went to the cinema.

Was	he she	tired	last at the	weekend?
Were	you they			

Yes,	I he she	was.	No,	I he she	wasn't.
	we you they	were.		we you they	weren't.

Asking and saying when things happened in the past

What did	you they he she	do on	Monday Tuesday Wednesday Saturday	morning? afternoon? evening?

When did	you they he she	go there?	Last week On Tuesday morning. At five o'clock. In May. In 1982.

Topics

Leisure activities, times of the day

Lexical items

- burglar busy camera cheque book decide great horse race listen to look at lovely lucky next night club race course radio see special stereo take (a taxi) taxi driver time (a great time) tired unfortunately weekend win wonderful

TEACHING GUIDE

This unit introduces the simple past tense using known verbs. Students are encouraged to talk about their own experiences as much as possible, so, if the circumstances demand it, you may want to introduce some new lexical items.

WARM-UP

Suggested warm-up activity: 3.

1 Present the past simple by asking students to listen to the conversation and to tick the activities that Richard and Carla did last Saturday. Check that everyone remembers the meaning of the vocabulary items; you may have to pre-teach *horse races*. Explain if necessary that they don't have to understand every word of the dialogue. Check that everyone understands *wedding anniversary*.

Tapescript

RICHARD:	Morning, Tom.
TOM:	Oh, hello, Richard. How are you? Did you have a good weekend?
RICHARD:	Yes, it was great – it was our tenth wedding anniversary on Saturday.
TOM:	Oh, really? Congratulations. Did you celebrate?
RICHARD:	Yes, we did. On Saturday morning we went shopping in Kowloon . . .
TOM:	Did you find anything nice?
RICHARD:	Yes – Carla bought me a Walkman – and I bought her a lovely silk dress. Then in the afternoon we went swimming in Repulse Bay with the children, and we went out for dinner in the evening.
TOM:	Where did you go?
RICHARD:	We went to the Mongolian Restaurant in Happy Valley – it was very good. And then we went to a night club. We didn't go to bed till two in the morning – we had a lovely time.
TOM:	And what did you do yesterday?
RICHARD:	We were very tired – so we didn't do anything special. How about you, Tom? Did you have a good weekend?

Answers

Last Saturday, Richard and Carla	went shopping.	T
	went to the cinema.	F
	went to the horse races.	F
	went swimming.	T
	had dinner in a restaurant.	T
	had dinner at home.	F
	went to the theatre.	F
	went to a night club.	T

2 Present the simple past productively by asking questions about Richard and Carla, and eliciting the reply *Yes, they did.* or *No, they didn't.* Make sure students understand the meaning of the contraction.
    Now get students to use the question form *Did they . . .?* by asking similar questions in pairs.

3 Present the question form *What did they do . . .?* by asking students to say again what Carla and Richard did at various times of the day on Saturday. Elicit replies using the simple past, and then get students to work in pairs to practise the question form. Write the cue sentence on the board and mark the stress and intonation.

> What did Carla and Richard do on Saturday morning? They went shopping.

Ask students to practise repeating the sentence in pairs. They should then practise similar stress and intonation patterns on the other sentences.

4 Practise the simple past question, affirmative and negative forms by asking students to work in pairs and find out what each other did last weekend. When they have finished talking to each other, they should find a new partner. Make sure they understand the sense of *It was all right. I didn't do anything special.* as a non-committal response to the question.

5 Practise the simple past by asking students to go round and complete the chart with different names. You may want to extend the list shown in the *Student's Book*. Students should start off by

asking Yes/No questions and then continue with Wh- questions. Point out the irregular past tense forms of be: was(n't)/were(n't).

WB 13.1

6 Practise writing by asking students to discuss with another student and then write a few sentences about what people did at the weekend. If you have time to organise correction in the class period, ask students to look at each other's sentences to check if they are correct. They should only mark a cross in the margin corresponding to the mistake in the sentence. Students should then look at their 'corrected' versions and try and find the mistakes.

7 Revise the present continuous by asking students to describe what's happening in the pictures of the story which are in the correct order. You may want to pre-teach race course and lucky, and explain, if necessary, that in some countries people bet on horse races. Then, without looking at 8, ask students to predict what the story might be about.

8 Practise reading for understanding text organisation by asking students to match the sentences with the pictures.

Answers

1 F, 2 C, 3 G, 4 A, 5 E, 6 B, 7 D

Ask students if they had predicted the story correctly. Then play the recorded version of the story and check that they've put the sentences in the correct order.

Tapescript

RICHARD:	How about you, Tom? Did you have a good weekend?
TOM:	No, it was terrible!
RICHARD:	Why? What happened?
TOM:	Well, I had nothing to do on Saturday afternoon, so I decided to go to the races. I left home at about two thirty and I took a taxi to Happy Valley. I arrived at the race course at about a quarter to three, and looked at the list of horses in the next race . . .
RICHARD:	Uh huh.
TOM:	. . . There was a horse called Seven Up at seven to one, so I decided to put seven hundred dollars on it.
RICHARD:	Seven hundred dollars – that's a lot of money!
TOM:	Well, yes. You see, seven is my lucky number.
RICHARD:	Oh, I see. Go on. Did Seven Up win the race?
TOM:	Well, I wanted him to . . . but unfortunately he finished seventh.

RICHARD:	Oh, no!
TOM:	And I lost seven hundred dollars . . . and that wasn't all!
RICHARD:	What do you mean!
TOM:	Well, of course, I had no money left and I felt terrible. So I went back home. When I arrived at my flat, the front door was open . . .
RICHARD:	Oh, no!
TOM:	Oh, yes! While I was at the races, burglars broke into my flat and they took my TV, my stereo, my camera . . .
RICHARD:	Oh, Tom, that's terrible. I am sorry!
TOM:	So am I.

Practise writing by asking students to write their own version of the story of Tom at the races. Point out the use of the linking words: and, but and so. Explain that so indicates result. Once again, you may like to ask students to correct each other's versions, and then hand them back. Go round and check that each story has been correctly marked.

9 Practise listening to specific information by asking students to read the questions before they listen to the dialogue. Pre-teach burglar. Ask students to describe the picture of Tom's flat and to predict what the listening passage might be about. Explain that they will not have to understand every word of the conversation.

Tapescript

POLICEMAN:	Now, Mr Kennedy – can you tell us what's missing?
TOM:	Well, as far as I can see, they took my stereo . . . my television . . . my camera . . . my cheque book and credit cards, and about 100 dollars in cash.
POLICEMAN:	I see. And, what time did you leave your flat this afternoon?
TOM:	At about half past two – I took a taxi to the races.
POLICEMAN:	And what time did you come home?
TOM:	At half past three.
POLICEMAN:	So you were only out for an hour?
TOM:	That's right.
POLICEMAN:	Did anyone know that you were at the races?
TOM:	No, I didn't tell anyone. Oh . . . well the taxi driver knew, of course.
POLICEMAN:	I see, Mr Kennedy. Thank you.

Answers

1 Stereo, television, camera, cheque book, credit cards, $100. 2 2.30 p.m. 3 3.30 p.m. 4 The taxi driver.

10 Practise writing by asking students to make a diary of their activities for the preceding day. Give an

example by writing your diary on the board. Include 'universal' activities such as: *I got up at. . . . ; I had breakfast/lunch at. . . . ; I went to bed at. . . .* Encourage students to write their daily diary in English in a special notebook. Collect their notebooks once a week and check for mistakes.

11 Practise asking and saying what you did and when by getting students to find other people who did the same things at the same time. To finish the activity, the students who did the same things at the same times should find more things which they all did at similar times in their lives.

12 Practise discriminating between consonant sounds in regular verb endings by getting students to listen and to write down the past tense forms in the correct columns. Then ask students to read out their lists.

Tapescript

visited	arrived	looked played wanted
listened	worked	watched decided danced
loved	liked	started phoned needed

Answers

/d/	/t/	/id/
arrived	looked	visited
played	worked	wanted
listened	watched	decided
loved	danced	started
phoned	liked	needed

By now, students should be able to produce all the irregular past forms of all the verbs in the list. Encourage them to add to the list when they come across new verbs.

Answers

go	→ went	come	→ came
have	→ had	get	→ got
do	→ did	speak	→ spoke
be	→ was/were	write	→ wrote
take	→ took	tell	→ told

WB 13.2, 13.3, 13.4

13 Practise listening for specific information by playing the recording and asking students to tick the places Richard's parents visited in Hong Kong. Remind students that they don't have to understand every word they hear. You may wish to draw attention to the Australian accent of the speakers.

Tapescript

RICHARD:	Hello, Mum – hello, Dad. Did you have a good day?
MRS KING:	Oh, yes – we had a wonderful time, didn't we, dear?
MR KING:	Oh, yes. It was lovely.
RICHARD:	What did you do?
MRS KING:	Well, first we took the Star Ferry to Kowloon – and we went shopping . . . Don bought five shirts and two suits . . .
MR KING:	No, dear – you did.
RICHARD:	Did you go to Tsimshatsui?
MRS KING:	Oh, yes – it was wonderful – everything was so cheap! Then we took the ferry back to Hong Kong Island, and we took the Peak Tram up to Victoria Peak . . .
MR KING:	I didn't like that . . . it was dangerous.
MRS KING:	Oh, nonsense, dear. It was perfectly safe – and the view from the Peak was fantastic. We had lunch up there . . .
RICHARD:	Did you like the food?
MRS KING:	Yes, it was very interesting . . . then we took a taxi to Repulse Bay and we sat on the beach . . .
RICHARD:	Did you go swimming?
MRS KING:	I didn't, but Don did.
MR KING:	Warm water – very nice.
MRS KING:	And then we went to Ocean Park to see the dolphins . . . and then we went to Aberdeen!
RICHARD:	Did you have dinner in a floating restaurant?
MRS KING:	Yes, we did! It was wonderful, very romantic . . .
MR KING:	. . . and the food was OK too.
MRS KING:	Oh, we had a wonderful time, didn't we dear?
MR KING:	Yes, dear.

Answers

	KEY	
1	Happy Valley Racecourse	
2	Sung Dynasty Village	
3	Tsimshatsui, shopping and hotel area	✔
4	Star Ferry	✔
5	Victoria Harbour	
6	Victoria Peak and Peak Tram	✔
7	Central District	
8	Nightmarket	
9	Ocean Park Oceanarium and Water World	✔
10	Floating Restaurants in Aberdeen	✔
11	Repulse Bay Beach	✔
12	Stanley Market	

14 Give further practice in the simple past question, and short answer forms, affirmative and negative,

by getting students to ask and say what Richard's parents did while they were in Hong Kong.

WB 13.5, 13.6

15 Get students to make notes and then talk about their own experiences in a place they have visited, perhaps on holiday or on business. Encourage them to think of the most memorable place they have visited in their lives.

16 Practise writing by asking students to write a brief account of their visit to the memorable place in 15. You may like to set this exercise for homework. If you decide to do it in class, try and correct as soon as the students have finished writing. Make a note of the errors and prepare a poster with all the errors explained. Put the poster on the wall in time for the next lesson. Ask students to look through their versions in their own time and try and correct their mistakes themselves without your help.

WB 13.7

LEARNING SKILLS

If your students have dictionaries, or intend to buy one, spend a few moments discussing why it is better to have an all-English dictionary rather than a bilingual one. Explain that it isn't always possible to translate a word exactly and that using an all-English dictionary helps people to think in English and to develop their reading skills. If necessary, explain what the various signs and abbreviations in the dictionary are. Ask them to look up the following words.:

> village, tea, concert, pub, traveller's cheque, cathedral

Then ask them to tell the class as much about the word as they can understand: e.g. 'Village' is a noun. It's a small town; there are houses and shops, perhaps a church and a school.
 Ask your students to note down three reasons why they are learning English. Get them to tell their partner, and then the rest of the class. Make a list of all the reasons why they are learning English.
 Ask them to look back over Units 7 to 13 and to note down six words which they think will be particularly useful to them. Ask them to explain why to the rest of the class.

PRONUNCIATION TAPESCRIPT

13.1 Listen and repeat.

/t/	/d/
town	down
tour	door
write	ride
bought	board

Now listen and tick the words you hear.

town   tour   ride   board

13.2 Listen to the endings and write these verbs in the correct column.

played /d/, looked /t/, stopped /t/, arrived /d/, danced /t/, loved /d/, travelled /d/, watched /t/

13.3 Listen to these words and tap the number of syllables.

businessman	(3)	restaurant	(2)
listening	(2)	evening	(2)
seventeen	(3)	vegetable	(3)

13.4 Listen and repeat. How many syllables are there in each of these words?

question	(2)	finished	(2)
information	(4)	different	(2)
comfortable	(3)	decided	(3)
Wednesday	(2)	magazine	(3)

STRUCTURE REVIEW TAPESCRIPT

13.1 Say the past tense of these verbs, like this:

play
played

decide
decided

Now you.

a) play	e) come	i) go
played	*came*	*went*
b) decide	f) visit	j) work
decided	*visited*	*worked*
c) listen	g) finish	k) have
listened	*finished*	*had*
d) look	h) take	l) invite
looked	*took*	*invited*

13.2 Say what happened or didn't happen, like this:

Did Bob leave at nine o'clock?
Yes, he did.

Did Carla arrive late?
No, she didn't.

Now you.

a) Did Bob leave at nine o'clock?
 Yes, he did.

69

b) Did Carla arrive late?
   No, she didn't.
c) Did the bank close at three o'clock?
   No, it didn't.
d) Did Nancy and Bob go to the cinema?
   Yes, they did.
e) Did Koji write a letter home?
   Yes, he did.
f) Did the film start at six fifteen?
   No, it didn't.

13.3 Answer the questions, like this:

Where did Bob go?
He went to America.

Now you.

a) Where did Bob go?
   He went to America.
b) What did Carla do?
   She wrote a letter.
c) What did Richard do?
   He watched TV.
d) Where did Diana go?
   She went to Venice.

e) What did Koji buy?
   He bought some clothes.
f) What did Nancy do?
   She stayed in bed.

13.4 Ask when people did things, like this:

Ask when Diana got home.
When did she get home?

Ask when Bob had dinner.
When did he have dinner?

Now you.

a) Ask when Diana got home.
   When did she get home?
b) Ask when Bob had dinner.
   When did he have dinner?
c) Ask when Richard went to work.
   When did he go to work?
d) Ask when Koji saw the film.
   When did he see the film?
e) Ask when Nancy came to New York.
   When did she come to New York?
f) Ask when Carla did the washing up?
   When did she do the washing up?

14 | Talking about the past (2)

UNIT SUMMARY

Functions

Asking and saying when things happened in the past

Structures

When	were	you they	born?	On 4th April, 1953.
	was	he she		In 1953.

When did	you they he she	start work? leave school?	On 1st March. In March. In 1959. Ten years ago. On Tuesday.

Talking about people's lives

Where Who What	did	you they he she	go? meet? study?

Asking and saying how long something lasted

How long did	you they he she	work there?	For two years.

Topics

Education, family, dates, travel, work

Lexical items

- about become be born child/children continent die discover fall in love fortnight get married give invent later part (n) probably reach sail sailor star (v) stay (v) study (v) think
- first next after that then finally

TEACHING GUIDE

This unit continues the presentation of the simple past with special reference to people's lives, education and careers. It may be useful at certain points during the unit to show pictures of well-known people so that students can talk about their lives. But as usual, make sure you refer as much as possible to the students' own lives and experiences. Teach them any words which are not covered by the passages but which are necessary to meet the students' particular requirements.

WARM-UP

Suggested warm-up activity: 11.

1 Practise reading for specific information by getting students to use the programme notes to fill in the form below. You may need to remind students where Kingston, Jamaica is; ask them to look at page 34. Explain if necessary, that RADA is one of the more important training institutes for actors in Britain. Martin Luther King was a black civil rights leader in America. For more information about him, read the passage in 6.

Answers

BOB ARMSTRONG

Date of Birth: ..*28th March 1956*..................
Place of Birth: ..*Kingston, Jamaica*..............
Nationality: ....*Jamaican*......................
Father's occupation: ...*Business man*..............
Mother's occupation: ...*Nurse*......................
Family: ....*2 sisters*........................

EDUCATION

From	To	
1967	1974	Munro Secondary School
1974	*1977*	College of Arts, Science and Technology, Kingston
1977	*1980*	RADA, London

WORK

From	To	
1980	*1982*	*The Bubble Theatre Co.*
1982	*1985*	*BBC TV - presenter of children's programmes*
NOW		

Is writing a musical about Martin Luther King

---

2 Practise listening for specific information by playing the radio interview and getting the students to fill in the form with details of Bob's education.

Tapescript

INTERVIEWER: . . . and with me in the studio I have Bob Armstrong. Bob's an actor and he's been working for the BBC in London. Now, Bob, you're living in London at the moment, but you're from Jamaica, aren't you?

BOB: Yes, that's right . . . I was born and raised in Jamaica – I suppose you could say I grew up there.

INTERVIEWER: And how did you come to be an actor – was it something you always wanted to do?

BOB: No, not really. I actually wanted to be a teacher . . . so I left school, er, secondary school when I was eighteen and went to college in Kingston to study English and Drama . . . that was in 1974. Now,

while I was at college, I did a lot of work in student productions, you know, things like singing and dancing, writing music, acting . . .

INTERVIEWER: So you got more and more interested in acting?

BOB: Yes, that's right. So when I went to London for a holiday – that was around, er, Christmas in 1976 – I applied for a place at RADA – that's the Royal Academy of Dramatic Art – and to my surprise, they offered me a place – starting in the autumn of 1977.

INTERVIEWER: And you were pleased about that.

BOB: Pleased! Absolutely delighted. So, when I finished my course at college in Jamaica in 1977, I went straight back to London – I was a drama student for three years – it was wonderful!

INTERVIEWER: And what brings you to the States? Are you working here – or are you over here for a holiday?

BOB: Er, both – well, partly holiday – but I'm writing a musical about Martin Luther King, so I thought I'd come over and find out some more about him.

INTERVIEWER: Well, I wish you the best of luck, and I hope you enjoy your stay. Bob Armstrong – thank you for joining us.

BOB: Thank you.

There is more information about Bob on page 22; students should look back and complete the form.

Answers See 1

3 Practise the structure *When did he . . .?* and giving dates (*on 28th March, 1956, in 1956*); present the structure *How long did he . . .?* and the use of *for . . .* with lengths of time, by getting the students to ask and answer questions about Bob. Write the example sentences on the board and mark in the stress and intonation pattern.

When did he join the Bubble Theatre Company?   In 1980.

How long did he work there?   For two years.

Go round and check that students are asking *informal* questions, e.g. *When was Bob born?* (not *What is his date of birth?*).

4 Practise the structures by asking students to copy the form and to use it as a basis for a pairwork dialogue. As they work in pairs, go round and give

any necessary vocabulary which isn't covered in the *Student's Book*.

5   Practise writing by asking students to write up the information about their partners. You may like to correct it by going round and looking at each version. Make a note of any mistakes you find, then write them up on the board without naming the students who made them. Students should then check their versions to see if they made the mistake.

6   Present the past simple forms of a number of common verbs by asking students to fill in the blanks. Encourage them to guess the meaning of unfamiliar past tense forms by a process of elimination.

Tapescript and Answers

Martin Luther King *was* born on 15th January 1929 in Atlanta, Georgia. In 1951, he *went* to Boston University, where he *studied* for four years. In 1952, he *met* Coretta Scott, and as soon as he *saw* her, he *fell* in love. They *got* married in 1953, and they *had* four children. In 1954, the Kings *left* Boston, and Martin *became* a minister at a Baptist Church in Montgomery, Alabama. Then he *started* working for the black freedom movement. Thousands of people *walked* to Washington to hear his famous speech at the Lincoln Memorial in 1963, and he *won* the Nobel Peace Prize in 1964. He *died* on 4th April 1968 in Memphis, Tennessee, from a gunshot wound.

7   Practise writing the infinitive and past tense of the verbs in 6.

Answers

became	→ become	(*irregular*)
died	→ die	(*regular*)
fell	→ fall	(*irregular*)
got	→ get	(*irregular*)
had	→ have	(*irregular*)
left	→ leave	(*irregular*)
met	→ meet	(*irregular*)
saw	→ see	(*irregular*)
started	→ start	(*regular*)
studied	→ study	(*regular*)
walked	→ walk	(*regular*)
was	→ be	(*irregular*)
went	→ go	(*irregular*)
won	→ win	(*irregular*)

This would be a good opportunity to check that the students have begun to organise their list of irregular verbs in a suitable way.

WB 14.1, 14.2

Note:
Explain that Einstein is famous for his theory of relativity, which gave rise to the equation $E = mc^2$.

8   Practise reading by getting students to find the answers to the questions. Students should do the exercise alone and then check their answers in pairs.

Answers

1	Ernest Hemingway	6	Bonnie Parker
2	Billie-Jean King	7	Marlon Brando
3	Neil Armstrong	8	Thomas Edison
4	George Washington	9	Joan Baez
5	Marilyn Monroe	10	Orville Wright

9   Practise writing questions and speaking by asking students to think of three famous people from their countries and to write questions about them. Get them to write the questions, then check they have written them correctly before playing the classroom quiz. They can use the questions in 8 as a model.

10   Practise writing by asking students to choose a famous person and to write a biography of him or her. If necessary, you may like to give them time to do this as homework. When they have finished, check that they have used the past simple correctly and then put the biographies up on the class notice board so everyone can read them. It is advisable to correct the written work *before* you put it up.

11   Practise reading and understanding text organisation by asking students to put the sentences in the correct order. Ask students not to worry too much about any difficult vocabulary at this stage.

Answers   E B G A D C F

Now get students to choose five words which they don't understand and ask them to decide what part of speech the words are. Then ask them to look for clues in the context as to the meaning. Then get them to write down a few words to describe what they think they might mean. They should then check their answers with another student. If they are not satisfied with their conclusions, tell them they can look up three of the words in the dictionary. Make sure they choose these words carefully.

Check the answers by playing the tape.

Tapescript

The first European sailors to reach America were probably the Vikings of Denmark and Norway. They visited America about a thousand years ago, in the eleventh century AD. Five hundred years later, European sailors again travelled across the Atlantic, and discovered America by mistake! In 1492, a Genoese sailor called Christopher Columbus sailed west from Spain and reached the Bahamas. He thought these islands were part of Asia, and so they were called the West Indies. Seven years later, another Italian, Amerigo Vespucci, sailed from Spain to South America. He discovered that this huge continent was not part of Asia, and he gave his name to the New World.

12 Practise reading for specific information and using the simple past by getting students to find out when the crossings were made to America, and then to ask and answer questions about them. Present *About . . . ago.* and revise *In . . . .* by eliciting the correct answers to the questions. Make sure people use both forms.

Answers

A Vikings: 1000AD.   B Christopher Columbus: 1492.   C Amerigo Vespucci: 1499.

WB 14.3

13 Practise listening for specific information by playing the tape and asking students to note how long Bob stayed in each place and to mark his route on the map. If there are any specific vocabulary problems, you may like to deal with them at the end of this exercise. Play the tape twice and allow them plenty of time to complete the activity.

Tapescript

NANCY:	Well, Bob, did you enjoy your tour?
BOB:	Yes, it was great!
NANCY:	Come on, let's hear about it.
BOB:	Well, first I went north to Boston by coach – I stayed in Boston for two days – it's a charming city. And next I flew to Chicago . . .
NANCY:	What did you think of Chicago?
BOB:	It's a very interesting city – of course it's very industrial, but there are wonderful museums and lots to do there. I liked it – I spent three days in Chicago. After that I flew to New Orleans for two days. That was wonderful.
NANCY:	Did you hear any jazz?
BOB:	Oh, yes – I even played in a couple of clubs!
NANCY:	Really? That's great!
BOB:	Then I went to Miami – and I spent four days lying on the beach.
NANCY:	Hmm. That's what I'd like to do right now. Go on.

BOB:	And finally I flew up to Washington – and I saw all the sights . . . the White House, the Lincoln Memorial . . . I was there for three days. And now here I am back in New York – and I'm really tired.
NANCY:	You're tired after a two-week holiday?
BOB:	Travelling is hard work!

Answers

14 Practise the structure *How long did . . . ?* by getting students to ask and answer questions about Bob's stay in Boston. Write up the cue sentence and mark in the stress and intonation pattern.

> How long did he stay in Boston?   For two days.

Get students to practise the correct pronunciation, stress and intonation of the question and response.

15 Practise writing by getting students to complete the sentences.

Answers

First he went to Boston for two days.
Next he flew to Chicago.
After that he flew to New Orleans.
Then he went to Miami.
Finally he flew to Washington.

Go round and correct their versions by marking each error with a cross in the margin. Ask students to see if they can spot the errors they have made.

WB 14.4

16 Practise the question form *When did . . . ?* and the reply *. . . ago* by getting students to ask and answer questions about Bob's tour. Make sure students realise that the time reference used with *ago* is from the present.

17 Practise use of the past tense by asking students to write down five important events in their lives

without writing the dates. Encourage them to think of very personal events which do not necessarily happen to everyone. After students have asked and answered questions about these events, they should write a few sentences about their partners. Correct them as in 15.

WB 14.5

18 Give further practice in using the past simple and the sequencing words in 15.

LEARNING SKILLS

Write the following passage on the board:

> When I bobbled that morning, it was a fuddly day.
> I put on my hirtle and goopies and went
> downstairs to have some wisket. But a pillet lay
> by the door; I was very froobied because I could
> recognise the dalking. It was from Bobby. The last
> time he dalked to me, it was doobiful news. I
> opened the pillet very quickly : . .

Ask students to decide what parts of speech the words which they don't recognise are. Are they nouns, verbs or adjectives? Explain that all the words underlined are nonsense words. Point out that you don't need to understand each word in order to understand the general sense of the passage.

PRONUNCIATION TAPESCRIPT

14.1 Listen and repeat.

/ɪ/	/iː/
live	leave
sit	seat
fill	feel
bin	been

Now listen and tick the words you hear.

leave   sit   feel   bin

14.2 Listen and write the words in the correct column

busy /ɪ/, cinema /ɪ/, city /ɪ/, eat /iː/, need /iː/, sink /ɪ/, TV /iː/, week /iː/

14.3 Listen and repeat. Tap the stressed syllables.

a) When were you born?
b) Where did you go to school?
c) How long did he stay there?
d) When did she start work?
e) When did he meet his wife?
f) How many children have they got?

Note:
After students have crossed out the unstressed words, draw their attention to these structure words that do not carry any stress in a sentence.

STRUCTURE REVIEW TAPESCRIPT

14.1 Say when people were born, like this:

When was Mozart born?
In 1756.

When was Buddy Holly born?
On the seventh of September 1936.

Now you.

a) When was Mozart born?
In 1756.
b) When was Buddy Holly born?
On the seventh of September 1936.
c) When was Picasso born?
In 1881.
d) When was Charlie Chaplin born?
On the sixteenth of April 1889.
e) When was Greta Garbo born?
In 1905.
f) When was Martin Luther King born?
On the fifteenth of January 1929.

14.2 Ask Carla questions about her life, like this:

Ask her when she was born.
When were you born?

Now you.

a) Ask her when she was born.
When were you born?
b) Ask her where she went to school.
Where did you go to school?
c) Ask her where she went to university.
Where did you go to university?
d) Ask her who she met at university.
Who did you meet at university?
e) Ask her when she got married.
When did you get married?
f) Ask her where her first job was.
Where was your first job?

14.3 Ask how long people did things, like this:

Ask how long Bob studied at RADA.
How long did he study at RADA?

Now you.

a) Ask how long Bob studied at RADA.
How long did he study at RADA?
b) Ask how long Carla lived in Rome.
How long did she live in Rome?
c) Ask how long Richard lived in Australia.
How long did he live in Australia?
d) Ask how long Diana worked in Manchester.
How long did she work in Manchester?
e) Ask how long Carla and Richard stayed in Italy.
How long did they stay in Italy?
f) Ask how long Nancy studied drama.
How long did she study drama?

15 | Looking ahead

UNIT SUMMARY

Functions

Talking about future plans and intentions

Structures

What	am	I	going to do	after the lesson? this evening? at the weekend? next year?
	are	you we they		
	is	he she		

I	'm	going to (*verb*).
You We They	're	
He She	's	

I	'm not	going to (*verb*).
You We They	aren't	
He She	isn't	

Are	you they	going to (*verb*)?
Is	he she	

Yes,	I	am.
	we they	are.
	he she	is.

No,	I	'm not.
	we they	aren't.
	he she	isn't.

Functions

Giving advice/instructions

Structures

You should	move the furniture out. wash everything. paint the ceiling first.

You shouldn't	pour water on a chip fire. smoke in bed. put butter on burns.

| First
Then
Next
After that
Finally | you should (verb). |
| | (imperative). |

Agreeing and disagreeing

I think so too.
No, I don't think so.

Topics

Clothes, rooms, household equipment, colours and patterns, instructions, emergency situations

Lexical items

- apron clothes pyjamas shorts swimming costume
- checked flowered plain spotted striped
- ambulance ashtray carpet ceiling cigarette cupboard curtain electric fire fat (n) fire first aid frying pan furniture iron (n) ironing board oil paintbrush plan (n) sheet shelf/shelves soap tennis racket towel
- burn catch fire cover (v) dry (v) fall asleep fall out fill hold move paint smoke switch off/on wash

TEACHING GUIDE

A large amount of new vocabulary is introduced in this unit; while the list above represents the lexical items that students will be required to use productively, students are not expected to learn all the words in the unit.

WARM-UP

Suggested warm-up activity: 14.

1   Practise the present continuous (see Units 5 and 7) by asking students to describe what the people in the pictures are wearing and holding. Make sure they understand the difference between *wear* and *hold*. Go round and check that each pair is using the structure properly, and then check their answers with the class as a whole. All the items in the word list are illustrated in the pictures, and

many of the words for clothes were introduced in Unit 7.

Answers

Diana's wearing blue jeans and a white pullover. She's holding a paintbrush.
Carla and Richard are wearing white T-shirts, white shorts, white shoes and white socks. They're holding tennis rackets.
Koji's wearing pyjamas. He's holding a book.
Nancy's wearing a black swimming costume and a towel.
Bob's wearing trousers, a blue shirt, a tie and a red apron. He's holding a frying-pan.

2   Present *going to* for talking about the future by asking students to guess the intentions of the

people in 1 from their clothes, etc. The phrases on the right-hand side will help them. Present the structure, then get students to practise in pairs.

Answers

Diana's going to paint the kitchen.
Carla and Richard are going to play tennis.
Koji's going to go to bed.
Nancy's going to go swimming.
Bob's going to cook a meal.

Present *Is (name) going to . . .? Yes, he/she is. No, he/she isn't.* using the same pictures. You may like to give further practice by bringing in some magazine pictures of 'action' shots and asking the students what they think is going to happen next.

WB 15.1

3 Present and practise the structure *What are you going to do after this lesson?* etc. by asking students to talk about their plans, first of all in pairs, then to other students. If you have time, you can ask them to take notes on what everyone they interview is going to do. You can then ask them to report their findings to the class as a whole, using *(name)'s going to. . . .*
   Check that everyone is using the short answers *Yes, I am./No, I'm not.* correctly. Practise writing by asking them to write sentences about their plans or about one or two of their colleagues' plans.

4 Practise the structure by asking students to mime something they're going to do (in groups of four). The rest of the group should try to guess *what* the activity is, and *when* its going to happen by asking questions; the student who is miming can only answer *Yes, I am./No, I'm not.*

WB 15.2, 15.3

5 Practise listening for specific information by playing the tape and asking the students to complete the chart. They can refer to the colour 'wheel'. Remind students not to try and understand every word, only the colours Diana is going to paint each room.

Tapescript

DIANA:	Fiona, sit down and have a cup of tea. I need your advice.
FIONA:	Why? What's the matter?
DIANA:	I'm going to decorate my flat.
FIONA:	What – all of it?
DIANA:	Yes, and I'm going to start with the kitchen. I want the kitchen to look bright and sunny, so I'm going to paint this

wall orange, and the other walls white . . .

FIONA:	And what about the ceiling?
DIANA:	The ceiling's going to be yellow – what do you think?
FIONA:	Mmm – sounds nice.
DIANA:	Then I'm going to start on the bathroom. The walls are going to be blue . . .
FIONA:	Isn't blue rather a cold colour?
DIANA:	Maybe, but the ceiling's going to be red!
FIONA:	Oh, well, it's your bathroom! What about the sitting room?
DIANA:	Well, I'd like white walls – and the ceiling's going to be green.
FIONA:	Very smart!
DIANA:	And then there's the bedroom. I want the bedroom to feel warm, so I'm going to paint the ceiling grey – and the walls are going to be pink.
FIONA:	How romantic!
DIANA:	Well, what do you think?
FIONA:	I think you're going to need some help!

Answers

	Walls	Ceiling
Kitchen	orange, white	yellow
Bathroom	blue	red
Sitting room	white	green
Bedroom	pink	grey

6 Practise *going to . . .* and colours, rooms, etc. by getting students to ask and answer questions about the colours of each room.

WB 15.4

7 Practise *going to* and present *She should* and *I think so too./I don't think so.* by discussing with students what Diana should buy for her flat. Discuss the colour scheme with individual students; then ask them to discuss it in pairs. Teach *plain, striped, flowered, spotted, checked* by referring to people's clothes.

8 Practise reading and listening to understand text organisation by asking students to read the instructions for decorating and then to listen to the conversation and to put the points in order. If there are any words the students don't understand tell them to decide what part of speech the word is, to look for clues in the context and to try and guess what the word means. If necessary, tell them they can look up *four* words in their dictionary.

Tapescript

DIANA:	Peter, I don't know much about decorating. Can you give me some advice?
PETER:	Well, first you should move the furniture out of the room.
DIANA:	What if I can't move it?
PETER:	If you can't move it, you should cover it with old sheets or newspapers.
DIANA:	I see.
PETER:	Next you should wash everything you're going to paint with soap and water. That's very important.
DIANA:	Uh huh.
PETER:	Then you can start painting. You should do the ceiling first . . . after that you should paint the walls . . . and finally you should paint the windows, doors, shelves and cupboards.
DIANA:	So it's ceiling, walls, woodwork?
PETER:	That's right. Good luck!

Revise the sequencing words and present *You should . . . .* by asking students to write out the instructions. Point out that written instructions are usually given in the imperative. Spoken instructions are more likely to use *You should. . . .*

Answers

First you should move the furniture out of the room. If you can't move it, you should cover it. Next you should wash everything you're going to paint with soap and water. Then you can start painting. You should do the ceiling first. After that you should paint the walls. Finally you should paint the windows, doors, shelves and cupboards.

9 Practise writing by asking students to write a paragraph describing their flat or house. Make sure they describe it as fully as possible. Go round and make a note of any mistakes you see, then discuss the mistakes with the class as a whole; encourage students to spot their own mistakes.

10 Practise reading for general sense by asking students to match the pictures with the paragraphs. Explain that it isn't necessary to understand all the words to do this exercise, but that they will need to learn most of them at some stage. Ask students to choose two or three words and to try and guess their meanings from the context. Now ask them to work in pairs and to check whether they have both tried to guess the meaning of the same words. Finally, make a list of all the unfamiliar words on the board and write up all the suggested meanings. Then tick the correct ones.

Answers 1 C, 2 A, 3 D, 4 B

11 Practise using the new vocabulary and *going to* by getting students to ask and answer questions about the situations illustrated and described in 10.

12 Practise *You should. . . ./You shouldn't. . . .* by asking students to describe what advice they would give to avoid the situations shown in 10. Ask them to write the sentences and then to check each other's versions for mistakes.

13 Practise reading for specific information by asking students to work in pairs and to read the passage to find out the answers to the questions. Explain once again that they don't need to understand every word. It probably isn't necessary to do any more vocabulary work, but if students are worried about not finding out the meaning of certain words, tell them to look three words up in their dictionaries: this will make them choose the words very carefully and restrict the vocabulary input.

Answers

STUDENT **A**'s questions:
You should put the burn under cold water and then take off anything tight. Next you should cover the burn and you shouldn't put any butter on it. Finally, you should call an ambulance.

STUDENT **B**'s questions:
First you should get everybody out of the house. Then you should send for the Fire Brigade. You shouldn't waste time trying to put the fire out. You should shut all the doors and windows.

14 Give further practice in giving advice by getting students to write down the numbers of the emergency services in their countries.

WB 15.5, 15.6, 15.7

LEARNING SKILLS

Ask students to note down the following words:

football, morning, presenter, life, European, oil, curtain, paint, actor, kitchen, bank, fire, ladies room, capital city, minister

Then explain that everyone has an active and a passive vocabulary. Our active vocabulary consists of words which we can *use* when speaking or writing. Our passive vocabulary consists of words which we *recognise and understand* when reading or listening. Ask students to look at the list above and to put A (for active) or P (for passive) against each of the words. Check their answers. Explain that the active/passive distinction will vary according to the student's particular needs. Ask them to look back at their list of content words and to decide whether they are active or passive items. Point out that active items should be revised more regularly than passive ones.

PRONUNCIATION TAPESCRIPT

15.1 Listen and repeat.

/n/	/ŋ/
sin	sing
win	wing
ran	rang
sun	sung

Now listen and tick the words you hear.

sin   wing   ran   sung

15.2 Listen and tick the words which contain the sound /ŋ/.

drink ✓   dinner   green   thanks ✓
morning ✓   night   going ✓   long ✓

15.3 Listen and underline the most important word in each of the answers.

a) Are you going to see her tomorrow?
   No, I'm going to see her <u>tonight</u>.
b) Do you like the green trousers?
   No, I like the <u>blue</u> ones.
c) Tom's got two brothers, hasn't he?
   No, he's got <u>three</u> brothers.
d) Does Bob live in New York?
   No, <u>Nancy</u> lives in New York.
e) Is Koji going to the theatre?
   No, he's going to the <u>cinema</u>.
f) Is your telephone number five two six – seven three double two?
   No, it's five two <u>nine</u> – seven three double two.

15.4 Listen to the questions again, and answer them yourself.

a) Are you going to see her tomorrow?
   No, I'm going to see her tonight.
b) Do you like the green trousers?
   No, I like the blue ones.
c) Tom's got two brothers, hasn't he?
   No, he's got three brothers.
d) Does Bob live in New York?
   No, Nancy lives in New York.
e) Is Koji going to the theatre?
   No, he's going to the cinema.
f) Is your telephone number five two six – seven three double two?
   No, it's five two nine – seven three double two.

STRUCTURE REVIEW TAPESCRIPT

15.1 Ask about people's plans, like this:

Bob's going to stay at home this evening.
Is Nancy going to stay at home too?

Now you.

a) Bob's going to stay at home this evening.
   Is Nancy going to stay at home too?
b) Richard's going to look for a new job next year.
   Is Carla going to look for a new job too?
c) Diana's going to go for a walk this afternoon.
   Is Koji going to go for a walk too?
d) Carla's going to watch TV tonight.
   Is Richard going to watch TV too?
e) Joe's going to play football tomorrow.
   Is Nina going to play football too?

15.2 Say what these people are going to do this evening, like this:

Is Bob going to see a film?
No, he isn't. He's going to stay at home.

Now you.

a) Is Bob going to see a film?
   No, he isn't. He's going to stay at home.
b) Is Nancy going to eat in a restaurant?
   No, she isn't. She's going to wash her hair.
c) Is Diana going to have dinner with friends?
   No, she isn't. She's going to visit her parents.
d) Are Carla and Richard going to take the children out?
   No, they aren't. They're going to play games at home.
e) Is Koji going to write to his wife?
   No, he isn't. He's going to phone her.

15.3 Give advice on keeping fit, like this:

Smoke.
You shouldn't smoke.

Eat lots of vegetables.
You should eat lots of vegetables.

Now you.

a) Smoke.
   You shouldn't smoke.
b) Eat lots of vegetables.
   You should eat lots of vegetables.
c) Go for a walk every day.
   You should go for a walk every day.
d) Eat lots of cakes and biscuits.
   You shouldn't eat lots of cakes and biscuits.
e) Drink strong coffee.
   You shouldn't drink strong coffee.
f) Go to bed early.
   You should go to bed early.

16 | Describing appearance

UNIT SUMMARY

Functions

Asking and saying what people look like

Asking and saying how old people are

Asking and saying what people are wearing

Asking and saying how tall people are

Giving compliments

Structures

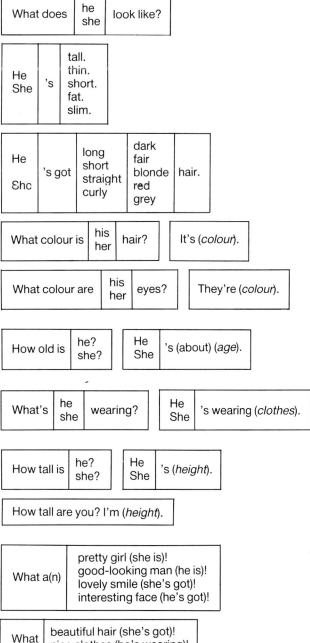

| What does | he / she | look like? |

| He / She | 's | tall. / thin. / short. / fat. / slim. |

| He / She | 's got | long / short / straight / curly | dark / fair / blonde / red / grey | hair. |

| What colour is | his / her | hair? | | It's (colour). |

| What colour are | his / her | eyes? | | They're (colour). |

| How old is | he? / she? | He / She | 's (about) (age). |

| What's | he / she | wearing? | He / She | 's wearing (clothes). |

| How tall is | he? / she? | He / She | 's (height). |

How tall are you? I'm (height).

| What a(n) | pretty girl (she is)! / good-looking man (he is)! / lovely smile (she's got)! / interesting face (he's got)! |

| What | beautiful hair (she's got)! / nice clothes (he's wearing)! |

81

Topics

Physical description: age, size, height, colour of hair and eyes, clothes

Lexical items

- blonde   brown   curly   dark   fair   fair-haired, etc.   fat   good-looking   hazel   long   nice   short   slim   straight   super   tall   thin   young
- aunt   beard   eye   face   girl   glasses   grandparents   hair   moustache   smile   uncle
- quite   very
- centimetre   foot/feet   inch   metre

TEACHING GUIDE

This unit revises familiar structures in the context of describing physical appearance.

WARM-UP

Suggested warm-up activity: 12.

1   Present the vocabulary of physical description by asking students to match the descriptions with the photographs. They should be able to match some of them quite easily without knowing all the words; others they will be able to guess by a process of elimination. Ask them if any of the descriptions fit any members of the class. Then check that students understand the meaning of all the new vocabulary items. Explain that *thin* is usually used in a negative sense (i.e. the person shouldn't be so thin) whereas *slim* is a neutral or positive description (i.e. the person is nice and slim). Point out the use of the modifiers *quite* and *very*, and make sure students understand what they mean.

Answers

A Victoria Wood
B Jerry Hall
C John Osborne
D Diane Keaton
E Michael Jackson
F Woody Allen

2   Practise the language of physical description by asking students to describe the people in 1 without looking at the written descriptions. Give the cue sentence *What does (Woody Allen) look like?* and elicit suitable responses. Then ask students to work in pairs: Student A covers the photo while

Student B covers the written description. Student A asks Student B: *What does . . . look like?* And Student B describes the person from the photo. Students should take turns in questioning and describing. Give further practice by asking students to describe each other.

WB   16.1

3   Revise *What's he/she wearing?* (see Units 7 and 15) by getting students to ask each other about the clothes the people in 1 are wearing. You may want to introduce some extra vocabulary at this stage. Extend this practice by talking about the clothes that the people in the class are wearing.

WB   16.2, 16.3

4   Present *How old is (name)?* by getting students to ask and say how old they think the people in the photographs are. Practise the structure by bringing a number of magazine pictures of people to class and getting students to ask and say how old these people are. Extend this practice by asking them to use the language for physical description which they have learnt in 1 to 4.

5   Practise the language of physical description by getting students to do the problem-solving activity in pairs. Suggest that students make a grid like the one shown in the *Student's Book*, and that they fill in as much information as they can. Explain the meaning of *younger*; *hazel eyes are greenish-brown*.

Answers

ROOM	201	202	203	204	205
NATIONALITY	Brazilian	Norwegian	Russian	German	Italian
MAN/WOMAN	woman	man	man	woman	man
AGE	29	39	54	42	31
COLOUR OF HAIR	red	brown	grey	fair	black
COLOUR OF EYES	green	blue	brown	hazel	grey

6 Give further practice in the structures generated by the problem-solving activity in 5 by getting students to check their answers orally. Go round each pair and make sure they are using the question forms correctly.

7 Practise writing by asking students to write sentences describing the people in each room. Give further practice in writing by asking students to write descriptions of the people in the magazine pictures you may have used in 4. Correct their versions individually, and then draw attention to any mistakes which the class as a whole is making.

8 Practise the language used for describing people by asking students to think of one of the characters in the book and to describe him/her to another student without looking at a picture. This activity can also be done with students describing other students in the same class, or describing well-known people.

9 Practise listening for general sense by playing the recording and asking students to make notes on the descriptions of Prince Charles and Princess Diana. They should then decide which description is the most accurate. Explain that they do not need to understand every word of the descriptions.

Tapescript

1 Er – well – Prince Charles I think is about . . . is between mid and late thirties – average size, average height – with brown hair. I don't know what colour his eyes are, and very conservative clothes I think, really, is my impression of him.

Princess Diana – she's quite a lot younger than Charles – she's twenty-one, twenty-two or something, em – pretty tall for a girl – and her hair is a nice blonde colour, and I think she's got blue eyes – and she wears some lovely clothes – em, much more adventurous than the ones normally worn by the Royal Family.

2 Well, Prince Charles I know was born in 1948, so he's either thirty-seven or thirty-eight – I know that because I was born in '48 too. Er – he's . . . about six foot, I think. He's slim – slimmer than he was – since he married, er, Princess Diana. He's got dark hair and I think blue eyes and he wears very, em, very conservative clothes, very smart usually.

Princess Diana I think is about twenty-four, twenty-five. She's tall and slim, very slim – some people say too slim – she's got blonde hair and blue eyes and she wears, er, very expensive, smart, casual clothes – sometimes, em, very stunning dresses . . . and, em, I think is very fashion-conscious.

3 Em, Prince Charles, em, he's about thirty-two I think – he's, er, he's quite slim – he isn't very tall, I'd say about . . . mm . . . five foot eight . . . em, hair colour – he's got, er, brown, brown to mousey hair – he's going a bit thin on top at the moment, actually – his eyes – I think they're – oh I think they're pale blue or grey, em, he dresses – oh, he's very straight – he's a bit boring, very establishment.

Em . . . Princess Diana – now she's younger – she's about twenty-four – er, she's very thin, very thin at the moment, she's dieted a lot, she's too thin. Em, she's, she's tall – she's taller than him – she's about . . . mm . . . five – five eight, five nine – she is tall – em, she's very blonde, very fair, lovely hair, er, and blue, very blue eyes and she, she dresses, she dresses very well – wears lovely hats – very pretty clothes.

Extend this practice by asking students to describe one famous person; get the others to decide which is the most accurate description.

10 Present *How tall are you? I'm one metre eighty/five foot eleven.* by asking students how tall they are and eliciting a suitable reply. They should practise the question form in pairs and with various students round the class. Explain that in Britain and America, people refer to someone's height in feet and inches, although sometimes in Britain, metres and centimetres are used. Point out that the plural form of *foot* is *feet*, but that when we talk about height, we usually use the singular form.

11 Practise listening for specific information by playing the recording and asking students to complete the form.

Tapescript

INTERVIEWER:	Ah, come in, Ms Wilson. Please take a seat.
TANIA:	Thank you.
INTERVIEWER:	You'd like to work as a model – is that right?
TANIA:	Yes, I would.
INTERVIEWER:	OK – first of all, could I have your personal details for our records? What's your first name?
TANIA:	Tania – that's T-A-N-I-A.
INTERVIEWER:	So that's Ms Tania Wilson. You're American, I guess?
TANIA:	Yes, I am.
INTERVIEWER:	And how old are you?
TANIA:	I'm twenty.
INTERVIEWER:	Uh huh . . . how tall are you?
TANIA:	I'm five foot seven.
INTERVIEWER:	Hmm – that's not very tall. We like out models to be taller than that – what colour is your hair?
TANIA:	Can't you see?

INTERVIEWER: Well, I can see that it's blonde now, but what colour is it really?

TANIA: It really is blonde – it's natural!

INTERVIEWER: Oh, I see. I'm sorry – you've got beautiful hair. And what colour are your eyes?

TANIA: They're blue-grey – it depends on the weather!

INTERVIEWER: All right. Now, Ms Wilson, I can't promise you any work – but I've got your details and if anything comes up, I'll give you a call . . .

Answers

```
Fifth Avenue Model Agency          794/523/5


NAME ___WILSON   Tania___    MS/M̶R̶S̶/M̶R̶

NATIONALITY ___American___   AGE _20_

HEIGHT ___5__ ft __7__ in

COLOUR OF HAIR ___blonde___

COLOUR OF EYES ___blue-grey___
```

12 Practise giving personal information by asking students to copy the form in the *Student's Book* and to use the conversation in 11 as a model for a role play in pairs.

WB 16.4, 16.5, 16.6

13 Present the structure *Who does he/she look like?* and *Who do you look like?* by asking students to talk about family likenesses. Ask students to show each other pictures of their families. This is an informal discussion, so try and avoid correcting too many mistakes; if there are any serious ones, talk to the class as a whole about them. Make sure they do not confuse *What does he/she look like?* (asking for a description) with *Who does he/she look like?* (asking for a name).

14 Present *What (a/an) + adjective + noun!* by paying compliments to students on their clothes, hair and other features. Ask them to go round the class giving each other compliments. Make sure they understand that *What* without the indefinite article is used for uncountable nouns, such as *hair*

and for countable nouns in the plural, such as *eyes*.

You may need to explain that if someone compliments you on one of your possessions, such as a watch or a necklace, it is not necessary in Britain and America to make a gift of this object to the person who is making the compliment.

15 Give further practice in writing about people's physical appearance by asking students to fill in the blanks in the passage with nouns and adjectives describing the physical appearance of the person of their dreams. Encourage them to be as light-hearted as possible.

WB 16.7, 16.8

LEARNING SKILLS

Remind students that they should try to think of ways to link an image, a sound or some kind of coding device to new words in order to help them recall the meaning. Write the following list on the board and check that everyone knows what they mean:

> slim, brown, nationality, dream, mother, student, memory

Ask students to think of some kind of code to link each word with its meaning. Then ask students to explain to the rest of the class what code they have chosen for each word and why.

PRONUNCIATION TAPESCRIPT

16.1 Listen and repeat.

/eə/	/ɜ:/
where	were
hair	her
fair	fur
pair	purr

Now listen and tick the words you hear.
fair   were   hair   pair

16.2 Listen and write the words in the correct column.

airletter /eə/, birth /ɜ:/, burn /ɜ:/, chair /eə/, hurt /ɜ:/, there/their /eə/, turn /ɜ:/, upstairs /eə/

16.3 Listen and mark the intonation with arrows.

a) She's got short fair curly hair.

b) He's got blue eyes, dark hair and a moustache.

c) He's tall and slim with brown hair.

d) She's got long straight dark hair.

16.4 Listen and repeat. Mark the stressed syllables.

a) What a beautiful woman!

b) What an interesting story!

c) What wonderful news!

d) What a good-looking man!

STRUCTURE REVIEW TAPESCRIPT

16.1 Ask what people look like, like this:

> I'm looking for my brother.
> *What does he look like?*

> I'd like to speak to Mrs Jones.
> *What does she look like?*

Now you.

a) I'm looking for my brother.
    What does he look like?
b) I'd like to speak to Mrs Jones.
    What does she look like?
c) I can't remember her name – she's an actress.
    What does she look like?
d) I can't find my children.
    What do they look like?
e) I want to find the man who took my wallet.
    What does he look like?
f) I'm looking for my new teacher – I don't know her name.
    What does she look like?

16.2 Ask questions about appearance, like this:

> Ask what he looks like.
> *What does he look like?*

Now you.

a) Ask what he looks like.
    What does he look like?
b) Ask about his clothes.
    What's he wearing?
c) Ask about the colour of his hair.
    What colour is his hair?
d) Ask about the colour of his eyes.
    What colour are his eyes?
e) Ask about his age.
    How old is he?
f) Ask about his height.
    How tall is he?

16.3 Give compliments, like this:

> Pretty girl.
> *What a pretty girl!*

> Beautiful clothes.
> *What beautiful clothes!*

Now you.

a) Pretty girl.
    What a pretty girl!
b) Beautiful clothes.
    What beautiful clothes!
c) Interesting person.
    What an interesting person!
d) Nice face.
    What a nice face!
e) Lovely eyes.
    What lovely eyes!
f) Good-looking woman.
    What a good-looking woman!

17 Seeing the difference

UNIT SUMMARY

Functions

Making comparisons

Structures

Comparison of adjectives

	Comparative	Superlative
large	larger	largest
small	smaller	smallest
high	higher	highest
low	lower	lowest
cheap	cheaper	cheapest
old	older	oldest
safe	safer	safest
cool	cooler	coolest
warm	warmer	warmest
cold	colder	coldest
fast	faster	fastest
slow	slower	slowest
quiet	quieter	quietest
hot	ho*tt*er	ho*tt*est
big	bi*gg*er	bi*gg*est
noisy	nois*i*er	nois*i*est
modern	more modern	most modern
dangerous	more dangerous	most dangerous
expensive	more expensive	most expensive
good	better	best
bad	worse	worst

The World Trade Center is	taller than	the Empire State Building.
You look		your father.

New York	is the	biggest	city in the USA.
Fifth Avenue		most expensive	street in New York.

Describing impressions

He She	looks feels sounds	ill. happy.
You	look feel sound	

86

Topics

Description of places, people, emotions

Lexical items

- angry big cheap cold cool dangerous expensive famous fast happy heavy high hot ill low noisy quiet sad safe slow warm worried
- feel look sound grow weigh
- airliner bridge (suspension bridge) building department store skyscraper statue street weather zoo

TEACHING GUIDE

This unit presents the language used for making comparisons, and both revises and introduces a number of useful adjectives.

WARM-UP

Suggested warm-up activity: 13.

1 Practise listening for specific information by playing the tape and asking students to circle or note down the words they hear. You can give the students some preparation for this exercise by asking them to look at the list of words *before* they listen and predicting which ones might refer to New York, and which ones to London. Explain if necessary that they are not expected to understand every word of the conversation, but it is better to make sure they understand the key words.

Tapescript

MARILYN:	Tell me, Bob, what do you think of New York?
BOB:	I love New York – I think it's a wonderful city. And there are so many people!
MARILYN:	Isn't London bigger than New York?
BOB:	In size, maybe, but there are more people in New York. The population is higher. And it feels very different. The tempo of life is much faster in New York and the streets are noisier . . . everyone's busy doing something – going somewhere – it's very exciting.
MARILYN:	Hmm. It's also quite dangerous. I hate travelling on the subway.
BOB:	Well, I suppose the subway *is* more dangerous than the London Underground, but I don't worry about it much.
MARILYN:	And London's got all the history, all those wonderful old buildings – all we have is skyscrapers.
BOB:	True, London is an older city, and some

of the buildings are very beautiful – but so are your skyscrapers.

MARILYN:	You like our skyscrapers?
BOB:	Yes, I do. And I love the food here – steak, salad, French fries . . . I think the food in New York is better than the food in London.
MARILYN:	What about the cost of living?
BOB:	Well, I suppose London is cheaper – prices here are quite high in New York at the moment – the dollar is very strong.
MARILYN:	I guess it doesn't rain so often here.
BOB:	Right – and it's much hotter than London . . .
MARILYN:	I think it gets too hot – 30° centigrade in summer. And New York is very cold in winter. Freezing cold.
BOB:	OK, London is warmer in winter, but it rains a lot – and I don't like the rain.

Answers

faster	older
better	more dangerous
higher	warmer
cheaper	noisier
hotter	bigger

2 Practise listening for specific information again by asking students to listen once more to the recording and to note down the words used to describe the various features mentioned in the *Student's Book*.

Answers

Size: bigger
Population: higher
Tempo of life: faster
Streets: noisier
Underground travel: more dangerous
Buildings: older
Food: better
Cost of living: cheaper
Weather: hotter, warmer

3 Practise comparative adjectives by asking students to make two lists.

Answers

faster	slower
better	worse
cooler	warmer
more modern	older
quieter	noisier
higher	lower
cheaper	more expensive
hotter	colder
smaller	larger/bigger
more dangerous	safer

Check the lists by saying an adjective and asking students to give the opposite adjective.

WB 17.1

Note:
Point out that *old* is the opposite of both *modern* and *young*.

4 Practise making comparisons by asking students to work in pairs, and to use their lists to make statements about the differences between New York and London. Make sure they use comparative adjective + *than* /ðən/.

5 Practise writing by asking students to work in pairs and to write eight sentences comparing New York and London, based on their work in 4. Go round and check that they are using the comparative forms correctly. Correct the errors of the class as a whole, and ask students to check their own work.

WB 17.2

6 Practise writing comparative adjectives by asking students to copy the list and to write the comparative forms (see the list in 1).

Explain that one-syllable adjectives usually form the comparative by adding -er. Some adjectives double the final consonant before adding -er (e.g. hotter, bigger). Adjectives ending in *y* change the *y* to *i* before adding -er (e.g. noisier). Most two-syllable adjectives and *all* longer adjectives form the comparative·with *more*. The only irregular comparatives presented in this unit are *good – better* and *bad – worse*.

Give further practice in making comparisons by asking students to compare towns they know well with London and New York. Ask them to discuss the differences in pairs. They may then change partners and continue the discussion. Finally, ask them to write a few sentences comparing their town with New York or London.

7 Present *looks* + comparative adjective by asking students to discuss the drawings in pairs. Make sure that students use the correct stress pattern for sentences such as *Yes, Tom looks fatter than Tim, but. . ..* Students should resist measuring the drawings until the end of the activity!

You may like to give further practice by asking students to look at photos of each other's families, to find out who all the people are and to make comparisons: *He/She looks taller/older, etc. than. . ..* Correct any errors with the class as a whole.

8 Present adjectives for describing feelings by matching the adjectives with the pictures and then eliciting sentences such as *Peter looks angry.* Practise with individual and then pairwork drilling. Then match the sentences with the reasons. Ask students to write a sentence about each person.

Answers

Peter looks angry because the phone is out of order.
Sophie looks ill because she's got a bad cold.
Roger looks worried because he can't find his cheque book.
Pamela looks tired because she's working very hard.
Daisy looks happy because she's going on holiday tomorrow.
Mike looks sad because his girlfriend is away.

9 Practise listening for specific information by playing the tape and asking students to check that their answers to 8 are correct.

Tapescript

PETER:	Oh, no! What's the matter with this phone! It's out of order again!
SOPHIE:	Oh, I feel terrible. I've got a very bad cold.
ROGER:	I can't find my cheque book – what am I going to do?
PAMELA:	Oh, dear. I've got so much work to do.
DAISY:	I feel great! I'm going on holiday tomorrow.
MIKE:	Oh, come back soon, darling. I miss you very much.

Then present the structure *Peter sounds . . . because . . ..*

10 Practise *You look. . ../You sound. . ..* and present *I feel. . ..* by getting students to say how others look and sound and to say how they feel. Write up the dialogue on the board and check that the pronunciation and intonation/stress patterns are correct. Ask students to come to the board and to mark in the pattern.

WB 17.3, 17.4

11 Present superlative adjectives and practise
listening for specific information by playing the
tape and asking students to find the places
mentioned on the map. Most of the places will be
familiar to your students and there should be no
difficulty with the superlative concept. Use the
Empire State Building (with the pictures here and
on page 98) to pre-teach *skyscraper* and *famous*
and establish that it's the most famous skyscraper
in the world. Point out the American spelling of
centre, i.e. *center*.

Tapescript

Washington DC is the capital of the United States,
but New York is the biggest city. It is also the
world's tallest city. The heart of New York is
Manhattan, where the buildings reach the sky.
The most famous skyscraper in the world is the
Empire State Building – 380 metres high with 102
floors. But the tallest building in New York is the
World Trade Center – its two towers are 415
metres high and the express lifts take only a few
seconds to reach the 110th floor. From here you
can see the whole of New York . . . Broadway is
the longest street in the city, and the home of New
York theatre. It is also the home of Macy's, the
largest department store in the world. But if
you're feeling rich and want to spend money,
then come to Fifth Avenue, which has the most
expensive shops in New York. Bridges and
tunnels link Manhattan with Brooklyn and
Queens on Long Island, and with the Bronx,
where you can visit the largest zoo in the USA.
And crossing the mouth of the Hudson River is
the longest suspension bridge in the world – the
Verrazano Narrows Bridge joins Long Island and
Staten Island. Beyond the bridge, at the entrance
to New York harbour, stands the most famous
statue in the world – the Statue of Liberty – often
called 'the grandest lady in the world'.

Practise superlative adjectives by asking
students to use the chart to make true sentences
about New York. You may want to play the tape
again. Explain that one-syllable adjectives usually
form the superlative by adding *-est*. Some
adjectives double the final consonant before
adding *-est* (e.g. hottest, biggest). Adjectives

ending in *y* change the *y* to *i* before adding *-est*
(e.g. noisiest). Most two-syllable adjectives and *all*
longer adjectives form the superlative with *most*.
The superlative of *good* is *best*; the superlative of
bad is *worst*. Emphasise that *all* superlatives are
preceded by the definite article: *the smallest, the
most expensive, the best.*

Play the tape again for students to check that
their sentences were true; then ask them to write a
sentence about each place in the chart.

Answers

New York is the biggest city in the USA.
The Empire State Building is the most famous
skyscraper in New York/the USA/the world.
The World Trade Center is the tallest building in
New York.
Broadway is the longest street in New York.
Macy's is the largest department store in New
York/the USA/the world.
Fifth Avenue is the most expensive street in New
York.
The Bronx has the largest zoo in New York/the
USA.
The Verrazano Narrows Bridge is the longest
suspension bridge in New York/the USA/the
world.
The Statue of Liberty is the most famous statue in
New York/the USA/the world.

12 Practise reading for specific information by asking
students to work in pairs and to read only the
information given to each one. Tell the students
who is A and who is B. Get them to ask and answer
questions about the illustrations. It isn't necessary
to correct all the errors at this stage, as this is a less
controlled activity. However, you may wish to
draw their attention to any serious mistakes after
they have finished their questions and answers.
They will probably need some assistance with
certain vocabulary items; encourage them to try
and guess the meaning of any unfamiliar words
from the context.

WB 17.5, 17.6

LEARNING SKILLS

Write the following passage on the board:

I was . . . in London in June 1940. I went to a . . .
not far from where I . . . until I was sixteen. My
first . . . was to make tea for the . . . on the local
newspaper. After a few years, I . . . my first article
for the . . .. Soon I was a . . . myself and wrote
about everything that happened in the district.
Then I . . . to try and get a job on a national . . . and
I began to . . . for *The Times*. . . . I was thirty-one, I

... my first book, which was very successful. I met Patricia two years later and we ... married in 1975. We have three ... and a large ... in the country.

Ask students to complete the passage, first by deciding what type of word could go in each blank, then by thinking of a suitable word. Point out once again that it isn't necessary to understand or even to see each word in order to understand what it means.

PRONUNCIATION TAPESCRIPT

17.1 Listen and repeat.

tallest building
largest city
most famous
most dangerous

Note:
The *t* in -est/most almost disappears before a consonant.

tallest animal
largest island
most interesting
most expensive

17.2 Listen and repeat.

coldest winter
most exciting
best university
most modern
longest river
fastest aeroplane

17.3 Listen and correct these statements, like this:

Madrid is the capital of Portugal.
No, it isn't. It's the capital of Spain.

Now you.

a) Madrid is the capital of Portugal.
   No, it isn't. It's the capital of Spain.
b) Tom is older than his sister.
   No, he isn't. He's younger than his sister.
c) New York is the biggest city in the world.
   No, it isn't. It's the biggest city in the USA.
d) London is larger than Tokyo.
   No, it isn't. It's smaller than Tokyo.
e) The plane leaves at four thirty.
   No, it doesn't. It leaves at three thirty.
f) He's got short dark hair.
   No, he hasn't. He's got short fair hair.

STRUCTURE REVIEW TAPESCRIPT

17.1 Talk about differences, like this:

Life is quite fast in New York
Yes, it's slower in London.

Now you.

a) Life is quite fast in New York.
   Yes, it's slower in London.
b) Clothes are quite cheap in New York.
   Yes, they're more expensive in London.
c) The summer is very hot in New York.
   Yes, it's cooler in London.
d) The streets are quite dangerous in New York.
   Yes, they're safer in London.
e) The food is very good in New York.
   Yes, it's worse in London.
f) The buildings are very modern in New York.
   Yes, they're older in London.

17.2 Make statements about New York, like this:

New York is a very big city, isn't it?
Yes, it's the biggest city in the United States.

Fifth Avenue has some very expensive shops, hasn't it?
Yes, it has the most expensive shops in New York.

Now you.

a) New York is a very big city, isn't it?
   Yes, it's the biggest city in the United States.
b) Fifth Avenue has some very expensive shops, hasn't it?
   Yes, it has the most expensive shops in New York.
c) Broadway is a very long street, isn't it?
   Yes, it's the longest street in New York.
d) The Empire State Building is a very famous skyscraper, isn't it?
   Yes, it's the most famous skyscraper in the world.
e) The World Trade Center is a very tall building, isn't it?
   Yes, it's the tallest building in New York.
f) The Bronx has a very large zoo, hasn't it?
   Yes, it has the largest zoo in the United States.

17.3 Say how people and things look, like this:

She's quite old.
Yes, but she looks young.

Now you.

a) She's quite old.
   Yes, but she looks young.
b) He's quite fat.
   Yes, but he looks slim.

c) He's quite short.
   Yes, but he looks tall.
d) The river is quite dangerous.
   Yes, but it looks safe.
e) The road is quite short.
   Yes, but it looks long.
f) These shoes were quite cheap.
   Yes, but they look expensive.

17.4 Say how people and things sound, like this:

   It isn't very noisy.
   No, it sounds very quiet.

Now you.

a) It isn't very noisy.
   No, it sounds very quiet.
b) He isn't very happy.
   No, he sounds very sad.
c) She isn't very well.
   No, she sounds very ill.
d) They aren't very old.
   No, they sound very young.
e) She isn't very happy.
   No, she sounds very worried.

18 Checking what you know

SUMMARY

Functions

In Units 13 to 17, students learnt how to:

Ask and say what happened in the past
Ask and say when things happened in the past
Ask and say how long something lasted
Talk about themselves: personal background
Talk about future plans and intentions
Give advice and instructions
Agree and disagree

Ask and say what people look like
Ask and say what people are wearing
Ask and say how old people are
Ask and say how tall people are
Give compliments
Make comparisons
Describe impressions

TOPICS

The topic areas covered have been:
Times of the day, leisure activities, education, family, dates, travel, work, clothes, rooms, household equipment, colours and patterns, instructions, emergency situations, description of people, places and emotions.

TEACHING GUIDE

WARM-UP

Suggested warm-up activities: 3, 8, 11, 12, 13 or 14.

WB

Students should be able to do the *Workbook* exercises at any stage in this revision unit.

1 Practise listening for specific information by playing the tape and asking students simply to note down the dates they hear. You may need to stop the tape after each date.

Tapescript

In 1860, London was a large city of two and a half million people. By 1910, London was the biggest city in the world with a population of five million. During that fifty years, there were many important changes in the city.

In the first half of the nineteenth century, transport was a big problem in London. One important means of transport was the horse bus. But it was too expensive for most people, and it was very slow. The other important means of transport was the River Thames. Many people travelled across London by steamboat on the river. But again, it wasn't very cheap, and if the weather was bad, it wasn't very safe. So thousands of people walked several miles to work every day.

Then the world's first underground railway opened in 1862. It was cheaper, safer and faster than the horse bus and the steamboat, and millions of people used it every year. Then Karl Benz invented the first motor car in 1885, and in 1907, two hundred motor buses came to London. Many people started travelling by bus, and people who were very rich bought their own cars.

Another important change came with electricity. In the first part of the nineteenth century, London had gas light. The streets were dark, dirty, and often dangerous. Things became much brighter when electric street lighting came to London in 1878. In the same year, people started using the telephone, and by 1891, the people of London could make phone calls to Paris. Five years later, in 1896, the first cinema opened in the centre of London, and people started going to the movies. At the turn of the century, a large number of theatres, hotels, restaurants and department stores opened, and by 1910, London was a modern city, very different from London in 1860.

Answers

EVENT	DATE
The first underground opened.	1862
Karl Benz invented the car.	1885
People started travelling by bus.	1907
Electric street lighting came to the city.	1878
People started using the telephone.	1878
The first cinema opened.	1896

2   Revise asking and saying when people did things in the past; students should check their answers by asking and answering questions about the changes in London between 1860 and 1910. Make sure they use *In . . ..* for dates, and *About . . . ago.* for the number of years.

3   Revise asking and saying what people did in the past by playing the tape again and asking students to say how people travelled at different times.

Answers

In 1860, they travelled by horse bus, by boat or on foot.
In 1890, they travelled by underground.
In 1910, they travelled by bus and by car.

4   Revise asking and saying what people did in the past by asking students to compare life in 1860 with life in 1910. Each student should take turns to make statements about life in the past. Go round and check one or two pairs to see that they are using the structures correctly.

5   Practise writing by asking students to write a short paragraph incorporating all the statements about life in the past which they formulated in 4. When they have finished they should pass their versions to another pair for correction. If you have time, you may like to ask students to write a similar paragraph about life in the past in their own towns.

6   Revise agreeing and disagreeing by asking students to discuss which are the most important of the inventions shown in their books. Explain that the *definite* article is used before singular nouns when referring to a class of things.

7   Revise giving advice and asking and saying what people are going to do by getting students to form groups of four and to decide which five items they should buy for their house, and in what order. Point out that the *indefinite* article must be used here because the discussion is about buying single items. When they are all ready, they should tell the class about their choice.

8   Practise reading for general sense by asking students to read the letter and to note down the topic(s) of each paragraph.

Answers

Paragraph 1: Appearance, Family
Paragraph 2: Past life, Future plans
Paragraph 3: Interests

Practise writing and revise language for giving personal information by asking students to write a letter about themselves using the same topic headings. They should make notes first of all, and then use the plan shown in their books as a model.
    This activity can be done for homework and corrected at a suitable moment during the next lesson.

9   Practise reading for specific information by asking students to work in fours, split into two pairs, A and B, and to follow the instructions in their books. Make sure they don't look at the other pair's information. Each pair should first of all answer the questions about Great Britain or Japan; if you like they can check their answers with other students who are reading the same passage. Ask them to note down their answers. They should then ask and answer questions about each pair's reading passage, and make comparisons between the two islands. If necessary, they should revise making comparisons by looking back at Unit 17.

10   Revise making comparisons by asking students to work in groups of six and to find out information about their own countries using the headings given in the FACTS AND FIGURES passages. This activity may take some time; you may like to ask them to do it for homework. If not, you can bring a reference book to class, and pass it round the groups. Encourage them either to find out about their own countries or to find out about countries which they do not know very much about. When everyone is ready, organise a class report on all the countries they have found out about.

LEARNING SKILLS

Write on the board or prepare an overhead projector transparency or photocopy of a short passage which has been cut in half.
    Ask students to work in pairs and to try and work out how each line finishes. You can make the exercise more creative by 'cutting' the passage closer to the left hand margin, or increasingly more creative by cutting the passage diagonally in half.
    Ask students to look back over their notes for Units 12 to 18 and to organise the new vocabulary into functions, topics or situations. Point out that they should now be organising their notes in this way all the time. Then ask them to choose ten or twelve words which are particularly relevant to their personal needs.

Example:

Here is a photograph of me. I'm
good! I'm tall and very thin,
brown hair and grey eyes. |
she's a social worker. My fa
company. I've got a brother
sisters, Emma and Rose. T
than me.

I'm 18, and I was born in
north-west of England, nea
school there for seven yea
moved to London, so I went
London. I left school last
and I'm going to be a doc
but I like it!

I don't have much free ti
I like going to the cinema d
I also like football and sail
Please write and tell me a
Best wishes.
            Pat

19 | Saying how you feel

UNIT SUMMARY

Functions

Asking and saying what things are called

Structures

What	's	this	called?
	are	these	

It's	a	finger.
	his	
	her	

They're	(his)	fingers.
	(her)	

Asking and saying what people think

I think	it's	amusing.
		great.
		lovely.
		terrible.
		ugly.
	they're	exciting.
		interesting.
		boring.
		silly.
		strange.

I don't mind	it.
	them.

It's	all right.
They're	

Agreeing and disagreeing

I agree.	So do I.
	I think so too.

I	disagree.
	don't agree.

No,	it isn't.
	they aren't.

95

Functions

Asking and saying how people feel

Making suggestions/giving advice

Sympathising

Structures

What's the matter?

I	don't feel very well.	
	feel	tired. sick. cold. hot.
	've got	a headache. backache. stomachache. toothache. earache.
My	foot leg arm shoulder hand	hurts.

Why don't you. . . ?			
If you ask me,	you we he	should	go to bed. lie down. get some exercise.
I think	she they		

How do you feel?	Oh, much better thank you.
	Not very well.

Oh, I *am* pleased.

Oh, I *am* sorry.

Topics

Parts of the body, emotional reactions, illnesses and ailments

Lexical items

- arm   back   ear   finger   foot/feet   hand   head   leg   mouth   neck   nose   shoulder   stomach   throat   toe
- amusing   boring   exciting   silly   strange   terrible
- backache   earache   faint   headache   hurt (v)   medicine   runny nose   sick   sore throat   stiff neck   stomachache   temperature   toothache
- keep (warm, cool)   lie down   stop (smoking)   take exercise   waste (time)

96

TEACHING GUIDE

This unit presents the language used to talk about physical and emotional feelings.

WARM-UP

Suggested warm-up activity: 8.

1 Present vocabulary items for parts of the body by asking students to work in pairs and to follow the instructions in their books. Student A has information which Student B does not have, and vice versa. When they have each labelled as many parts of the body as possible, they should work together and exchange information. Present *What's this called?/What are these called?* with two or three students to give them the model; then ask them to practise in pairs. Note that, for the purposes of this exercise, the indefinite article is used when we are referring to a part of the body of which there is more than one, e.g. It's *a* finger; the definite article is used when we are referring to a part of the body of which there is only one, e.g. It's *the* nose. Explain that, when referring to 'real' people rather than diagrams, possessive pronouns should be used with parts of the body (*her nose, his fingers, my arm*, etc.).
2 Practise the vocabulary for parts of the body by getting students to ask and say which parts of the sculpture they think represent the various parts of the body.

WB 19.1

3 Practise listening for general sense by playing the tape and asking students to listen and decide whether the people talking like the picture or not. Ask them simply to place a tick or a cross in the chart. Remind students that they don't need to understand every word.

Tapescript

1 Well, I think it's boring, I mean, I—I don't really see the point of it, it just looks like a lot of bricks that have just been left behind by somebody.

2 I agree, I think it's very silly. It's just white bricks on the floor.

3 I think it's great. It takes a lot of imagination to come up with something like that.

4 I don't see the point of it. It—it's terrible, it's just a waste of money.

5 It's quite amusing really. Of course that depends on your point of view, but I quite like it.

6 I think it's very strange, I mean, it's just a pile of bricks, isn't it?

Answers

Speaker	likes?
1	✗
2	✗
3	✓
4	✗
5	✓
6	✗

4 Present expressions for saying what you think by asking students to remember which of the expressions shown in their books they heard on the tape. Ask them to tick or note down the ones they heard, then play the tape again so they can check their answers.

Answers

I think it's	amusing. ✓		I don't mind it.
	great. ✓		
	lovely.		It's all right.
	terrible. ✓		
	ugly.		I agree. ✓
	exciting.		
	interesting.		I don't agree.
	boring. ✓		disagree.
	silly. ✓		
	strange. ✓		

5 Practise using the expressions for saying what you think, by asking students to tell each other what they think of the sculpture. Make sure everyone understands the *degree* of feeling in the different expressions; you may need to use more examples to convey the various nuances.
6 Practise using the expressions for saying what you think by asking students to think of things which they find amusing, exciting or strange. They should then work in pairs and ask their partner if he/she agrees. Go round each group and check they are using the expressions correctly.

WB 19.2

7 Practise listening for specific information by playing the tape and asking students to write down the parts of the body they hear.

Tapescript

1 WOMAN: Oh dear, you don't look very well. What's the matter?

MAN:	It's my stomach. I feel sick.	
WOMAN:	Oh, I *am* sorry. Would you like me to close the window?	
MAN:	No, I'd like some fresh air. I've got a headache as well.	
WOMAN:	Why don't you lie down?	
MAN:	Yes, that's a good idea.	

2
SICK PERSON:	(sneezes.)	
FRIEND:	Bless you. What's the matter? Are you all right?	
SICK PERSON:	No, I don't feel very well. I've got a headache.	
FRIEND:	Oh, I *am* sorry. Would you like an aspirin?	
SICK PERSON:	Yes, if you've got one. I feel hot and I've got a sore throat as well.	
FRIEND:	I think you're going to get flu. Why don't you go to bed?	
SICK PERSON:	Yes, that's a good idea.	

3
YOUNG MAN:	What's the matter? Are you all right?	
OLD MAN:	My leg hurts.	
YOUNG MAN:	Oh, I *am* sorry. Why don't you sit down for a moment?	
OLD MAN:	Yes. Ah, that's better. Oh, ow, oh!	
YOUNG MAN:	What's the matter now?	
OLD MAN:	My shoulder hurts as well.	
YOUNG MAN:	Would you like me to call the doctor? You're much too old to play football.	
OLD MAN:	I'm not that old . . . Ow!	

Answers

Dialogue	Part of the body
1	stomach, head
2	head, throat
3	leg, shoulder

8 Present the language for asking and saying how you feel, and for making suggestions, by asking students to complete the dialogue with suitable phrases from the list.

Answers See Dialogue 1 above.

When they have listened to Dialogue 1 again, check that everyone understands what the key phrases mean. Point out that *Why don't we . . .?* was presented in Unit 5.

9 Practise the language for asking and saying how you feel, and for making suggestions, by getting students to use Dialogue 1 as a model to act out Dialogue 2. Go round and check that everyone is using the structures and vocabulary correctly. Ask students to change partners and then get them to act out Dialogue 3. Point out that the article must be used with *headache*.

Make sure they use the correct stress and intonation pattern with *Oh, I am sorry*. If necessary, explain that *am* is not contracted in order to emphasise the speaker's sympathy.

10 Present further expressions for saying how you feel by playing the tape and asking students to tick or note down the expressions they hear. At this stage they don't need to understand every word of the dialogues.

Tapescript

1
DOCTOR:	Now, what seems to be the matter, Mr Barlow?	
MR BARLOW:	Well, it's my back, actually. I've got constant backache and a stiff neck at the moment. And my shoulder hurts as well.	
DOCTOR:	Uh huh. I see. Does it hurt when you bend over?	
MR BARLOW:	Yes, it does.	
DOCTOR:	And when did this start?	
MR BARLOW:	About a week ago.	
DOCTOR:	Do you do any sport or physical exercise?	
MR BARLOW:	No, but I did some gardening a couple of weekends ago.	
DOCTOR:	I see . . .	

2
DOCTOR:	Come in and sit down, Mrs Collins. What seems to be the problem?	
MRS COLLINS:	Oh, I just don't feel very well at the moment. Nothing special, but I just feel tired all the time.	
DOCTOR:	I see.	
MRS COLLINS:	I get very bad headaches every so often and I often feel sick.	
DOCTOR:	And do you ever feel faint?	
MRS COLLINS:	Yes, sometimes. And I've got this terrible cough . . .	
DOCTOR:	Do you smoke?	
MRS COLLINS:	No. Well, yes. Not many.	
DOCTOR:	How many a day?	
MRS COLLINS:	Oh, eight or nine.	
DOCTOR:	And do you get much exercise?	
MRS COLLINS:	No, not much. I stay indoors most of the time.	
DOCTOR:	Well, I don't think it's serious but . . .	

Answers

Dialogue	Symptoms
1	backache, stiff neck, shoulder hurts
2	tired, bad headaches, sick, faint, cough

WB 19.3

11 Practise *If you ask me/ I think he/she should . . . .* by getting students to work in pairs and to choose the best advice for each person. Remind students that they should agree or disagree as well, using *Yes, that's a good idea. No, I think . . . .*

12 Practise reading for general sense by asking students to look at the labels for various medicines and to decide which one(s) would be suitable for each of the people who are ill. Of course, they don't need to understand every word of the text, but there should be enough clues to allow them to make appropriate choices.

Answers

MR BARLOW: Paracetamol, Deep Heat.
MRS COLLINS: Paracetamol, Veno's.

13 Practise listening for general sense by playing the tape and asking students to check their answers to 11.

Tapescript

1 DOCTOR: I think you should lie flat for at least twenty-four hours, just to rest your back.
MR BARLOW: All right.
DOCTOR: It's very important to keep warm as well. The cold will make your shoulder worse.
MR BARLOW: I see.
DOCTOR: And I think you should use some ointment on your back and shoulders. Just rub it in twice a day. If it still hurts a lot, take a couple of aspirin.
MR BARLOW: All right, thank you.

2 DOCTOR: Well, I don't think it's serious, but the first thing you've got to do is take more exercise. You should go for a long walk every day and get some fresh air.
MRS COLLINS: All right.
DOCTOR: I'm a bit concerned about your cough, so here's a prescription for some cough medicine. Take it

twice a day, and keep away from other people.
MRS COLLINS: I see.
DOCTOR: If you still feel sick, don't eat anything for a day except some soup. I'll put some pills for your stomach on the prescription as well. Oh, and one more thing . . .
MRS COLLINS: Yes?
DOCTOR: I think you should give up smoking . . .

Answers

The doctor suggests that the first person should lie flat for 24 hours, keep warm, rub some ointment in and, if necessary, take some aspirin. The second person should take more exercise, take some cough medicine, not eat anything for a day except soup, and give up smoking.

14 Practise giving advice and making suggestions by asking students to write a few sentences describing what the three people should do to get better. Students may like to work in pairs for this activity.

15 Practise the language used for asking and saying how you feel by getting students to work in pairs and act out the role play.

WB 19.4, 19.5

LEARNING SKILLS

Ask students to think of three things which they should do in class and three things which they shouldn't do. For example, *I should try and join in as much as possible. I shouldn't look up every word I don't understand in the dictionary.* Go round the class asking each student for their advice on how to be a good learner, and write it up on the board. Then ask students to decide which are the ten most useful pieces of advice.

Remind students of the importance of regular revision. Point out that it is often better to revise new vocabulary and structures just before you go to bed, and to check it shortly after you have got up in the morning.

PRONUNCIATION TAPESCRIPT

19.1 Listen and repeat.

/əʊ/	/aʊ/
no	now
phoned	found
load	loud
known	noun

Now listen and tick the words you hear.

found   known   no   loud

19.2 Listen and write these words in the correct column.

show /əʊ/, town /aʊ/, brown /aʊ/,
shower /aʊ/, low /əʊ/, toe /əʊ/, south /aʊ/,
comb /əʊ/

19.3 Listen and say you're sorry or pleased, like this:

I don't feel very well.
Oh, I am sorry.
But at least I don't feel sick.
Oh, I am pleased.

Now you.

a) I don't feel very well.
   Oh, I am sorry.
b) But at least I don't feel sick.
   Oh, I am pleased.
c) I've got a dreadful headache.
   Oh, I am sorry.
d) And my shoulder hurts.
   Oh, I am sorry.
e) But my back's much better.
   Oh, I am pleased.
f) And my leg doesn't hurt any more.
   Oh, I am pleased.

STRUCTURE REVIEW TAPESCRIPT

19.1 Say what things are called, like this:

What's this called?
It's a painting.

What are these called?
They're trees.

Now you.

a) What's this called?
   It's a painting.
b) What are these called?
   They're trees.
c) What are these called?
   They're teeth.
d) What's this called?
   It's a handbag.
e) What's this called?
   It's an armchair.
f) What are these called?
   They're eyes.

19.2 Say what you think, like this:

What do you think of this picture?
I think it's interesting.
How about these clothes?
I think they're great.

Now you.

a) What do you think of this picture?
   I think it's interesting.
b) How about these clothes?
   I think they're great.
c) Do you like these people?
   I think they're amusing.
d) What do you think of this statue?
   I think it's ugly.
e) Do you like this music?
   I think it's lovely.
f) How about this food?
   I think it's terrible.

19.3 Say what the matter is, like this:

What's the matter?
I feel sick.

What's the matter?
I've got a headache.

Now you.

a) What's the matter?
   I feel sick.
b) What's the matter?
   I've got a headache.
c) What's the matter?
   I feel hot.
d) What's the matter?
   I've got toothache.
e) What's the matter?
   I've got earache.
f) What's the matter?
   I feel tired.

19.4 Give people advice, like this:

Jack's got a headache.
If you ask me, he should take some aspirin.

Now you.

a) Jack's got a headache.
   If you ask me, he should take some aspirin.
b) My back hurts.
   If you ask me, you should lie down.
c) My daughter's got a temperature.
   If you ask me, she should keep away from other people.
d) I've got a cough.
   If you ask me, you should take some cough medicine.
e) Sarah's got flu.
   If you ask me, she should keep warm.
f) The children feel sick.
   If you ask me, they should eat nothing.

20 Doing the right thing

UNIT SUMMARY

Functions

Asking and saying what people have to do

Structures

What	do	I you we they	have to	do?
Where				go?
When	does	he she		leave?

I You We They	have	to	go to the airport. change in Athens. label your baggage.
He She	has		

I You We They	must		water the plants. turn off the gas. empty the dustbin.
	need have (got)	to	
He She	must		
	needs has (got)	to	

Please You must	show your tickets.

Saying what people mustn't do

You mustn't smoke in this room!

Asking for permission

Giving and refusing permission

	Yes, you can.
Can I smoke?	No, I'm afraid it's not allowed.

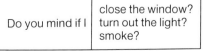

Do you mind if I	close the window? turn out the light? smoke?

Structures

Not at all – go ahead.
I'm sorry, it's not allowed.
I'd rather you didn't.

Topics

Travel arrangements, household arrangements, baggage

Lexical items

- change   check in   confirm   depart   fasten   label   land (v)   reconfirm   return (flight)   seat belt   take off   terminal
- cancel milk   empty dustbin   pack suitcase   turn off electricity   water plants
- baby carriage   bottle (of perfume)   briefcase   duty-free goods   pipe   typewriter   wheelchair

---

TEACHING GUIDE

This unit introduces the language used for air travel.

WARM-UP

Suggested warm-up activity: 12.

1   Practise listening for specific information by playing the tape and asking students to complete the missing information on the travel itinerary. Explain that not all words need to be understood in this dialogue.

Tapescript

TRAVEL AGENT:	Hello, it's Ms Pye, isn't it?
DIANA:	That's right. Is my ticket ready yet?
TRAVEL AGENT:	Yes it is. Here we are. Now, it's for London to Heraklion, via Athens. You have to change at Athens.
DIANA:	Oh, I see. There's no direct flight.
TRAVEL AGENT:	No, I'm afraid not. But there's hardly any delay in Athens. You leave from London Heathrow airport on flight number BA 562.
DIANA:	Heathrow . . . BA 562. And that will be Terminal One?
TRAVEL AGENT:	That's right – Terminal One. You have to check in at 11.30 in the morning, and you leave at 12.30. All right?
DIANA:	Check in at 11.30, leave at 12.30. OK.
TRAVEL AGENT:	Now, you arrive in Athens at 18.05 in the evening. And then you have to change. You have to go to the West Terminal for flight number OA 512 leaving at 19.00.
DIANA:	I see. OA 512 . . . leaving at 19.00

	from the West Terminal. And what time does it get to Heraklion?
TRAVEL AGENT:	At 19.50. Oh, there's just a couple more things: you have to label your baggage and you have to reconfirm your return flight and check-in times.
DIANA:	When do I have to do that?
TRAVEL AGENT:	About 72 hours before you leave. So, there you are. Have a nice trip.
DIANA:	Thank you. I will.

Answers

ITINERARY FOR: Ms D Pye

THU 02 MAY 1985 LONDON to HERAKLION via: . . Athens . . . .

FLIGHT No. BA562 ECONOMY CLASS

AIRPORT: . London Heathrow . . .   TERMINAL: . . 1 . . . .

CHECK-IN: . . . 11·30 . . . .

DEPART: . 12·30 . Hrs   ARRIVE . 18·05 . Hrs ATHENS (East)

CHANGE FLIGHTS AT: . . Athens . .   TO FLIGHT No: OA 512

                                                     TERMINAL: . West .

DEPART: . 19·00 . Hrs   ARRIVE: . 19·50 . Hrs HERAKLION

All times shown are local. Baggage must be labelled; for allowance, see ticket. We advise ONWARD/RETURN flights and CHECK-IN times are reconfirmed **72 hrs** ahead.

2   Present *Which airport does she have to leave from?* by checking the answers to 1 with the students. Ask the questions shown in the *Student's Book*, and elicit short answers. Then get students to work in pairs and to ask and answer the questions themselves. Make sure they are using the question form correctly. Explain any unfamiliar vocabulary items.

Answers See 1

3 Present *You have to . . . .* by choosing one of the students and acting out the dialogue between the travel agent and Diana. Write up the first person question form of *Which terminal does she have to go from?* i.e.

> Which terminal do I have to go from?

and elicit the first person question form of the other questions in 2. Then ask one student to help you act out the conversation; you should play the role of the travel agent. You can use the questions and the travel itinerary to help you. Then ask students to work in pairs and to act out the dialogue themselves.

If you have time, you can give further practice in the structures presented so far by asking students to work in pairs and to prepare a travel itinerary similar to the one shown in 1, but to a destination of the students' own choice. They can use it for role play practice with students from other groups.

4 Present some vocabulary and expressions for talking about household arrangements by asking students to match the verbs with the nouns on the list, and then say what Diana has to do before she leaves. Present *She must . . . ., She's got to . . . .* and *She needs to . . . .* by asking students to repeat the list of arrangements using the different structures.

Explain that, in this case, the four structures mean the same thing: *has got to* is the colloquial form of *has to*.

Answers

She	must has (got) to needs to	water the plants. cancel the milk and the newspapers. pack her suitcase. tell the police. empty the dustbin. find her passport. turn off the electricity and gas. buy some traveller's cheques.

Ask students if they can think of any other things you have to do before you go away.

5 Practise reading for specific information and using the structures presented so far in this unit by asking students to complete the letter. If you'd like to make the exercise simpler, write up the missing words on the board and ask the students simply to put them in the correct position.

Answers

Dear Ms Pye,

       We are writing to confirm your travel arrangements from London to _Heraklion_ . Your flight leaves from _Heathrow_ airport at _12·30_ Hrs. You _have_ to check in at Terminal _1_ at _11·30_ Hrs. Your journey from London to _Athens_ is on flight number _BA 562_ . When you get to Athens you _must_ change planes and go to _West_ Terminal. Your journey to _Heraklion_ is on flight OA 512 at _19·00_ Hrs. You arrive in Heraklion at 1950 Hrs.

       We remind you that you _have/need_ to _label_ your baggage and that you _have/need_ to reconfirm your return flight and _check-in_ times at least _72_ hrs ahead.

       We hope you have a pleasant trip.

       Yours sincerely,

A. Winterbottom

A. Winterbottom

If you have asked students to prepare their own travel itinerary in 3, you can ask them to write a similar letter giving details about the journey they have planned.

WB 20.1, 20.2

6 Practise reading for general sense by asking students to look at the airport signs and to work out what they mean. Revise *You must(n't) . . . ..* (see Unit 12) by asking them to explain the signs using this structure. Explain, if necessary, that signs giving instructions often use the imperative.

Answers

| Please show boarding card/ticket at this point | You must show your boarding card/ticket at this point. |

| Do not leave your baggage unattended | You mustn't leave your baggage unattended. |

| No Smoking | You mustn't smoke. |

| Passengers only may proceed beyond this point | You mustn't go/proceed beyond this point, if you are not a passenger. |

You mustn't enter.

| KEEP EXIT AREA CLEAR | You must keep the exit area clear. |

WB 20.3, 20.4

7 Practise listening for specific information by playing the tape and asking students to put a cross by the items which passengers cannot take on the plane as hand baggage.

Tapescript

ASSISTANT:	Good morning, madam. Can I have your ticket please?
PASSENGER 1:	Here you are. Can I take my typewriter on the plane with me?
ASSISTANT:	I'm afraid not. You have to check it in, I'm afraid.
PASSENGER 2:	It's all right if I keep my camera with me, isn't it?
ASSISTANT:	Of course, sir. No problem.
PASSENGER 3:	My husband can't manage without the wheelchair – can we take it on to the plane?
ASSISTANT:	Yes, of course – don't worry. The airline staff will help you.
PASSENGER 4:	There's no problem about the baby carriage, is there?
ASSISTANT:	Not at all, sir. I'll call someone to help you carry it on the plane.
PASSENGER 5:	Look, I can't check this in. It's a very expensive musical instrument. Can I take it on the plane with me?
ASSISTANT:	I'm sorry, sir, but it's not allowed. You have to check it in or buy another ticket.
PASSENGER 5:	That's ridiculous.
PASSENGER 6:	Well, it's only a little stuffed donkey.
ASSISTANT:	It may be little to you, but it's too big for the plane. I can't let you take it on as hand baggage, I'm afraid.

Answers

The passengers can't take the following items on the plane as hand baggage: typewriter, guitar, donkey.

8 Present asking for and giving permission by asking students *Can I take . . . as hand baggage?* and eliciting the response *Yes, you can./No, I'm afraid it's not allowed.* Make sure the intonation pattern for the negative response is polite. Give further practice in the structures by suggesting other items such as large suitcases, heavy camera equipment, a bicycle, etc.

9 Present *Do you mind if I . . .?* by asking students to match the pictures with the requests.

Answers   1C, 2A, 3B

10 Present *I'd rather you didn't./I'm sorry, it's not allowed./Not at all – go ahead.* by playing the tape and asking students to match the responses with the pictures and requests in 10. Explain that *I'd*

rather you didn't. is a personal preference, and that *I'm sorry, it's not allowed.* is a prohibition coming from a source other than the speaker.

Tapescript and Answers

MAN:	Excuse me, do you mind if I sit by the window?
WOMAN:	Well, I'd rather you didn't.
WOMAN:	Excuse me, do you mind if turn the light on?
MAN:	Not at all – go ahead.
MAN:	Excuse me, do you mind if I smoke?
STEWARDESS:	I'm sorry, it's not allowed.

WB 20.5, 20.6

11 Practise listening for general sense by playing the recordings of in-flight announcements and asking students to decide at what point during the flight they would be heard. Explain the meaning of *take-off* and *landing*.

Tapescript

1 You may now smoke if you wish, except in the toilets and in the no-smoking section. For your safety and comfort during the flight we recommend that you keep your seat belts fastened while you are seated.

2 In a few minutes we shall be landing at Athens, where the temperature is twenty-eight degrees centigrade. Please fasten your seat belts, put the back of your seats in the upright position, and make sure that your tables are folded back. Kindly extinguish your cigarettes and refrain from smoking until you are in the airport building.

3 Ladies and gentlemen, welcome to Athens. You are kindly requested to remain seated with your seatbelts fastened until the plane has completely stopped, the engines turned off and the doors have been opened. Please be sure to take with you all your hand baggage and personal belongings, and do not forget to tell our ground staff if you are making a connection with another flight. We hope you have enjoyed your flight and look forward to seeing you again on board.

4 Good afternoon, ladies and gentlemen. Captain Davies and all of us welcome you on board our flight BA 562 to Athens. Please fasten your seatbelts, do not smoke and make sure that your seats are in the upright position and your tables are folded back. We will be taking off in about five minutes. Thank you.

Answers

1 after take-off
2 before landing
3 after landing
4 before take-off

12 Practise the structures presented in this unit by playing the recording again and asking students to write sentences on what you can, must or mustn't do according to each announcement.

Answers

1 You can smoke but you mustn't smoke in the toilets and no-smoking section.
2 You must fasten your seatbelts, put the back of your seats in the upright position, and make sure tables are folded back. You mustn't smoke until you're in the airport building.
3 You must remain seated. You must take your hand baggage with you. You must tell the ground staff if you're making a connection with another flight.
4 You must fasten your seatbelts and make sure the seats are in the upright position and your tables are folded back. You mustn't smoke.

13 Practise the structures presented in this unit in a different context by asking students to describe what they can, must or mustn't do during the English class. When they have prepared a few sentences in pairs, they should compare their list with another pair and draw up a second list including all the sentences. The group of four with the largest number of points on their list is the winner.

14 Practise reading for general sense by asking students to work in pairs and to read the two passages. They should not look at each other's passage. Their first task is to match the headings to the paragraphs. Explain that, once again, they are unlikely to be able to understand every word of the reading passages, but that this is not necessary in order to grasp the general sense. Point out also that the vocabulary is very often found in the context of air travel.

Answers

STUDENT **A**

Electronic equipment:	International regulations forbid . . .
Reading:	On international flights . . .
Hand baggage:	Put your hand baggage . . .
Drinks:	On short flights . . .
Smoking:	Non-smoking sections . . .

Payment:	For Tourist Class passengers . . .
Duty-free goods:	On all our transcontinental and European flights . . .
Meals:	Special religious, health . . .
Baggage in the hold:	International regulations require . . .
Comfort:	Flying makes you . . .

The role play activity will oblige the students to understand a little more about each of their reading passages; go round and help each student with suitable answers to the questions. When everyone has done the role play once, you should explain any necessary vocabulary, correct any serious errors you may have heard, and ask students to change partners. If you'd like them to change roles, they will also have to start the activity from the beginning by reading the second passage.

LEARNING SKILLS

Play a conversation in advanced level English; ask students the following questions:
How many speakers are there?
Are they male or female?
What is the situation? Where are they?
What roles are the speakers playing?
What is the relationship between the speakers? Do they know each other well? Are they friends?
You will find that students will be able to answer most of the questions even if the passage is quite advanced. The aim of the activity is to give the students practice in inferring as much information about a listening comprehension passage as possible. You may like to do this activity regularly for the rest of the course. Always emphasise how much they have understood, rather than how little.

PRONUNCIATION TAPESCRIPT

20.1 Listen and repeat.

/ɒ/	/ʌ/
boss	bus
lock	luck
wrong	rung
collar	colour

Now listen and tick the words you hear.

colour   lock   bus   wrong

20.2 Listen and write these words in the correct column.

money /ʌ/, donkey /ɒ/, cough /ɒ/, worry /ʌ/, sorry /ɒ/, nothing /ʌ/, long /ɒ/, onion /ʌ/

20.3 Listen and mark the stress on these words.

traveller	recorder
announcement	terminal
arrangements	commercial
typewriter	dictionary
timetable	revision

STRUCTURE REVIEW TAPESCRIPT

20.1 Say what these people have to do, like this:

Where do I have to go?
You have to go to Terminal 1.

Now you

a) Where do I have to go?
You have to go to Terminal 1.
b) When do I have to check in?
You have to check in by eleven a.m.
c) What do I have to do after that?
You have to go through passport control.
d) Where do I have to wait?
You have to wait in the departure lounge.
e) Where do I have to change planes?
You have to change planes in Athens.

20.2 Say what you must or mustn't do, like this:

I don't want to speak to her.
But you must speak to her.

I'd like to leave my car here.
But you mustn't leave your car here.

Now you.

a) I don't want to speak to her.
But you must speak to her.
b) I'd like to leave my car here.
But you mustn't leave your car here.
c) I think I'm going to be late.
But you mustn't be late.
d) I haven't got time to see the doctor.
But you must see the doctor.
e) I want to leave at five o'clock.
But you mustn't leave at five o'clock.
f) I'm not going to have a holiday this year.
But you must have a holiday this year.

20.3 Say what people can or cannot do, like this:

Can I park here?
No, I'm afraid it's not allowed.

Can I sit here?
Yes, you can.

Now you.

a) Can I park here?
No, I'm afraid it's not allowed.

b) Can I sit here?
   Yes, you can.
c) Can I smoke?
   No, I'm afraid it's not allowed.
d) Can I use the telephone?
   Yes, you can.
e) Can I unfasten my seatbelt?
   Yes, you can.
f) Can I pay in dollars?
   Yes, you can.

20.4 Ask people if you may do things, like this:

You want to change seats.
Do you mind if I change seats?

Now you.

a) You want to change seats.
   Do you mind if I change seats.
b) You want to turn on the light.
   Do you mind if I turn on the light?
c) You want to sit by the window.
   Do you mind if I sit by the window?
d) You want to smoke a cigar.
   Do you mind if I smoke a cigar?
e) You want to pay by cheque.
   Do you mind if I pay by cheque?
f) You want to listen to some music.
   Do you mind if I listen to some music?

21 Making things clear

UNIT SUMMARY

Functions	Structures

Functions

Making suggestions

Structures

How / What	about	a T-shirt? / some chocolates? / something to read?

Agreeing/disagreeing with suggestions

Yes, that's a good idea!

No, I don't think so.

Asking for and giving reasons

Why	do	you / they	want to go to the first floor?
	does	he / she	

To buy					a	dress. / shirt.
Because	I / we / they	want	to buy		some	trousers. / clothes.
	he / she	wants				

It's too small.   It's not big enough.

I / We / They	want	something	more expensive. / bigger. / smaller. / longer. / shorter. / cheaper.
He / She	wants		

Asking and saying which one(s) you want

How about	this one?		No,	that one.
	these ones?			those ones.

The	big / red / cheap	one. / ones.

Functions

Saying what kind of thing you want

Structures

Something to	eat. drink. wear. read.

Topics

Shopping items and gifts, shops and services, clothes, colours

Lexical items

- bag basement cassette cassette player chocolates floor (first floor) ground (floor) hat present
- baker's butcher's greengrocer's petrol station travel agent's

TEACHING GUIDE

This unit deals with the language used when shopping; in this context, known language is revised (see Unit 7), and more complex transactions are introduced.

WARM-UP

Suggested warm-up activity: 11.

1 Present *something to . . .* by playing the tape and asking students to note down what Bob wants to buy for his family and friends. Explain that the structure is used when you need to describe something in very general terms. Write up the model answer *something to eat* and ask students to check their answers with each other by saying *He/She'd like something to . . ..*

Tapescript

BOB:	I must do some shopping today. I've got to buy some presents for my mother and father and some friends before I go. Something typical of New York.
NANCY:	How about a hot dog?
BOB:	Nancy, be serious!
NANCY:	Well, what would your mother like?
BOB:	Maybe something to eat . . . but not hot dogs!
NANCY:	OK, we can think of something. And what about your father?
BOB:	Hmm – I think he'd really like something to read.
NANCY:	We'll find him a good book. All right – who's next?
BOB:	Well, there's Jenny. Maybe I could get her a record or something like that.
NANCY:	Does she like clothes?
BOB:	Yes, that's a good idea. I'll get her something to wear. And that leaves Tom. What can I get him?
NANCY:	How about something to drink?
BOB:	Yes . . . but nothing alcoholic. He doesn't like wine or beer.
NANCY:	That's fine! Is that all?
BOB:	Yes, I think so.

Answers

Mum: something to eat

Dad: something to read

Jenny: something to wear

Tom: something to drink

Point at other articles in the classroom and say whether they are something to eat, drink, wear or read. You may also introduce phrases such as *something to write with, something to play cassettes on*, etc. if you think the students have grasped the concept of the structure.

2 Practise *something to . . .* by asking students to point at the articles in the illustration and say what kind of thing they are. If possible, bring to class a few magazine pictures showing things to eat, drink, wear, read, etc.; hold them up and ask students to say what kind of things they are.

Answers

Hat, T-shirt: something to wear
Book, magazine: something to read
Whiskey, apple juice, mineral water: something to drink
Chocolates, biscuits: something to eat

3 Practise listening for specific information by
playing the rest of the dialogue and asking the
students to note down what Bob decides to buy for
each person. All the items are illustrated in 2;
explain that *cookies* is American English for
biscuits.

Tapescript

BOB:	Yes, I think so.
NANCY:	So you think your mother would like something to eat?
BOB:	Yes, I think so.
NANCY:	Well, how about some chocolates?
BOB:	No, I don't think so. She doesn't like them.
NANCY:	Then what about some cookies? What do you call them? Biscuits?
BOB:	Yes, that's a good idea! I'll get Mum some biscuits.
NANCY:	And something to read for your father – would he like a book about New York?
BOB:	Yes, he'll love that!
NANCY:	OK, and you think Jenny would like something to wear?
BOB:	Yes, I think so.
NANCY:	How about a hat?
BOB:	No, I don't think so. She doesn't like hats.
NANCY:	What about a T-shirt?
BOB:	Yes, that's a good idea! And then – something non-alcoholic for Tom.
NANCY:	They make some very good apple juice in upstate New York.
BOB:	Can I get that in town?
NANCY:	Sure.
BOB:	Great! Let's go shopping!

Answers

Mum:	biscuits
Dad:	book about New York
Jenny:	T-shirt
Tom:	apple juice

4 Present the language for making and accepting or
rejecting suggestions by getting the students to put
the sentences in the right order.

Answers

And you think Jenny would like something to wear?
Yes, I think so.
How about a hat?
No, I don't think so. She doesn't like hats.
What about a T-shirt?
Yes, that's a good idea.

Play the tape for 3 again so that students can
check their dialogues. Then ask them to practise

the dialogue in pairs. Go round and check that
students are using the correct stress and intonation
patterns.
5 Practise writing by asking students to complete
the dialogue without looking at their notes; they
should then look back at their notes from 3 and the
expressions in 5 to check.

Answers

NANCY:	So you think your mother would like something to eat?
BOB:	Yes, I think so.
NANCY:	Well, how about some chocolates?
BOB:	No, I don't think so. She doesn't like them.
NANCY:	Then what about some cookies?
BOB:	Yes, that's a good idea!

6 Practise the structures presented so far in this unit
by getting students to act out the conversations
between Bob and Nancy about the other people.
Students should look back at their notes for 1 and
3.

WB 21.1, 21.2

7 Practise reading for specific information by asking
students to look at the store guide and to note
down the departments where Bob and Nancy can
get each article, and the floor number.

Answers

biscuits:	Food, in the Basement
book:	Books, on the Ground Floor
T-shirt:	Ladies' fashions on the First Floor, or Sportswear, on the Fifth Floor
apple juice:	Food, in the Basement

Ask students to check their answers by getting
them to ask and say where Bob and Nancy can get
each item.
8 Present *To . . ..* and Because *I want to . . ..* by
getting students to think of things they would like
to buy in the department store and to note down
the floor number of the department. They should
show each other their list of floor numbers and ask
and say why they want to go to each floor. Present
the exchange with one or two students to begin
with, then ask students to practise in pairs.
Explain that *To . . ..* is the short answer, but that
Because I want to . . .. is equally appropriate.
9 Practise asking for and giving reasons by asking
students to think of things to do in the various
shops and services listed in the *Student's Book*.
Ask them to work in pairs and to ask and say why
they each want to go to the different places. Go
round and check that everyone is using the correct
structures.

10 Practise listening for specific information by playing the tape and asking students to note down the articles that Bob wants to see in the shop. Before you play the tape, check that students remember the words for each of the items illustrated in the *Student's Book*.

Tapescript

ASSISTANT:	Can I help you, sir?
BOB:	Yes, I'm looking for some trousers.
ASSISTANT:	Yes, sir. Which ones would you like . . . how about these ones?
BOB:	Yes, they're very nice – how much are they?
ASSISTANT:	Twenty-four dollars, sir.
BOB:	Twenty-four dollars? No, they're too expensive. I don't want to spend that much. Could I see the T-shirt over there?
ASSISTANT:	This one, sir? Here you are.
BOB:	Thank you . . . I don't think this one is big enough. Have you got a larger one?
ASSISTANT:	I'm sorry, not in that colour. What about the green one?
BOB:	No, I don't like the colour. All right, can I have a look at that shirt over there? The blue one.
ASSISTANT:	Certainly, sir.
BOB:	Thank you – yes, I like this one very much. How much is it?
ASSISTANT:	Fourteen dollars ninety-five.
BOB:	OK, I'll have that. And can I see the pullover on your right? Up there.
ASSISTANT:	Here you are, sir.
BOB:	Oh, it's a bit too short. Have you got a longer one?
ASSISTANT:	Yes, sir. How about this one?
BOB:	Great. That's perfect. OK, so that's the blue shirt and the pullover.
ASSISTANT:	That's twenty-two dollars fifty in all.

Check their answers and then play the tape again; ask students which articles Bob buys.

Answers

He wants to see: trousers, T-shirt, shirt, pullover. He buys the shirt and the pullover.

Discuss with the students the reasons why Bob doesn't buy the other articles.

Answers

The trousers are too expensive. The T-shirt isn't big enough and he doesn't like the colour.

11 Practise the structures presented so far in this unit by asking students to work in pairs and role play the situations described on their role cards. Students can use the clothes in 10 as a basis for this activity; if possible, bring in magazine pictures of various shopping items for the role play. Mark prices on the items, and place them where everyone can see them. Act out the role play as a model with a student in front of the class, then ask students to do the role play themselves. If you have time to collect a large number of pictures, it is a good idea to spread them around the room in 'departments' so that when students change roles and partners, they can also change department.

Remind students that *this* and *these*, *that* and *those* are usually accompanied by a pointing gesture.

12 Practise reading for general sense by asking students to match each paragraph with a picture. This is one of the more difficult reading passages so far in this book, so remind students once again if necessary that they don't have to understand every word.

Answers

Flight bag A	Disc camera C
Cassette clock radio B	Cassette player D

Ask students to re-read the passage quickly and to note down any words which they recognise. Give a brief explanation of meaning of some of the lexical items and then ask them to do 13.

13 Practise reading and using the structures presented in this unit by asking students to discuss which of the articles described in 12 would be suitable gifts for people in the class. If students don't find anything suitable in the shopping catalogue, they can choose from the items presented in the magazine pictures used in 11.

14 Practise writing by asking students to write a few sentences explaining their choice. Students can do this exercise individually or in pairs. If they do it individually, they can compare their versions with their partners. Go round and mark any mistakes discreetly with a mark in the margin. Students must re-read the line and look for the mistake.

LEARNING SKILLS

Ask students to look for passages in English which they expect to find interesting. Encourage students to bring to class any material which appeals to them, e.g. leisure interests, science and technology, films and songs. It is worthwhile spending a little time every so often allowing the students to read or listen to something which particularly interests them. You should go round and help them if there are any vocabulary difficulties, but you should explain that there may be too much new information for the students to understand everything. If possible, use some of this material to supplement your work on the coursebook. Simple tasks which are graded to the students' level can always be organised: noting down familiar-looking words, recognising familiar-sounding words, putting words in order according to where they appear in the passage. It is important to encourage students to look at and listen to authentic English as much as possible, even if they don't understand every word.

PRONUNCIATION TAPESCRIPT

21.1 Listen and repeat.

/ʃ/	/tʃ/
wash	watch
sheep	cheap
cash	catch
ship	chip

Now listen and tick the words you hear.

ship   sheep   watch   cash

21.2 Listen and tick the sentence you hear.

a) Some people live on ships.
b) The mother watched her children.
c) He hit me on the chin.
d) Did you cash it?

21.3 Listen and say what you'd like, like this:

Would you like a blue shirt?
No, I'd like a green one.

Now you.

a) Would you like a blue shirt?
 No, I'd like a green one.
b) Would you like these trousers?
 No, I'd like those ones.
c) Would you like a large hamburger?
 No, I'd like a small one.
d) Would you like this car?
 No, I'd like that one.
e) Would you like an expensive hotel?
 No, I'd like a cheap one.
f) Would you like a short holiday?
 No, I'd like a long one.

21.1 Make suggestions about presents, like this:

I don't know what to get Ken.
How about a book?

And what shall I get Felicity?
What about some perfume?

Now you. Use *How about* and *What about* in turn.

a) I don't know what to get Ken.
 How about a book?
b) And what shall I get Felicity?
 What about some perfume?
c) What can I buy for Antonio?
 How about a pen?
d) And I must get something for Maria.
 What about some tea?
e) I'd like to find something for Kim.
 How about a camera?
f) I don't know what to get for Stewart.
 What about some clothes?

21.2 Ask for reasons, like this:

Ask why Bob wants to go to the library.
Why does he want to go to the library?

Ask why Diana wants to buy some aspirin.
Why does she want to buy some aspirin?

Now you.

a) Ask why Bob wants to go to the library.
 Why does he want to go to the library?
b) Ask why Diana wants to buy some aspirin.
 Why does she want to buy some aspirin?
c) Ask why Richard wants to leave early.
 Why does he want to leave early?
d) Ask why Nancy wants to get up early.
 Why does she want to get up early?
e) Ask why Koji wants to go home.
 Why does he want to go home?
f) Ask why Carla wants to visit her parents.
 Why does she want to visit her parents?

21.3 Say what's wrong with things, like this:

So it's not big enough?
No, it's too small.

So it's too expensive?
Yes, it's not cheap enough.

Now you.

a) So it's not big enough?
 No, it's too small.
b) So it's too expensive?
 Yes, it's not cheap enough.
c) So it's not long enough?
 No, it's too short.

d) So it's too modern?
   Yes, it's not old enough.
e) So it's not fast enough?
   No, it's too slow.
f) So it's too short?
   Yes, it's not tall enough.

21.4 Make suggestions about clothes, like this:

I'm looking for some trousers.
How about these ones?

No, I don't like them.
How about those ones?

Now you.

a) I'm looking for some trousers.
   How about these ones?
b) No, I don't like them.
   How about those ones?
c) And I need a shirt.
   How about this one?
d) No, it's too expensive.
   How about that one?
e) Have you got any socks?
   How about these ones?
f) They're not long enough.
   How about those ones?

22 Describing objects

UNIT SUMMARY

Functions

Asking and saying where things are

Structures

It's	at the top / in the corner / on the right / on the left / in the middle / at the bottom	(of . . .).

Describing objects

What	's it / are they	like?		It's / They're	tall. / small. / large. / heavy. / light. / thick. / thin.

What shape	is it? / are they?		It's / They're	square. / round. / rectangular.

What colour	is it? / are they?		It's / They're	blue. / green. / red. / pink.

Asking and saying what things are made of

What's it / What are they	made of?

It's / They're	made of	glass. / wood. / metal.

Topics

Description of places, buildings, objects: shape, size, material

Lexical items

- church circle corner handbag light (*adj*) opera house police station rectangle, rectangular round (*adj*) square (*n* and *adj*) thick triangle, triangular turning (take the first turning)
- above across behind below bottom into out of past round through top under
- canvas cardboard glass leather metal nylon paper plastic wood
- lost stolen

TEACHING GUIDE

This unit presents the language used for describing objects; encourage students to use objects in the classroom for further practice.

WARM-UP

Suggested warm-up activity: 4.

1 Present the prepositional phrases given in the diagrams using people and objects in the classroom. Then ask students to look at the large photograph and to describe the exact position of the items listed. The diagrams serve to illustrate the meanings of the prepositional phrases; students can refer to them during the activity.

Answers

The woman in blue is on the left of the photo, near the orange car. She's next to the man in white.
The man who's wearing glasses is on the right of the photo, in front of the underground map.
The car is on the left of the photo, opposite the underground station.
The man in the brown jacket is on the left of the photo, behind the woman in blue.
The map of the underground is on the right of the photo, below/under the sign.

2 Practise using various prepositional phrases by asking students to look at the large photograph, and to decide where the small photographs come from.

Answers

Looking from left to right:

- This is part of the back of the orange car on the left of the large photo.
- This is part of the sign above the underground map on the right of the large photo.
- This one's on the right of the large photo. It's the bicycle in front of the underground map.
- This one's in the middle of the large photo. It's a picture of the two girls in front of the underground station.
- This sign is on the left of the large photo. It's above the 'Covent' sign.
- This comes from the left of the large photo. It's the window at the top of the building in the corner.

3 Practise using the various prepositional phrases by asking students to work in pairs. Student A chooses another object in the large photograph; Student B asks questions to guess which object

Student A is thinking of. When they have finished, they should change roles and partners.

4 Practise writing by asking students to write a detailed description of where the small photographs in 2 are taken from. Go round and correct each student's version individually.

5 Practise listening for specific information and following instructions by playing the tape and asking students to draw the picture which is being described. You may need to play the tape twice before asking students to check their drawings with their partners.

Tapescript

Have you got a piece of paper and a pencil? I'll describe the picture. In the middle of the picture is a large triangle and above the triangle is a small circle. Below the triangle is a larger circle. In the top right-hand corner is a small square and below the small square is a large rectangle and below the rectangle in the bottom right-hand corner is a small circle again. In the bottom left-hand corner is a small rectangle and above that a square and above that in the top left-hand corner is a small triangle.

Answer

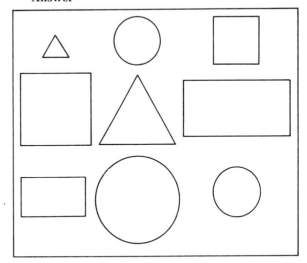

6 Practise giving instructions and using various prepositional phrases by asking students to draw their own pictures and, without showing them, to describe them to their partners. When they have finished, you may like to correct any common errors. Then ask them to change roles and partners.

WB 22.1

7 Practise listening for specific information by

playing the tape and asking students to match the six places with the letters on the map.

Tapescript

1	MAN 1:	Er, excuse me please, can you tell me the way to the, er, police station?
	MAN 2:	Er, yes, er, turn right here into Long Acre, this is, that's the main street there.
	MAN 1:	Aha.
	MAN 2:	Go a few yards along and the next turning on the right is Bow Street . . .
	MAN 1:	Yes.
	MAN 2:	Turn right there and the police station is just a few yards along on the left-hand side.
	MAN 1:	Thank you, er, very much.
2	WOMAN 1:	Hello, em, I wonder please, could you tell me the way to the church?
	WOMAN 2:	Oh, yes, um, just go round the corner to the right into James Street and right down towards the market. Then turn right into King Street and if you go through the edge of the market you'll find the church between King Street and Henrietta Street.
3	MAN 1:	Can you tell me the way to the bookshop please?
	MAN 2:	Er, yeah, if you turn right into James Street, and then walk through the market, it's er, it's at the bottom on the right-hand side, opposite the church.
	MAN 1:	Oh, great, thanks.
4	MAN:	Excuse me, can you direct me to the London Transport Museum?
	WOMAN:	Oh, yeah, um, well, you turn right out of the tube, then you turn right into James Street, then you go right on down James Street, right through the market and then you turn left into Henrietta Street and, er, the museum is just there.
	MAN:	Oh, thank you.
5	WOMAN:	Ah, pardon me, would you be kind enough to direct me to the Opera House?
	MAN:	Sure, it's very easy from here. You just go straight along Long Acre and then turn right down Bow Street and it's on your right-hand side almost opposite the police station.
	WOMAN:	Oh, yeah, thank you.
6	MAN:	Can you tell me please, how to get to the theatre?

	WOMAN:	The theatre, oh yes, um, well you turn right out of the station and you continue all the way along Long Acre as far as Bow Street. Then you turn right into Bow Street, um, and then left, next left, into Russell Street and Drury Lane Theatre is—is just there on your right.

Answers

1	Police Station	C	4	Museum	E
2	Church	A	5	Opera House	B
3	Bookshop	F	6	Theatre	D

Explain, if necessary (see Unit 4), that the district of Covent Garden used to be the site of the fruit and vegetable market. The market has now moved to another site in London, but the local authorities have restored the old market buildings and turned them into a lively centre full of shops, restaurants and bars. There are also a number of actors and musicians performing in the market square.

8 Practise using various prepositional phrases by asking students to complete the blanks.

Answers

1 The police station is on the right of the market, opposite the Opera House.
2 The church is on the left of the market, next to King Street.
3 The book shop is in the market, opposite the church.
4 The museum is on the right of the market, in the corner of the square.
5 The theatre is on the corner of Russell Street and Catherine Street.

WB 22.2

9 Practise giving directions by asking students to work in groups of four. Student A should choose a place on the map and give directions to it without saying what it is; the others should follow the directions. When Student A has finished, another student in the group should give directions to another place on the map. Remind students that they learnt many of these expressions for giving directions in Unit 10.
10 Practise listening for specific information and following directions by playing the tape and asking students to follow the route on the map.

Tapescript

	KOJI:	Hello, Diana!
	DIANA:	Oh, Koji – something terrible's happened. I've lost my handbag.
	KOJI:	Your handbag!
	DIANA:	Yes – and I don't know where I've left it.

KOJI:	How?
DIANA:	Well, I came out of the tube station, and then I went for a walk along Long Acre and I went to the Opera House – you know, to collect the tickets . . .
KOJI:	Oh, I know where that is, yes.
DIANA:	And I went down Bow Street past the police station, and I don't know if I still had it with me or not – it was just over my shoulder . . .
KOJI:	You cannot remember?
DIANA:	No.
KOJI:	Oh.
DIANA:	And then I went into the market, and I stopped off and had a cup of coffee . . .
KOJI:	Yes.
DIANA:	And I think I must have had it then but I got money out of my pocket – I didn't get money out of my handbag to pay. And then I wandered into a bookshop and I didn't buy anything in the bookshop, so I still don't know if I had the handbag in the bookshop or not . . .
KOJI:	Oh.
DIANA:	And then I went along James Street to the tube – to come to meet you.
KOJI:	I tell you what – we, er, what is the English word? We'll retrace . . .

Answer

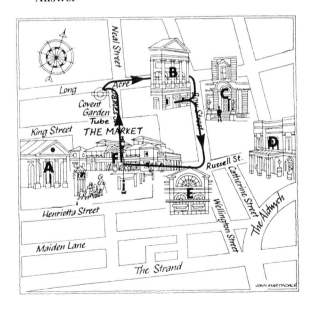

11 Practise writing by asking students to write a few sentences describing the route Diana took. Go round and check that everyone is using the prepositional phrases correctly; the simple past is probably the most likely tense for this activity.

12 Practise speaking by asking students to think about what Diana might have had in her handbag. If you like, you can ask one or two students to empty out their bags and use the articles for vocabulary building or revision.

▄▄ Practise listening for specific information by playing the tape and asking students to check whether they had guessed correctly. The pre-listening activity should have helped prepare the students for the listening comprehension task, so they shouldn't have too much difficulty with this activity.

Tapescript

POLICEMAN:	Right, miss—er, when did you lose this handbag?
DIANA:	Er, I lost it about half an hour ago, sergeant.
POLICEMAN:	Uh huh, yes. And, er, can you describe the contents, please?
DIANA:	Em, well, it's got a diary, it's got my wallet, my driving licence is in it, em, a lace handkerchief . . .
POLICEMAN:	Handkerchief, yes . . .
DIANA:	A notebook . . .
POLICEMAN:	A notebook . . .
DIANA:	Em, a pen and a lipstick and a comb . . .
POLICEMAN:	Comb, yes.
DIANA:	And it's got my cheque book, my keys, my credit cards – everything I need.
POLICEMAN:	And, er, what is the bag itself like?
DIANA:	Oh, it's a small, square, shabby, black leather handbag.
POLICEMAN:	Black leather handbag, yes. And, em, miss – when did you last have it?
DIANA:	I last had it, sergeant, in the bookshop.
POLICEMAN:	In the bookshop.
DIANA:	Yes.
POLICEMAN:	I see.

13 Present vocabulary used for describing objects and
▄▄ practise listening for specific information by playing the tape again and asking students to note down any words used to describe the handbag and when she last saw it.

14 Practise listening for specific information by
▄▄ playing the tape again and asking students to complete the chart. The activities in 12 and 13 should have prepared the students for this listening task, but you may decide to play the tape two or three times to allow the students plenty of opportunity to complete the chart accurately.

Answers See chart on page 119.

15 Practise listening for specific information by
▣ playing the tape and asking students to complete
the chart for the other three missing articles.
   They should listen once and tick the words and
expressions they hear; then they fill in as much of
the chart as possible. Play the tape again and ask
them to listen and check.

Tapescript

1 MAN: Ah, ah, can you help me please?
  POLICEMAN: Er, yes, sir?
  MAN: I, I've lost, um, a briefcase.
  POLICEMAN: Ah just a moment, sir. One brief-case, yes . . .
  MAN: Yes.
  POLICEMAN: What colour was it?
  MAN: It's brown, a brown leather brief-case.
  POLICEMAN: I see, and where did you lose it, sir?
  MAN: Well, I, I think it was on the tube last night.
  POLICEMAN: Oh, on the tube last night, yes . . .
  MAN: Yes. On the way home.
  POLICEMAN: What was in the briefcase, sir?
  MAN: Well it had some papers, a lot of papers.
  POLICEMAN: Papers.
  MAN: Work, you know.
  POLICEMAN: Yes. And what time was this?
  MAN: Oh, er, well, it was quite late last night. Oh it had, er, there were two books inside it as well.
  POLICEMAN: Two books.
  MAN: Yes.
  POLICEMAN: Yes. And what time did you say it was, sir?
  MAN: Well, it was quite late, it was, er, after 11 o'clock.
  POLICEMAN: After 11 o'clock . . .

2 POLICEMAN: Uh, can I help you, madam?
  WOMAN: Oh, er, yes I hope so. I, I've had a suitcase stolen.
  POLICEMAN: Oh, a suitcase. Er, where was it stolen from?
  WOMAN: It was stolen from my car actually.
  POLICEMAN: I see, and where was your car, madam?
  WOMAN: Um, it was parked in the market.
  POLICEMAN: In the market.
  WOMAN: Yes, that's right.
  POLICEMAN: Now can you describe the case to me please?
  WOMAN: Um, yes, it was green, um . . .
  POLICEMAN: Green . . .
  WOMAN: Plastic . . .
  POLICEMAN: Plastic . . .
  WOMAN: Actually . . .

POLICEMAN: Yes, and er, what was in the case, madam?
  WOMAN: Er, well, it had quite a lot of clothes . . .
  POLICEMAN: Clothes.
  WOMAN: And um, er, some shoes, yes . . .
  POLICEMAN: Shoes, yes.
  WOMAN: And a lot of jewellery.
  POLICEMAN: Jewellery. I see. Um, what time did you last see the case, madam?
  WOMAN: Um, well it was there obviously when I parked my car, um, well, I just, now, it went some time yesterday, probably in the after-noon.
  POLICEMAN: I see, what time did you park the car?
  WOMAN: Er . . .

3 POLICEMAN: Er, is anything the matter, madam?
  WOMAN: Oh, officer, yes, I've lost my bag.
  POLICEMAN: Oh dear, where did you lose it?
  WOMAN: Well, I think it was in a restaurant in King Street, earlier on today.
  POLICEMAN: I see. What kind of bag was it, madam?
  WOMAN: Well, it was a large canvas shoulder bag.
  POLICEMAN: Canvas shoulder bag.
  WOMAN: Yes and er, you want me to . . .
  POLICEMAN: What was in it?
  WOMAN: Oh, what was in it? Oh, it had everything. It had my diary, my purse containing quite a lot of money in traveller's cheques.
  POLICEMAN: I see.
  WOMAN: All my files, er, my pen which I had only just purchased and was very expensive.
  POLICEMAN: Yes, now you say it was in a restaurant in King Street.
  WOMAN: I believe so, that's where I had my lunch.
  POLICEMAN: Er, you've been back to the restaurant?
  WOMAN: Oh, indeed I have, but there's no sign of it now.

16 Practise vocabulary and structures used for
describing objects by asking students to role play
one of the conversations in the police station.
After they have finished, correct any mistakes and
then ask them to change partners and roles and to
choose another conversation to role play.

17 Practise using the language for describing objects
by asking students to work in pairs; Student B

Answers to 14 and 15

Article	Lost or Stolen	Description	Contents (if any)	Last seen
Handbag	Lost	small, square, black, leather	diary, wallet, driving licence, handkerchief, notebook, pen, lipstick, comb, chequebook, keys, credit cards	in bookshop, half an hour ago
Briefcase	lost	brown, leather	papers, 2 books	on tube, last night
Suitcase	stolen	green, plastic	clothes, shoes, jewellery	in car, in market, yesterday
Bag	lost	large, canvas	diary, purse, files, pen	in restaurant in King Street, lunchtime

thinks of an object and Student A asks Yes/No questions to guess what it is. They should change roles when they have finished.

WB 22.4, 22.5, 22.6, 22.7, 22.8

LEARNING SKILLS

Play one of the listening passages in the book and ask students to follow the transcript; ask them to underline all the words which are stressed. Then get them to write all these words in a list. Ask them if these words represent the main ideas of the passage?

The aim of this activity is to show that the stressed words in English carry the main information about a passage. It is better to play only a short extract from a listening passage (i.e. about five or six lines).

Ask students to look at their vocabulary lists for the last unit. Get them to look at each word they have noted down and to say the word to themselves as they think of a suitable link image. This will help them recall the word in the future.

PRONUNCIATION TAPESCRIPT

22.1 Listen and repeat.

/b/	/p/
buy	pie
bought	port
bill	pill
back	pack

Now listen and tick the words you hear.

pill port buy pack

22.2 Listen and repeat.

a) Put the packet of biscuits back in the cupboard.
b) The pub is behind the bookshop.
c) Bring me a bottle of Perrier, please.
d) Peter baked an apple pie.
e) It's a big brown plastic bag.
f) Penny bought bread, bananas, and pears.

22.3 Listen and answer all the questions with this sentence:

No, she bought two bottles of milk last night.

The sentence is the same, but the stressed word will be different each time.

a) Did she buy three bottles of milk last night?
   No, she bought two bottles of milk last night.
b) Did she drink two bottles of milk last night?
   No, she bought two bottles of milk last night.
c) Did she buy two bottles of milk last week?
   No, she bought two bottles of milk last night.
d) Did he buy two bottles of milk last night?
   No, she bought two bottles of milk last night.
e) Did she buy two glasses of milk last night?
   No, she bought two bottles of milk last night.
f) Did she buy two bottles of milk this morning?
   No, she bought two bottles of milk last night.

STRUCTURE REVIEW TAPESCRIPT

22.1 Ask what things are like, like this:

Ask what Diana's handbag is like.
What's it like?

Now you.

a) Ask what Diana's handbag is like.
   What's it like?
b) Ask what Koji's suitcase is like.
   What's it like?
c) Ask what Bob's house is like.
   What's it like?
d) Ask what Nancy's books are like.
   What are they like?
e) Ask what Richard's office is like.
   What's it like?
f) Ask what Carla's clothes are like.
   What are they like?

22.2 Say what shape things are, like this:

What shape is the room?
It's square.

What shape are the windows?
They're rectangular.

Now you.

a) What shape is the room?
   It's square.
b) What shape are the windows?
   They're rectangular.
c) What shape is the table?
   It's round.
d) What shape are the boxes?
   They're square.
e) What shape is the garden?
   It's rectangular.

22.3 Ask what things are made of, like this:

Mary gave me a lovely ring.
Oh, really? What's it made of?
Silver. And George gave me some handkerchiefs.
Oh, really? What are they made of?
Silk.

Now you.

a) Mary gave me a lovely ring.
   Oh, really? What's it made of?
b) Silver. And George gave me some handkerchiefs.
   Oh, really? What are they made of?
c) Silk. And Penny gave me a beautiful jacket.
   Oh, really? What's it made of?
d) Leather. And my father gave me a suitcase.
   Oh, really? What's it made of?
e) Canvas. And Mum gave me some cups and
   saucers.
   Oh, really? What are they made of?
f) China. And Peter gave me a clock.
   Oh, really? What's it made of?
   Glass and metal.

23 Explaining what to do

UNIT SUMMARY

Functions

Giving instructions

Structures

How do you	boil an egg? make a pot of tea? start a car?

First you . . .. Then you . . .. Next you . . .. After that you . . .. Finally you . . ..

Giving advice

Always Make sure you Don't forget to	slow down in bad weather. look in your mirror before you change lanes.

Never Don't	get too close to the car in front.

Topics

Public notices and signs, traffic regulations, parts of the car, first aid, tourism

Lexical items

- accident advice aeroplane bleed brakes breathe bus stop button cash desk casualty check damage engine escalator forest frontier headlights helmet injure injury keep calm kiss-of-life mirror motorcycle operation panic park (n and v) petrol (cap, pump) police porter press protect public (in public) rest area remove replace safety belt shake (hands) silence slow down take out tank traffic lights tyre vehicle victim warn windscreen

TEACHING GUIDE

This unit presents the language used for giving advice and instructions; the list above represents the lexical items that students will be required to use productively.

WARM-UP

Suggested warm-up activity: 10 or 14.

1 Present the vocabulary for giving various instructions by asking students to look at the signs and to decide where they might find them.

Answers 1C, 2D, 3A, 4B, 5F, 6E

2 Practise listening for recognition by playing the tape and asking students simply to tick the expressions they hear.

Tapescript

PORTER:	Move along, now. Mind your backs, please. Mind your backs . . .
PATIENT:	Good morning, I've come to see Doctor Garbitt.

RECEPTIONIST:	Yes, do you have an appointment?
PATIENT:	I'm afraid not.
RECEPTIONIST:	I'll just see if he has time to see you. Do sit down.
PATIENT:	Thank you.
CUSTOMER:	I've come to collect the photographs.
ASSISTANT:	Yes, madam. Have you got the ticket?
CUSTOMER:	Here you are.
ASSISTANT:	Wait here please. I'll just go and fetch them.
MAN:	Come in. Ah, Mrs Hill. How nice to see you. Please take a seat.

Answers

Please follow me. (Arriving for an appointment.)
Come in. ✓ (Arriving for an appointment.)
Do sit down. ✓ (In a waiting room.)
Wait here please. ✓ (In a shop.)
Please fasten your seatbelts. (On an aeroplane.)
Mind your backs please. ✓ (In a station.)

Point out that the imperative is commonly used for giving instructions; however, you may need to explain that in situations where personal contact is involved, it is necessary to be more tentative in order to be more polite (see Units 10 and 11).
Ask students to discuss the situations in which you would expect to hear the instructions.

3 Practise giving instructions by asking students to discuss what kind of instructions they expect to find in the situations shown in their books.

Answers

In a library: Silence.
At a petrol station: No smoking. Pay at the cash desk.
In a park: No cycling. Do not walk on the grass.
On an aeroplane: No smoking. Fasten your seatbelts.
On a train: Do not lean out of the window.
In a forest: Do not drop lighted cigarettes.

4 Practise giving instructions by asking students to say what the various signs mean.

Answers

A Cross

B Turn left

C No smoking   E Keep dry
D Take your shoes off

5 Practise reading for general sense by asking students to match the sentences with the pictures. You may need to pre-teach some of the vocabulary items; however, the illustrations should be self-explanatory.

Answers   1C, 2E, 3D, 4A, 5F, 6B

6 Present *Always . . .* and *Never . . .* by asking students to complete the sentences.

Answers

Never drink and drive.
Always stop when the lights are red.
Always look out for people walking at night.
Always wear a helmet on a motorcycle.
Never drive fast near a school.
Always keep your car in good condition.

7 Present *Make sure . . . .* and *Don't forget to . . . .* by asking students to work in pairs and to write sentences giving advice on how to keep the car in good condition. The sentences and labels accompanying the illustration should provide the students with any necessary vocabulary; however, they may want to look up some of the difficult vocabulary in their dictionaries. Go round and check for any mistakes.

8 Practise listening for specific information by
📼 playing the tape and asking students to compare the advice they gave in 7 with that given by the mechanic.

Tapescript

Well, now let me see, you should always make sure that the windscreen is clean. You should check the windscreen wipers and replace them regularly— yes, and don't forget to check the brakes. Now the mirrors should always be clean and so should the lights—always make sure the lights are working. Oh, and check the indicators are working properly too. Now then, you should change the oil regularly and make sure there's enough water in the radiator. Oh, and don't forget to check the battery. Then, er, check the tyre pressures, make sure the tyres are pumped up and you should never drive a car with tyres that are worn smooth. Oh, yes, and very important, make sure you've got enough petrol for your journey.

Answers

Extra advice:
Check the windscreen wipers.
Clean the mirrors.
Check the indicators.
Check the battery.

WB   23.1, 23.2, 23.3

9   Practise reading for general sense by asking
students first of all to put the pictures in the right
order and then to match the instructions to the
pictures. Explain that they don't need to
understand every word; however, if they ever
drive a car in an English-speaking country, this
vocabulary will be quite useful.

In order to put the pictures in the right order,
you may first need to do some work in the class
deciding what exactly is happening in each
picture and looking ahead to the instructions.
Don't be afraid to give students clues.

Answers

G   Press button to choose petrol.
F   Remove petrol cap.
B   Take out petrol pump and place in tank.
A   Fill petrol tank.
E   Replace petrol pump.
D   Replace petrol cap.
C   Pay at cash desk.

10   Practise writing a sequence of instructions by
asking students to write the instructions out in
full. Revise *First of all, . . . Then . . . After that, . . .*
Next . . . Finally, . . . which were presented in Unit
13.
11   Practise reading for general sense by asking
students to work in pairs; each student should
read one of the passages. Explain that they are not
expected to understand every word, merely to
understand the general sense and to find the
relevant information to write a list of instructions.
After each student has read the instructions, they
should work together to work out a sensible order
of priority. When each pair has finished, ask
students to suggest suitable instructions and write
them on the board. Encourage students to discuss
their choice of instructions and the order as much
as possible.

WB   23.4

12   Practise giving advice by asking students to work
in four groups and to read the role cards. Students
should discuss their topics before circulating to
ask for and give advice. Make sure each group uses

appropriate language both for asking for advice
and for giving advice.

If possible, when each group has prepared its
advice, ask students to form new groups consisting
of one member from each of the old groups. This
will allow everyone to hear the advice given by
each of the groups.
13   Practise reading for general sense by asking
students to decide which information is true and
which is false.

Answers

1   False. Tips are usually between ten and fifteen
per cent of the charge.
2   True.
3   True. In London, you are not even allowed to
smoke inside the station.
4   False. Hats are not a necessary part of everyday clothing.
5   False. You're likely to make a lot of people
very angry if you do this.
6   True. Also known by some as the 'right'
(i.e. correct!) side of the road.
7   False. But the driver will be very pleased if
you do.
8   False. This sign, seen near escalators, is only
designed to safeguard animals.
9   True. The left-hand side is for people in a
hurry.
10   False.
11   True. Policeman are usually very helpful.
12   False.

Practise listening for general sense by playing
the tape of English people talking about customs
in their country. The language will naturally be
advanced level, but the students should be able to
manage without too much trouble since they will
have been well prepared for the activity.

Tapescript

MAN:	'Never tip waiters, porters or taxi drivers.'
WOMAN:	Well . . .
MAN:	That's not true, is it?
WOMAN:	No, it isn't. If you don't tip them they won't do anything for you.
MAN:	So you ought to tip them.
WOMAN:	Yes.
MAN:	All right.
WOMAN:	'You should shake hands when you meet a person for the first time.'
MAN:	Well, that's true, men do that anyway.
WOMAN:	I suppose you do a bit, yes, all right, yes.
MAN:	Er . . .
WOMAN:	What about that one? 'You mustn't smoke on an underground train.'
MAN:	That's true. You can't do that.

WOMAN:	Good thing too. Yes.
MAN:	'Don't forget to wear a hat when you go out.'
WOMAN:	I haven't got one.
MAN:	I never do that. Er. 'Never stand at the back of a queue. Always go to the front.'
WOMAN:	If you do that you'll be punched in the face.
MAN:	I think you will. I don't think you can do that in England. And 'Make sure you drive on the left.'
WOMAN:	I don't . . .
MAN:	That's true.
WOMAN:	I don't know my left from my right anyway.
MAN:	You would do if you drove on the wrong side. Um, 'When you . . .
WOMAN:	Number 7.
MAN:	. . . get off a bus, you must thank the driver.' No, you mustn't do that.
WOMAN:	You'd probably get run over.
MAN:	You'd get run over. 'If you see the sign DOGS MUST BE CARRIED, you must have a dog.'
WOMAN:	That's not true, I read it all the time.
MAN:	That's not true. No.
WOMAN:	Er . . .
MAN:	'You should stand on the right of an escalator in the underground.'
WOMAN:	Oh that's right.
MAN:	Is that true?
WOMAN:	That really makes me angry, yes, if people don't do that.
MAN:	All right.
WOMAN:	Er. 'Never eat all the food on your plate. Always leave something.'
MAN:	That's nonsense.
WOMAN:	No, that's very silly.
MAN:	You don't have to do that.
WOMAN:	No.
MAN:	'Ask a policeman for directions if you're lost.'
WOMAN:	Ah, yes, that's a very good idea to do. Yes.
MAN:	Is that wise?
WOMAN:	Yes that's wise.
MAN:	All right.
WOMAN:	Yes.
MAN:	'Take off your shoes when you go into someone's home.' No you mustn't do that.
WOMAN:	I don't think they'd appreciate that.
MAN:	No.
WOMAN:	No.

14 Practise writing by asking students to make a list of six pieces of advice for people visiting their country for the first time. Then ask them to discuss their list with another student.

Alternatively, you may like to ask them to write

a similar list of true and false pieces of advice, and to ask other students to read it through and decide which is true and which is false.

WB 23.5

LEARNING SKILLS

Ask students to revise some of the expressions used when asking for information about words which you presented in Unit 11 (see Learning Skills, page 61). Get them to choose three or four words which they don't understand, or don't know how to pronounce, and then ask them to go round the class using the expressions to help them answer their queries.

PRONUNCIATION TAPESCRIPT

23.1 Listen and repeat.

/ɪə/	/eə/
here	hair
ear	air
cheer	chair
beer	bear

Now listen and tick the words you hear.

ear   chair   hair   bear

23.2 Listen and repeat.

/ɪə/	/eə/
appearance	airport
near	millionaire
theatre	their
year	wear

23.3 Listen and repeat. Mark the stressed syllables.

a) Don't touch the cooker!

b) Stop making that noise!

c) Keep away from the fire!

d) Don't leave the building!

e) You mustn't say anything!

f) Please shut the door!

STRUCTURE REVIEW TAPESCRIPT

23.1 Give advice, like this:

What must you always do when crossing a road?
Always find a safe place.

What must you never do?
Never cross a busy street.

Now you.

a) What must you always do when crossing a road?
Always find a safe place.
b) What must you never do?
Never cross a busy street.
c) What must you always do?
Always wait for the traffic to stop.
d) What must you always do?
Always look round for traffic.
e) What must you never do?
Never run across the street.
f) What must you always do?
Always walk straight across.

23.2 Remind people to do things, like this:

What shall I do about the newspapers?
Don't forget to cancel them.

And what about the electricity?
Make sure you turn it off.

Now you. Use *Don't forget to* and *Make sure you* in turn.

a) What shall I do about the newspapers?
Don't forget to cancel them.
b) And what about the electricity?
Make sure you turn it off.
c) What shall I do about the plants?
Don't forget to water them.
d) And what about the dustbin?
Make sure you empty it.
e) And I must find my passport.
Don't forget to take it.
f) I haven't got any traveller's cheques.
Make sure you buy some.

23.3 Give instructions, like this:

How do you make a pot of tea?
First, you boil some water.

What do you do then?
Then you warm the pot.

Now you.

a) How do you make a pot of tea?
First, you boil some water.
b) What do you do then?
Then you warm the pot.
c) What do you do next?
Next you put the tea in the pot.
d) What do you do after that?
After that, you pour the boiling water on the tea.
e) And finally . . .?
Finally, you pour the tea.

23.4 Tell people to do things, like this:

Oh, you're driving very fast!
Please slow down.

Now you.

a) Oh, you're driving very fast!
Please slow down.
b) I can't hear you.
Please speak louder.
c) I can't read your writing.
Please write more clearly.
d) Don't stand there.
Please sit down.
e) There's no hurry.
Please take your time.
f) Don't wait outside.
Please come in.

SUMMARY

Functions

In Units 19 to 23, students learnt how to:

Ask and say what things are called
Ask and say what people think
Agree and disagree
Ask and say how people feel
Sympathise
Make suggestions and give advice
Ask and say what people have to do
Ask and say what people mustn't do
Ask for permission
Give and refuse permission

Say what kind of thing they want
Ask for and give reasons
Offer help
Say what they want
Ask and say which one(s) they want
Ask and say where things are
Ask for and give directions
Describe objects
Ask and say what things are made of
Give instructions

Topics

The topic areas covered have been:
Parts of the body, emotional reactions, illnesses and ailments, travel arrangements, household arrangements, baggage, shopping items and gifts, shops and services, clothes, colours, description of places, buildings, and objects, shape, size, material, public notices and signs, traffic regulations, parts of the car, first aid, tourism

TEACHING GUIDE

WARM-UP

Suggested warm-up activities: 4, 8, 10, 11, 12, or 14.

WB

Students should be able to do the *Workbook* exercises at any stage of this revision unit.

1   Revise asking and saying what people think by asking students to look at the paintings and to match them with their titles. They should check their answers with another student. Then ask them to write down three reasons why they like one of the paintings. They should then go round the class looking for someone else who likes the same painting; ask them to discuss why they both like it. Encourage them to think of as many reasons as possible why they like the painting.

Answers

A The Girls on the Bridge
B Man Lying on a Wall
C Mother and Children

2   Revise asking and saying what people think by getting students to find other students who dislike the same painting as they do. They should choose which painting they dislike, then write down three reasons why they dislike it. They should then find someone else who dislikes it and discuss their reasons.
    Revise asking and saying what people think, by getting students to find as many people as possible who like and dislike the same paintings. They should then think of three more things they like and three more things they dislike.

3   Practise writing by asking students to choose one of the paintings and to write a short description of

it. Students will also revise saying where things are, describing objects, and saying what things are made of. The descriptions can be as simple as they like, but the more ambitious students may wish to add more details about their emotional reactions to the painting. Ask them to correct each other's descriptions.

4 Revise asking and saying what you must and mustn't do and asking for and giving permission by getting students to work in two groups and to follow the instructions in their books. Make sure they don't look at each other's passages. First of all they should match the headings to paragraphs.

Answers

GROUP **A**
Baggage: Paragraph C
Check-out time: Paragraph A
Taxi service: Paragraph E
Newspapers: Paragraph B
Mail and messages: Paragraph F
Credit cards: Paragraph D

GROUP **B**
Laundry and dry cleaning: Paragraph B
Dogs: Paragraph D
Keys: Paragraph E
Valuables: Paragraph F
Packed lunches: Paragraph A
Cheques: Paragraph C

Students should then find a member of the other group and act out the situations. For the first role play, students in Group A should be the hotel guests and students in Group B should be the hotel staff. When they have finished, they should change roles.

5 Revise giving instructions, by asking students to read the sentences taken from a recipe for onion soup, and to match them with the illustrations. You may need to pre-teach some of the vocabulary, e.g. *oven*, *slice*, *bowl*, *stock*, *boil*, *egg yolk*, *grate*, but encourage students to guess unfamiliar words from the context.

Answers   A1, B5, C6, D3, E4, F2.

6 Revise giving instructions by asking students to put the sentences in a suitable order.

Answer

D Chop three large onions and fry them in oil.
C Add ¾ litre of stock and bring to the boil.

B Put some slices of bread in a deep bowl.
F Pour the soup into the bowl and grate some cheese on top.
A Put it in the oven to brown the top.
E Take it out of the oven and mix in the yolk of an egg and a small glass of Madeira.

Point out that the Madeira isn't essential but gives a very pleasant flavour to the whole dish. You can use a sweet vermouth if you like.

Then play the tape so students can listen and check.

Tapescript

For this recipe you need three or four large onions, some slices of bread, some stock – chicken stock is ideal, but it doesn't really matter – the yolk of an egg and some Madeira wine – about half a small glass is enough. So, first of all you chop the onions and fry them in a little oil. While the onions are cooking, put some slices of bread in a deep bowl, a layer to cover the bottom and then another layer on top. When the onions are ready, add about three-quarters of a litre of stock to the onions and bring to the boil again. After that, you may want to add some salt and pepper. Next, pour the soup into the bowl over the slices of bread and grate some cheese on top. Then you put the whole thing in the oven or under the grill to brown the top. Finally, you take it out and mix in the yolk of an egg and the Madeira. Then serve immediately. And that's the gratinée – a great meal for cold winter nights!

7 Revise giving instructions by asking students to write a recipe of their own. It doesn't matter if the recipe is very simple. Then ask everyone to read their recipes out to the rest of the class.

8 Revise asking for and saying what people want, describing objects, asking and saying which one(s) they want by getting students to work in pairs and to prepare the SHOPPING GAME. The rules are explained in the *Student's Book*. As they play the game, you should go round and check that everyone is following the rules and using suitable language.

LEARNING SKILLS

Ask students to perform the vocabulary building activity explained in the Learning Skills for Unit 10 on three or four adjectives of their choice.

Ask them to check that their notes are organised under suitable function, topic or situation headings.

Ask them to choose ten or twelve words which they think are particularly useful to them. Get them to explain their choice of words to the rest of the class.

25 | Leading up to the present

UNIT SUMMARY

Functions

Asking and saying what people have done

Structures

Present perfect tense

Have	you they	(ever) been to America?
Has	he she	

Yes,	I we they	have.	No,	I we they	haven't.
	he she	has.		he she	hasn't.

I You We They	've haven't	been to America.
He She	's hasn't	

	Verb	Past simple	Past participle
I R R E G U L A R	be buy come eat go have know meet read /iː/ see take write	was/were bought came ate went had knew met read /e/ saw took wrote	been bought come eaten gone/been* had known met read /e/ seen taken written
R E G U L A R	book like listen live play stay visit watch work	booked liked listened lived played stayed visited watched worked	booked liked listened lived played stayed visited watched worked

*Note: been = gone and come back
gone = gone and not come back

128

Functions

Asking and saying how long people have done things

Structures

How long	have	they you	lived there?
	has	he she	

For seven years.
Since 1983.

Talking about personal experience

Who	's the	ugliest prettiest best worst most luxurious most expensive best looking most interesting	person town village film book restaurant	you've ever	been to? seen? visited? read?
What					

Topics

Sightseeing, town facilities, leisure activities

Lexical items

- architecture atmosphere before boating boutique café club comedy district exhibition fashionable fine freedom friendly horse riding luxurious noise once popular relax roller skating thriller traffic trip

---

TEACHING GUIDE

This unit introduces the present perfect tense:
a) for referring to the *indefinite past* (with *ever, never, before*);
b) with *for* and *since* to refer to actions which began in the past and continue into the present.

WARM-UP

Suggested warm-up activity: 8 or 13.

1   Practise reading for general sense by asking students to match the paragraphs with their titles. The students are likely to recognise only certain words in the texts, but this should be sufficient to enable them to perform the exercise. You may like to do some vocabulary building on the texts, but it is better to limit the number of new words to be explained to five or six. You may also want to ask students to choose the five or six new words themselves and to try and work out the meaning on their own before looking them up in the dictionary.

Answers

A Central Park
B Greenwich Village
C Empire State Building
D St Patrick's Cathedral
E Statue of Liberty

2   Present the present perfect tense by playing the tape and asking students to tick the places that Bob has visited. Students here are asked simply to distinguish between an affirmative and a negative response without having to understand every word.

Tapescript

NANCY:	Well Bob, what've you been doing since you've been in New York? Have you been to Central Park yet?
BOB:	Yes I have, I went there last week.
NANCY:	And have you seen the Frick Museum?

BOB:	No I haven't, not yet.	
NANCY:	And have you visited China Town?	
BOB:	Yes, I have. I had lunch there yesterday.	
NANCY:	And have you been down Wall Street?	
BOB:	Wall Street? No, no, not yet. I haven't.	
NANCY:	And have you seen the Met, the Metropolitan Museum?	
BOB:	Ah yes, yes. I went there at the weekend. It was great.	
NANCY:	And then there's the Guggenheim Museum.	
BOB:	No, I haven't been there yet.	
NANCY:	Have you been to the top of the World Trade Center?	
BOB:	The World Trade Center? No, not yet. I haven't.	
NANCY:	And then there's the Empire State Building.	
BOB:	Ah yes, yes. I went right up to the top, wonderful view.	
NANCY:	And have you visited the Statue of Liberty?	
BOB:	Oh yes, yes. That was the first thing I did in New York, been all around it, up and down.	
NANCY:	And have you seen the famous Times Square?	
BOB:	Yes, I've been there, been through it several times.	

Answers

CENTRAL PARK ✓ , FRICK MUSEUM, CHINATOWN ✓ , WALL STREET, METROPOLITAN MUSEUM ✓ , GUGGENHEIM MUSEUM, WORLD TRADE CENTER, EMPIRE STATE BUILDING ✓ , STATUE OF LIBERTY ✓ , TIMES SQUARE ✓

3 Present *Has he been to . . .? Yes, he has./No, he hasn't.* by checking the answers to 2 with the class. Give a few clear examples of the model questions and replies and then ask students to practise the structure in pairs.

4 Present *Have you been to . . .? Yes, I have./No, I haven't.* by asking students to write down a list of places in the town where you are now, or perhaps a large city which everyone has visited. Give the model question and answer exchange by asking one student *Have you been to/visited/seen . . .?* and eliciting the responses *Yes, I have.* or *No, I haven't.* Then ask students to look at each other's lists and to ask and say where they've been. Go round and check that everyone is using the structure correctly. Practise writing by asking students to write down a few sentences describing where people have/haven't been, or what they have/haven't seen/visited. Correct each student's work individually.

5 Practise using the present perfect by getting students to ask and say if they've been to the places shown in their books. You can obviously extend this list to include a variety of cities and countries all over the world. Try and make the places as relevant as possible to the students.

6 Practise listening for general sense by playing the tape and asking students simply to decide if the speakers have been to New York before. Explain that they are not all native English speakers.

Tapescript

1	INTERVIEWER:	Excuse me, I wonder if you'd mind telling me, is this your first visit to New York?
	MR SCHMIDT:	Yes, it is.
	MRS SCHMIDT:	That is correct.
	INTERVIEWER:	Oh, oh it is. And what sort of places have you seen so far?
	MR SCHMIDT:	We have seen . . .
	MRS SCHMIDT:	Oh we have been everywhere, many places.
	MR SCHMIDT:	The Statue of Liberty.
	INTERVIEWER:	Oh yeah.
	MR SCHMIDT:	Aha.
	MRS SCHMIDT:	We've eaten hot dogs.
	INTERVIEWER:	Oh, you have.
	MR SCHMIDT:	Very delicious . . .
	INTERVIEWER:	Did you enjoy them?
	MR SCHMIDT:	Very much.
	MRS SCHMIDT:	Yes, yes. We've stayed in—in many of the good hotels in New York.
	MR SCHMIDT:	Yes they're very comfortable.
	INTERVIEWER:	Oh good, I'm very glad to hear.
	MR SCHMIDT:	Very good food . . .
2	INTERVIEWER:	Ah, hello, could you tell me, is this your first visit to New York?
	PAUL MATHIEU:	My first visit? No I have been here once before but that was business, I am here now on holiday.
	INTERVIEWER:	Oh, I see and what have you been doing since you've been here?
	PAUL MATHIEU:	I've been here, em, all over the city. I've been, er, seeing everything I can.
	INTERVIEWER:	And what about food? Have you been eating here?
	PAUL MATHIEU:	Yes, I have. I—I've a great passion for Chinese food so I go to Chinatown.
	INTERVIEWER:	Oh, good. And anything else?
	PAUL MATHIEU:	Well, I've been writing a lot of postcards, sending them home.
	INTERVIEWER:	Oh, I see. Thank you very much.
3	INTERVIEWER:	Excuse me, is this your first visit to New York?

CARMEN GONZÁLEZ:	Yes, this is the first time I've been in New York.
INTERVIEWER:	Oh, and er, what sort of places have you seen?
CARMEN GONZÁLEZ:	Oh, I have seen everything except the museums. I'm not interested in the paintings.
INTERVIEWER:	Oh, oh, I see and, and, what else have you done?
CARMEN GONZÁLEZ:	I've listened to a pop concert in Central Park.
INTERVIEWER:	Oh.
CARMEN GONZÁLEZ:	And I bought a T-shirt with the Empire State Building on it.
INTERVIEWER:	Aha.
CARMEN GONZÁLEZ:	I have met some very nice people.
INTERVIEWER:	Oh, I'm very pleased to hear that. Thank you.

4	INTERVIEWER:	Excuse me, I'm doing a survey. Could you tell me please, is this your first visit to New York?
	PAT McCARTHY:	My first visit to New York? Oh no, not at all.
	INTERVIEWER:	Oh, I see. Well, can you tell me where you've been?
	PAT McCARTHY:	Well, I've been everywhere.
	INTERVIEWER:	Oh really? Well, what sort of thing have you been doing?
	PAT McCARTHY:	Well, I've just booked some tickets for the theatre. I watched a ball game.
	INTERVIEWER:	Oh, of course, I realise, you're American. Where are you from?
	PAT McCARTHY:	As a matter of fact I'm from here, right here in New York. I'm a policeman, er, at the moment I'm off duty, but I live and work here in New York, in the Bronx.
	INTERVIEWER:	Oh, really.

Answers

1 Mr and Mrs Schmidt ✗
2 Paul Mathieu ✓
3 Carmen González ✗
4 Pat McCarthy ✓

Check their answers by asking students to say if the speakers have been to New York before. You may need to teach *once, twice, three/four times,* etc. if you wish to extend the discussion by asking students if they have been to New York themselves, and if so, how many times.

7 Practise listening for specific information by playing the tape and asking students to note down what the speakers have done in New York. The students are simply required to link each speaker with the appropriate phrases in their books. You may like to stop the tape after each speaker has finished.

Tapescript See 6.

Answers

Mr and Mrs Schmidt: have taken a trip round the Statue of Liberty, eaten hot dogs and stayed in many of the good hotels in New York.
Paul Mathieu: has written some postcards and had lunch in Chinatown.
Carmen González: has listened to a concert in Central Park, bought a T-shirt and met some nice people.
Pat McCarthy: has booked tickets for the theatre and watched a ball game; is in fact an off-duty policeman from the Bronx!

Students should then practise the structures by saying what the speakers have done. Present the past participles of various verbs and ask students to practise using them in pairs.

8 Practise verb forms by asking students to match the infinitives listed in the book with their past participles, and to decide which of the verbs are irregular.

Answers

Regular		Irregular	
Infinitive	**Past Participle**	**Infinitive**	**Past Participle**
listen	listened	buy	bought
book	booked	eat	eaten
watch	watched	take	taken
stay	stayed	have	had
		meet	met
		write	written

This is a suitable moment to remind students of the past simple forms of these verbs as well. You can ask them to complete the chart on page 156 in their books, and encourage them to add to the list when they come across new irregular verbs.

9 Practise using past participles by asking students to complete the postcard.

Answers

been, lived, met, done, eaten, had, taken, watched

If you have time, ask students to write a similar postcard describing what they've done and where they've been in the town where you are at the moment.

WB 25.1

10 Present *How long has he/she known/lived/etc . . .? For/Since . . .* by getting students to answer the

131

questions. Get one student to ask the questions and give the model replies yourself. Then ask students to practise in pairs.

11 Practise *How long . . .? For/Since . . .* by getting students to ask and answer the questions in their book. Make sure everyone has understood that you use *for* with a length of time, and *since* with a fixed point in time.

12 Practise *for* and *since* by asking students to look back at the paragraphs in 1 and to answer the questions. Explain that it isn't necessary to understand every word of the paragraphs to perform the exercise.

Answers

A Since 1863	D Since 1879
B Since the 1840s	E Since 1885
C Since 1931	

Ask students to write full answers and to use *for . . . years.*

WB 25.2, 25.3

13 Practise listening for general sense by playing the tape and asking students to note down what the speakers like and dislike about New York.

Tell students that all the vocabulary they need is above the chart in their books, and check that they understand all the words. Then ask students to listen and simply place the items in the right boxes.

Tapescript

1	INTERVIEWER:	Could I ask you what you think of New York?
	MRS SCHMIDT:	Oh, the food is the best we have ever eaten.
	MR SCHMIDT:	Oh, yeah, and the people are the friendliest, yes.
	MRS SCHMIDT:	The traffic though is the worst we have ever seen. Terrible.
	MR SCHMIDT:	And the noise, noise, I dislike the noise very much.
2	INTERVIEWER:	I wonder, could you tell me what you think of New York?
	PAUL MATHIEU:	Oh, yes, certainly. I love the atmosphere, er, the music in the streets, er, the noise, er, colour, er, but the, er, the architecture is the worst I've ever seen.
3	INTERVIEWER:	Could you tell me what you actually think of New York?
	CARMEN GONZÁLEZ:	I love the buildings. They are very beautiful, and the food is very good, and the taxi drivers are very friendly, but the subway is the most dangerous I have ever travelled on.

4	INTERVIEWER:	Tell me, what do you really think of New York?
	PAT McCARTHY:	New York? It's a great city. I like the people, the shops, the restaurants, the theatres—must be the best in the world. There's only one thing I really dislike and that's the weather. It's just too hot.
	INTERVIEWER:	Thank you.

Answers

	Likes	Dislikes
1 Mr and Mrs Schmidt	food, people	traffic, noise
2 Paul Mathieu	atmosphere, music in streets	architecture
3 Carmen González	buildings, food, taxi-drivers	subway
4 Pat McCarthy	people, shops, restaurants, theatre	weather

Practise writing by asking students to write a few sentences saying what the speakers like and dislike. Check that they all remember how to form the superlative of adjectives (see Unit 17).

14 Practise using the present perfect and revise the superlative by asking students to talk about their experiences using the chart in their books. They should start off working in pairs and then should ask other members of the class. Finally they should report back to the rest of the class.

WB 25.4

15 Practise using the present perfect and making suggestions by asking students to look at the entertainments page of their local paper and to discuss what they might like to see. Encourage them to talk about their likes and dislikes and then to make plans to go and see something in their groups. Be prepared to supply further vocabulary if necessary.

LEARNING SKILLS

Whenever students start to read a passage, particularly passages which are not simplified for language learners, ask them to think about the following questions:
What does the title tell you about the passage?

What do you know about the topic?

Does the topic interest you?

Can you think of five questions which you expect to be answered in the passage?

When they have read the passage, get students to reflect on whether their questions were answered or not. This activity encourages students to prepare themselves for reading. If students are well-prepared for reading, they are likely to understand more.

PRONUNCIATION TAPESCRIPT

25.1 Listen and repeat.

/v/	/f/
view	few
of	off
leave	leaf
very	ferry

Now listen and tick the words you hear.

few   leave   very   off

25.2 Listen and tick the sentence you hear.

a) They've left the office.

b) I've had a wonderful holiday.

c) We lived here for a long time.

d) You won a lot of money!

25.3 Listen and repeat.

a) How long have you lived in the village?

b) He's the tallest man I've ever seen.

c) He's never had time to decorate the house.

d) Have you ever been to Africa?

e) I think they've known each other for a very long time.

f) She's seen Mike, but she hasn't spoken to him.

STRUCTURE REVIEW TAPESCRIPT

25.1 Say what you've done. Answer the questions, like this:

Have you been to America?
Yes, I have. or *No, I haven't.*

Now you.

a) Have you been to America?
....

b) Have you seen *Superman*?
....

c) Have you worked abroad?
....

d) Have you eaten spaghetti?
....

e) Have you had a holiday in the mountains?
....

f) Have you stayed in the Hilton Hotel?
....

25.2 Listen to two people answering the same questions. Say what they have or haven't done, like this:

Have I been to America? Yes, I have.
He's been to America.

Superman? No, I haven't seen it.
She hasn't seen Superman.

Now you.

a) Have I been to America? Yes, I have.
He's been to America.

b) Superman? No, I haven't seen it.
She hasn't seen Superman.

c) Have we worked abroad? Yes, of course we have.
They've worked abroad.

d) Spaghetti? We eat spaghetti every day.
They've eaten spaghetti.

e) Have I had a holiday in the mountains? No, I haven't.
She hasn't had a holiday in the mountains.

f) The Hilton Hotel? No, we haven't stayed there.
They haven't stayed in the Hilton Hotel.

25.3 Ask people how long, like this:

Ask how long Nancy has lived in New York.
How long has she lived in New York?

Now you.

a) Ask how long Nancy has lived in New York.
How long has she lived in New York?

b) Ask how long Koji has been in England.
How long has he been in England?

c) Ask how long Carla has worked in Hong Kong.
How long has she worked in Hong Kong?

d) Ask how long Bob has had a car.
How long has he had a car?

e) Ask how long Richard has liked football.
How long has he liked football?

f) Ask how long Diana has played the piano.
How long has she played the piano?

25.4 Say how long, like this:

How long has Bob known Nancy?
Since 1982.

How long has Diana known Koji?
For two weeks.

Now you.

a) How long has Bob known Nancy?
Since 1982.

b) How long has Diana known Koji?
For two weeks.

c) How long has Richard known Carla?
For ten years.

d) How long has Carla been a journalist?
Since 1975.

e) How long has Bob been an actor?
Since 1980.

f) How long has Diana lived in her flat?
For six months.

26 Talking about recent events

UNIT SUMMARY

Functions

Asking and saying what people have or haven't done yet

Structures

Have	you we they	
Has	he she	had breakfast yet?

	I we they	have.			I we they	haven't.
Yes,	he she	has.		No,	he she	hasn't.

I We You They	haven't	had lunch. gone to work. been running.
He She	hasn't	

Asking and saying what has just happened

I We You They	've	just	got up. left home. arrived.
He She	's		

Topics

Routine activities, news items

Lexical items
- abroad appointment break down careful celebrate clean (v) climb cut (v) dentist do (homework) editor make (the bed) manager middle class news order (v) receive socialist tooth/teeth voter

TEACHING GUIDE

This unit introduces the present perfect used to talk about what has just happened or what you've done or haven't done yet. There is not a great deal of new

vocabulary, so use this opportunity to revise some items which have already been presented.

WARM-UP

Suggested warm-up activity: 7.

1 Practise listening for general sense by playing the
🔲 tape and asking students to tick the things which
Carla has already done.

Tapescript

LEE:	Hi, Carla. You look well. I haven't seen you for some time.
CARLA:	Hello, Lee. It's nice to see you. You're looking very well too.
LEE:	So what's your secret?
CARLA:	Actually, I go running every day now. I usually go before lunch, but I haven't been today. I'm going later on this afternoon.
LEE:	And how's your work?
CARLA:	Busy, as usual. But interesting. I met Henry Binham this morning. I'm doing an article on him for next week's magazine. He was very nice.
LEE:	Really?
CARLA:	Oh, and I had lunch with your old friend Terry Kline as well.
LEE:	Terry! How is he?
CARLA:	Fine, just fine.
LEE:	And are you going to have a holiday this year?
CARLA:	Well, I wanted to talk to the editor this morning to ask her for some time off next month, but she was too busy.
LEE:	So you haven't been away yet this year?
CARLA:	No. Look, I'm in a dreadful hurry. I'm on my way to see my bank manager and then I've got to pick the children up from school and do some shopping.
LEE:	I see! I don't usually see you around here during the day.
CARLA:	No, but I've just been to see my dentist. He lives two blocks from here. Are you at home this evening?
LEE:	Yes.
CARLA:	Can I give you a ring? About eight?
LEE:	Yes, OK.
CARLA:	Great! Oh, I'm going to be late. Bye!

Answers

Wednesday	Aug 10 ✓

10am Meet Henry Binham — my office. ✓
11.30 Talk to editor about holiday.

Lunch 12.45 — with Terry Kline. ✓
2 pm Dentist! ✓
3pm Appointment with bank manager.
3.45 Pick up children from school.
Do the shopping
Evening Go running ??

---

2 Practise *Has she done . . . yet? Yes, she has./No, she hasn't.* by getting students to ask and say what Carla has done. Explain that the present perfect can be used to describe actions which have taken place in the recent past, as well as to describe people's experience (Unit 25). Point out that *yet* is used in questions, and in negative replies (*No, I haven't done it yet.*). Explain that *been* means 'gone and returned', whereas *gone* means 'gone and not returned'.

WB 26.1

3 Practise *Have you . . . yet? Yes, I have./No, I haven't.* and revise *going to* for plans and intentions by asking students to make a list of all the things which they all intend to do today. Point out that this should be a list compiled by the class as a whole, and that the *Student's Book* only contains examples of possible things to be done. Get students to ask and say what they've done or haven't done yet. If there are things which they haven't done yet, get them to say when they're going to do them. Give a few model exchanges by saying what you have or haven't done and asking another student. Then get students to find out what others have or haven't yet done.

4 Practise writing by asking students to write a few sentences saying what the others have or haven't done in the class. They should use the example in their books as a model.

WB 26.2, 26.3

5 Present *He's just . . .* by asking students to describe what has just happened in the pictures. Revise *He/she's going to . . .* by asking them to suggest what is going to happen next. You may like to ask students to work in groups of three or four and to try and link all the pictures into a story.

6 Practise using the present perfect by asking students to think of something which has just happened and to mime it to the others in the group. You may need to mime something to show them how to do this activity; mime something simple such as: *You've just received a letter with some very good news.* and get students to guess what has happened. Students can either mime some of the situations in their books, or you can ask them to write down a situation on a piece of paper; collect the pieces of paper and redistribute them to one member of each group. Remember that situations which are badly mimed will generate much more language than those which are clear and well-performed! Help students not to be afraid of making fools of themselves!

WB 26.4, 26.5

7 Practise listening for general sense by playing the
🔲

tape. Students can only hear one side of this telephone conversation so ask students to try and imagine what the other person is saying.

Tapescript

> CARLA: Hello, Lee. This is Carla . . . What's the matter, Lee? You sound ill! . . . Why? What's happened? . . . But Lee, you looked all right when I saw you this afternoon! Have you called the doctor? . . . But you must – I mean, it's not normal for that to happen . . . It's not very hot at the moment. Is Kim with you? . . . Where's she gone? . . . Do you know when she's coming back? . . . Oh, that's not long to wait – but really, Lee, you should look after yourself. I think you should take a holiday . . . Don't be silly – of course you've got time. You're working too hard at the moment . . .

8   Practise writing by asking students to complete the dialogue with what they imagine Lee is saying.

Answers

Lee's responses would probably be something like this:

CARLA: Hello, Lee. This is Carla.
LEE: Hello, Carla.
CARLA: What's the matter, Lee? You sound ill!
LEE: Oh, I don't feel very well.
CARLA: Why? What's happened?
LEE: I felt very ill when I was out shopping, and I fainted in the supermarket.
CARLA: But Lee, you looked all right when I saw you this afternoon! Have you called the doctor?
LEE: No, I haven't. I didn't think it was serious enough to worry the doctor.
CARLA: But you must – I mean, it's not normal for that to happen.
LEE: It's probably just the heat.
CARLA: It's not very hot at the moment. Is Kim with you?
LEE: No, she isn't.
CARLA: Where's she gone?
LEE: I think she's gone to the shops. I didn't get all the shopping.
CARLA: Do you know when she's coming back?
LEE: In about half an hour I expect.
CARLA: Oh, that's not long to wait – but really, Lee, you should look after yourself. I think you should take a holiday.
LEE: Oh, I haven't got time.
CARLA: Don't be silly – of course you've got time. You're working too hard at the moment.

Ask the students to role play their dialogues three times with different partners. They should compare their versions when they have finished. Remind them that there are many possible versions, but that they should all be grammatically correct.

9   Practise using the present perfect by asking students to role play the situation in their books in pairs.

10 Practise reading for general sense by asking students to match the headlines to the photographs. Remind students that newspaper headlines are usually in a fairly compressed style of language, missing out little words such as articles because there isn't enough room to print the whole sentence. Explain that the present simple form is used in headlines to express the recent past.

Answers   1B, 2C, 3D, 4A

11 Practise reading for general sense by asking students to match photograph and headline with the articles. Explain that they will not understand every word, but that they will recognise enough to do the exercise. Point out that the present perfect is very often used in news items to report events which have just happened, the consequences of which are still in the present. When they have finished, it is important to emphasise how much they have understood, rather than how little.

Answers   1Bb, 2Cd, 3Dc, 4Aa

12 Practise reading for specific information by asking students to answer the questions. Again, they do not need to understand all the words in the news items; this activity gives useful practice in searching for answers to questions in an advanced level text.

Answers

1   Three.
2   Supporters of the socialists in the towns.
3   The middle class voters of the country areas.
4   Twenty-seven.
5   Forty.
6   To be careful on the way home from their holidays.
7   For forty years.
8   Five.

Then ask students to write the headlines out in full using the present perfect tense. Suggest that they refer to the news items for useful phrases.

Answers

1 The Socialists have won the regional elections.
2 A film star has married for the fifth time.
3 Twenty-seven people have died on the roads during the holiday weekend.
4 A US State official has arrived in Portugal.

13 Practise speaking and listening by asking students to discuss what items they expect to hear in the radio news for today. You may like to tune in to the national news in their own language if you're teaching a monolingual class, and then ask them to predict which items are likely to be included in the BBC news. Point out that the World Service News usually presents items of international importance. You may also like to try other English-speaking news services. Ask students to listen to the news at home and check whether the items they predicted appeared or not.

LEARNING SKILLS

By now, students should have realised that it isn't necessary to understand every word in a passage; often you can guess its general sense by using a number of simple techniques.

Explain to them that when you come across an unfamiliar word:

you decide what part of speech it is;
you look for clues to its meaning in the context;
you guess what the word means;
you read on and revise or confirm your guess.

Give students a passage of English which is slightly above their present level and ask them to read the passage using the techniques above whenever they come across an unfamiliar word.

Ask students to discuss whether they read the following material in the same way: a novel, a newspaper, a telephone directory, a political brochure, a dictionary. If they don't read them all in the same way, how do they read each one? Explain that there are various ways of reading, according to the type of material and the purpose of the reader.

PRONUNCIATION TAPESCRIPT

26.1 Listen and repeat.

/dʒ/	/j/
jet	yet
joke	yolk
juice	use
jaw	your

Now listen and tick the words you hear.

jet   your   yolk   juice

26.2 Listen and tick the words which contain the sound /dʒ/.

angry	bridge ✓	change ✓
check	dog	going
high	just ✓	suggest ✓
vegetable ✓		

Listen and repeat.

/j/ university   USA   useful   year   you

26.3 Listen and repeat. Underline the most important words, and cross out the other words.

a) ~~The~~ man ~~at the~~ door ~~was about~~ sixty . . .
b) . . . ~~and he had a~~ letter ~~in his~~ hand.
c) ~~The~~ man ~~said he was~~ sorry ~~to~~ trouble ~~us~~ . . .
d) . . . ~~and~~ asked ~~if we could~~ help ~~him.~~
e) ~~He~~ wanted ~~to~~ deliver ~~the~~ letter . . .
f) . . . ~~but he~~ couldn't find ~~the~~ house ~~he was~~ looking ~~for.~~

We hear the sound /ə/ fifteen times. In the words _he_, _him_ and _his_, the sound /h/ is almost dropped in unstressed words.

STRUCTURE REVIEW TAPESCRIPT

26.1 Say what people have or haven't done, like this:

Has Bob had breakfast yet?
Yes, he has.

Has Diana left for work yet?
No, she hasn't.

Now you.

a) Has Bob had breakfast yet?
   Yes, he has.
b) Has Diana left for work yet?
   No, she hasn't.
c) Has Richard taken the children to school yet?
   No, he hasn't.
d) Has Koji bought any presents yet?
   Yes, he has.

e) Have Joe and Nina gone to bed yet?
   No, they haven't.
f) Has Nancy got up yet?
   Yes, she has.

26.2 Say what you haven't done yet, like this:

Can I see you for a minute?
No, I haven't finished the exercise yet.

Now you.

a) Can I see you for a minute?
   No, I haven't finished the exercise yet.
b) Come and have lunch.
   No, I haven't revised Unit twenty-five yet.
c) Can you help me?
   No, I haven't looked at my notes yet.
d) Are you ready?
   No, I haven't had my coffee yet.
e) Are you coming with us?
   No, I haven't bought the teacher a drink yet.

26.3 Ask if people have done things yet, like this:

Ask if Angelo has done his homework yet.
Has he done his homework yet?

Now you.

a) Ask if Angelo has done his homework yet.
   Has he done his homework yet?
b) Ask if Maria has arrived yet.
   Has she arrived yet?
c) Ask if Lee and Tim have seen the newspaper yet.
   Have they seen the newspaper yet?
d) Ask if Manuel has bought a motorbike yet.
   Has he bought a motorbike yet?
e) Ask if Günther and Luigi have changed classes yet.
   Have they changed classes yet?
f) Ask if Anna has met the teacher yet.
   Has she met the teacher yet?

27 Talking about the future (1)

UNIT SUMMARY

Functions

Asking and saying what the weather will be like

Structures

Future simple tense

What will	it the weather	be like tomorrow?

It'll be	rainy. sunny. cloudy. snowy.	There'll be	rain. sunshine. cloud. snow.

Will it be	rainy? sunny? cloudy? snowy?	Yes, it will. No, it won't.

Will there be	rain? sunshine? cloud? snow?	Yes, there will. No, there won't.

Talking about plans for the future

If it's	rainy sunny	(I expect) (I think)	I we they he she	'll	stay at home. go for a walk.

I We You They He She	won't have to stay at home. 'll be able to go out.

Topics

The weather, seasons, leisure activities

Lexical items

- cloud cloudy rain rainy snow snowy sun sunny sunshine
- spring summer autumn winter
- decorate early enjoy expect few go for a walk instead late match (football match) party quick

TEACHING GUIDE

This unit introduces the use of the future simple for making predictions and for discussing open conditions. Remind students that the present continuous is used for future arrangements (see Unit 9) and *going to . . .* is used for plans and intentions (see Unit 15).

WARM-UP

Suggested warm-up activity: 11.

1   Present *What will it be like in . . .? It'll be cold/warm*, etc. by asking students to look at the map and the chart showing the weather forecast. Then ask them what the weather will be like in a variety of different places and elicit suitable answers. The weather symbols should explain the meaning of the new words, but you may want to check that everyone has understood. Explain, if necessary, that the initials next to the cities in the chart refer to *sunny, cloudy, snowy,* and *rainy*. Get students to ask and say, in pairs, what the weather will be like. Then introduce *There'll be rain*, etc. in the same way. Make sure everyone understands that you say *There'll be rain/sunshine/snow in . . .* but *cloud over . . .*
2   Practise *will be* and revise the comparative form of adjectives by asking students to compare the temperatures of different places on the chart. You may like to ask them to write down five or six sentences. Go round and correct them individually.
3   Practise listening for specific information by playing the tape and asking students to put suitable symbols by each place name. You may like to do this as a class activity on the board. (Madeira is the only place named which is not on the map.)

Tapescript

. . . And here's the weather forecast for anyone heading for the continent on holiday this weekend. Generally it will be very sunny with temperatures reaching thirty degrees Celsius in Munich, Prague, Geneva and Vienna, and thirty-two degrees in Rome, Madrid and Barcelona. The hottest place in Europe will be Athens, where it'll be thirty-three degrees Celsius. There'll be a bit of cloud over Berlin but it'll still be warm – about twenty-five degrees, and Warsaw will be about the same. But there's some rain heading across the Atlantic, which will reach Madeira and Lisbon tomorrow – it'll still be quite warm though, at twenty-two degrees Celsius. London and Paris will start cloudy and uncomfortably warm, I'm afraid, and will have rain in the afternoon or early evening, but it won't last long. Coldest places over the weekend will be Edinburgh where there'll be rain, and Copenhagen where there'll be some cloud, turning to rain later on in the day. Temperatures won't get much above eighteen degrees Celsius, slightly below the seasonal average. And that's all from me, back to the studio.

Answers

Munich ☼		Berlin ☁	
Prague ☼		Warsaw ☁	
Geneva ☼		Madeira ☔	
Vienna ☼		Lisbon ☔	
Rome ☼		London ☁ ☔	
Madrid ☼		Paris ☁ ☔	
Barcelona ☼		Edinburgh ☔	
Athens ☼		Copenhagen ☁ ☔	

4   Present *Will it be . . .? Yes, it will./No, it won't.* by asking students to check their answers to 3 in pairs. Present the structures by asking a student *Will it be sunny in Paris?* and eliciting the responses *Yes, it will.* or *No, it won't.* Then get students to practise the structures in pairs. Repeat the procedure for *Will there be . . .? Yes, there will./No, there won't.*
5   Practise the future simple by asking students to say what the weather will be like tomorrow in their country. Then revise the names of the months and present *autumn, spring, summer, winter* with further practice of the future simple.
6   Practise writing by asking students to prepare a weather forecast for your region. If they want to be sure about their forecast, they can check in a local newspaper and then write it in English.

WB   27.1, 27.2, 27.3

7   Practise listening for specific information by playing the tape and asking students to write R or S in the chart according to what the speakers will probably do if it's rainy or sunny.

Tapescript

JOHN: Have you got any plans for the weekend, Geoff?

GEOFF: No, nothing special. I'll probably stay at home and do some work. I've got so much to do.

JENNY: But it'll be lovely weather, Geoff. You can't stay at home! I think I'll go to the beach.

GEOFF:	Well, so will I if it's sunny. I can do some work there. But what will you do if it rains, Jenny?	
JENNY:	Oh, I don't know. Perhaps I'll go to the cinema or visit a museum. I don't know yet. What about you, John?	
JOHN:	I think I'll go for a long walk in the country if it's sunny and maybe play some tennis in the evening. But if it rains . . . well, I think I'll stay in bed.	
JENNY:	What! All weekend?	
JOHN:	Well, I've had a very busy week!	

Answers

	GEOFF	JENNY	JOHN
go to the beach	S	S	
go for a walk in the country			S
play tennis			S
stay at home and work	R		
visit a museum		R	
go to the cinema		R	
stay in bed			R

Get students to check their answers with each other, using the structure *Geoff thinks he'll . . . if it's sunny*, etc. Make sure they realise that the *if* clause is in the present simple.

8 Practise *If + present simple/future simple* by getting students to talk about their plans for the weekend. Explain that you use the conditional structure when you're speculating about possible actions and activities in the future, and *going to . . .* when you've already made up your mind what you're going to do before you begin speaking. Get students to ask and say what they'll probably do and what they're definitely going to do at the weekend. They should go round and find two people who have the same plans, and then find one more thing which they'd all like to do together. Students should keep a note of these plans for work they will be doing in 13.

WB 27.4, 27.5

9 Practise listening for specific information by playing the tape and asking students to write K or D by the things Koji and Diana are planning to do at the weekend. Then ask students to make a schedule of Koji's and Diana's plans.

Tapescript

DIANA:	What are your plans for the weekend, Koji?	
KOJI:	Well, tomorrow I think I'll go to Beaulieu – is that how you pronounce it?	
DIANA:	Yes, that's right. Oh, it's lovely – you'll enjoy yourself.	
KOJI:	Yes, I've heard it's very interesting. I'll take a train or a coach in the morning . . . and I can have lunch in a pub. What about you?	
DIANA:	Well, tomorrow I'm not doing anything special during the day, but I'm having dinner in a restaurant with some friends in the evening, and then we're off to a party. What are you doing in the evening?	
KOJI:	Oh, nothing in particular. I'll probably go and see a film.	

Answers

Koji's plans:
Saturday morning – go to Beaulieu by train or coach, have lunch in a pub. Saturday evening – see a film.
Diana's plans:
Saturday evening – have dinner in a restaurant with friends, go to a party.

10 Practise listening for specific information by playing the tape and asking students to make notes on the things Koji and Diana are going to do together. Ask students to check their answers in pairs, and then write sentences about Koji and Diana's plans. Go round and check for any mistakes.

Tapescript

DIANA:	Look, I've got an idea! Why don't you come and have dinner with me and my friends on Saturday . . .?	
KOJI:	Well, that would be lovely – but are you sure your friends won't mind?	
DIANA:	Of course not – they'll be pleased to meet you! They're very nice – I'm sure you'll like them. And then we'll go to the party together afterwards.	
KOJI:	I'd love to – thank you, Diana.	
DIANA:	And then we'll take my car and we'll go to Beaulieu on Sunday. It'll be much quicker than going by train or coach. And what's more, there'll be fewer people visiting the place on Sunday . . .	
KOJI:	That's true.	
DIANA:	But we won't stay late at the party on Saturday night . . . if we leave early on Sunday morning, we can have lunch on the way. What do you think?	

KOJI: That sounds wonderful!
DIANA: That's settled, then. We'll meet at the restaurant tomorrow evening – I'll give you the address.

Answers

On Saturday evening, Koji and Diana are going to have dinner in a restaurant. After that, they're going to go to a party. On Sunday morning, they're going to drive to Beaulieu and have lunch on the way.

11 Practise listening for specific information by playing the tape and asking students to put a cross on their notes for 10, by the plans which Koji and Diana will have to change.

Tapescript

. . . that's all the news for today. And now for the weather this weekend: it looks like rain over most of the country, although there'll be a few sunny patches on Sunday; temperatures will be about fifteen to eighteen degrees Celsius with a gentle wind from the south-west bringing the rain. Traffic news: Hampshire police advise motorists not to use the A31 near Winchester as there are some roadworks which will cause problems for traffic in both directions. One last piece of information. Beaulieu House is closed this weekend, but will be open from Tuesday onwards. So if you're going to Beaulieu tomorrow or Sunday, I'm afraid you'll be disappointed. Open again as from Tuesday. And that's all from the newsdesk.

Get students to check their answers by saying what Koji and Diana won't be able to do and what they'll probably do instead.

Answers

They won't be able to go to Beaulieu because it'll be closed this weekend.
They won't be able to go for a drive because it'll be rainy.
They'll probably see a film instead.
They'll have to stay inside.

12 Practise discussing the future by asking students to work in pairs and to act out the dialogue between Koji and Diana when they change their plans.
13 Practise reading for general sense by asking students to think about their plans for the weekend which they discussed in 8. Then ask them to read their horoscope and to discuss what they won't be able to do and what they'll do instead. They should begin this exercise in pairs, and then go round the class asking how other students will change their plans. Most of the

vocabulary in the reading passage will be recognised by the students; however, you may need to explain any unfamiliar words in the individual horoscopes. It is probably better not to explain all the unfamiliar words to all the students, only those which are relevant to the individual students.

WB 27.6

LEARNING SKILLS

Encourage students to listen to the radio news in English by asking them to discuss the news which is likely to appear in today's bulletin. Ask them to think about important international events. You may want to help them by letting them read the morning's newspaper headlines. Ask students to listen to the BBC World Service News and to say whether their predictions were correct or not.

PRONUNCIATION TAPESCRIPT

27.1 Listen and repeat.

/l/	/r/
lane	rain
lock	rock
flight	fright
glass	grass

Now listen and tick the words you hear.

fright   glass   lock   lane

27.2 Listen and repeat.

a) The children played in the field.
b) What will it be like in Lisbon tomorrow?
c) It'll be cloudy, with rain later.
d) Will you arrange another French lesson?
e) I'll leave the record player in the living room.
f) Lee's writing a letter to his girlfriend.

27.3 Listen and repeat the answers.

a) Shall we play tennis tomorrow?

Yes, if it's sunny.
b) Can you do the shopping?

Yes, if I'm not too busy.
c) Will you phone the restaurant?

Yes, if I can find the number.
d) Will you give me a lift to the station?

Yes, if the car will start.
e) Would you like to go to the theatre tonight?

Yes, if we can get tickets.
f) Shall I make an omelet for supper?

Yes, if we've got enough eggs.

27.4 Listen to the questions in 27.3 again, and answer them yourself.

a) Shall we play tennis tomorrow?
   Yes, if it's sunny.
b) Can you do the shopping?
   Yes, if I'm not too busy.
c) Will you phone the restaurant?
   Yes, if I can find the number.
d) Will you give me a lift to the station?
   Yes, if the car will start.
e) Would you like to go to the theatre tonight?
   Yes, if we can get tickets.
f) Shall I make an omelet for supper?
   Yes, if we've got enough eggs.

STRUCTURE REVIEW TAPESCRIPT

27.1 Say what the weather will be like, like this:

Will it be sunny tomorrow?
Yes, it will.

Will there be snow tomorrow?
No, there won't.

Now you.

a) Will it be sunny tomorrow?
   Yes, it will.
b) Will there be snow tomorrow?
   No, there won't.
c) Will there be rain tomorrow?
   No, there won't.
d) Will it be cloudy tomorrow?
   Yes, it will.
e) Will there be sunshine tomorrow?
   Yes, there will.
f) Will it be rainy tomorrow?
   No, it won't.

27.2 Say what you'll do, like this:

What shall we do tomorrow?
If it's sunny, we'll go for a walk.

Now you.

a) What shall we do tomorrow?
   If it's sunny, we'll go for a walk.
b) What shall we do this evening?
   If it's rainy, we'll stay at home.
c) What shall we do at the weekend?
   If it's cloudy, we'll do some decorating.
d) What shall we do in the mountains?
   If it's snowy, we'll go skiing.
e) Where shall we have lunch?
   If it's sunny, we'll sit in the garden.
f) What shall we do in London?
   If it's rainy, we'll visit a museum.

27.3 Say what people won't be able to do, like this:

I hope it won't rain.
No, if it rains we won't be able to go to the open-air concert.

Now you.

a) I hope it won't rain.
   No, if it rains we won't be able to go to the open-air concert.
b) I hope there won't be too much traffic.
   No, if there's too much traffic we won't be able to arrive in time.
c) I hope we won't arrive too late.
   No, if we arrive too late we won't be able to see our friends.
d) I hope there won't be too many people.
   No, if there are too many people we won't be able to sit at the front.
e) I hope we won't sit too far away.
   No, if we sit too far away we won't be able to hear the music.

Talking about the future (2)

UNIT SUMMARY

Functions

Making requests

Agreeing to and refusing requests

Offering to do things

Accepting and refusing offers

Making suggestions

Talking about plans

Structures

Can Could Will	you	be quiet, speak louder, bring us the bill,	please?

Yes,	of course. certainly.

I'm sorry, I'd rather not.

I'll open the window (,shall I?) Shall I open the window?

Oh, thank you very much. Yes, please.

No, it's all right. I'd rather you didn't.

Why don't we . . .? I think we should . . ..

We're going to . . ..

Topics

Banking, numbers

Lexical items

- bank clerk   champagne   currency   exchange rate   fluently   foreign   loud
  note (pound note)   outing   picnic   report (n)   surprise   turn down (radio)   turn on (light)

TEACHING GUIDE

This unit focuses on useful formulae for making requests and offering to do things. It both revises language presented in Units 10 and 11 and extends practice of the future simple.

WARM-UP

Suggested warm-up activity: 3.

1 Practise reading by asking students to fill in the dialogue with suitable responses from the list. You may like to ask students to complete the dialogue before they have looked at the responses given.

Tapescript and Answers

KOJI:	I'd like to change some money, please.
CLERK:	Yes, sir. Do you have foreign currency or traveller's cheques?
KOJI:	Traveller's cheques. I'd like to change 15,000 yen into pounds sterling, please. What's the exchange rate?
CLERK:	324 yen to the pound. Will you sign the cheques please?
KOJI:	Yes, of course. Could I borrow your pen?
CLERK:	Yes, certainly. And could you date the cheques?
KOJI:	Yes, it's the twenty-fifth today, isn't it?
CLERK:	That's right. Could you give me your passport, please?
KOJI:	Here you are.
CLERK:	Thank you. That will be £46.30. How would you like it?
KOJI:	In five-pound notes, please.

Play the tape and ask students to listen and check.

When the students have finished the exercise, they might like to act out the dialogue in pairs. Explain that bank clerks in Britain usually ask *How would you like it?* to find out the kind of notes which the customer requires.

2 Practise recognising numbers by playing the tape and asking students to correct the exchange rates. They may find it easier if they copy out the list of exchange rates before you play the tape. If students work in pairs, student A can dictate the list to student B, giving both students practice in recognising and writing numbers.

Tapescript

Austrian Schilling twenty-seven point eight. Belgian Franc seventy-nine point eight. Canadian Dollar one point seven nine. Danish Krone fourteen point two. French Franc twelve point oh eight. German Mark three point nine. Dutch Guilder four point three. Irish Punt one point two three. Italian Lira two thousand five hundred and twenty. Japanese Yen three hundred and twenty-four point eight four. Norwegian Krone eleven point three seven. Portuguese Escudo two hundred and twenty-seven point oh two. Spanish Peseta two hundred and twenty-six point six three. Swedish Krona eleven point five. US Dollar one point three oh.

Answers

AUSTRIA	Schilling	27.8
BELGIUM	Franc	79.8
CANADA	Dollar	1.79 (Corrected)
DENMARK	Krone	14.2
FRANCE	Franc	12.08 (Corrected)
GERMANY	Mark	3.9
HOLLAND	Guilder	4.3 (Corrected)
IRELAND	Punt	1.23
ITALY	Lira	2520
JAPAN	Yen	324.84
NORWAY	Krone	11.37 (Corrected)
PORTUGAL	Escudo	227.02
SPAIN	Peseta	226.63 (Corrected)
SWEDEN	Krona	11.5 (Corrected)
USA	Dollar	1.30

3 Present *What's the exchange rate for . . .?* and practise saying numbers by getting students to ask and say what various exchange rates are. Point out that decimals are pronounced e.g. *eleven point three nine, three hundred and twenty-four point eight four, twenty-seven point eight.*

4 Practise the dialogue in 1 by asking students to work in pairs and to role play the situation described in their books.

WB 28.1, 28.2, 28.3

5 Present making requests by asking students to match the requests with the pictures.

Answers 1D, 2A, 3C, 4B

Then ask students to decide which of the responses would be suitable. In some cases, more than one may be suitable.

Answers

1f Is that better?
1c Can you hear me now?
2a Yes, certainly.
3b Sorry!
4a Yes, certainly.

Explain to students that *Could you . . .?* is slightly more polite than *Will you . . .?* but that the degree of politeness usually depends on the intonation.

6 Practise listening for general sense by playing the tape and asking students to decide what the situation is. Ask the students how well the speakers know each other.

Tapescript

1. WOMAN 1: Yes, I put it in the post this morning.
   WOMAN 2: Oh, good. Then I'll get it tomorrow or the day after, then.
   WOMAN 1: Yes, I hope so. By the way, I haven't taken a copy.
   WOMAN 2: Well, I'll do one for you, then.
   WOMAN 1: Yes, please. But could you also give me a ring when you receive it?
   WOMAN 2: Yes, certainly. Don't worry. It will get here all right.

2. MAN: But it's only for a day or two.
   WOMAN: I'm sorry, I'd rather you didn't.
   MAN: Oh, why not? I'll bring it back. I won't keep it for long.
   WOMAN: No, I'm sorry but . . .
   MAN: Well, could I borrow it just for tonight, then?
   WOMAN: I'm sorry, but it's not mine.

3. WOMAN: It's certainly very . . . interesting. Why don't you put some red over here?
   MAN: Like this?
   WOMAN: Yes . . . but . . . well, could you do this line again, do you think?
   MAN: Is that better?
   WOMAN: Well . . .

4. MANAGER: It's half past nine!
   ASSISTANT: Yes, I know.
   MANAGER: Could you tell me why you're so late, then?
   ASSISTANT: Sorry!
   MANAGER: I'm warning you, this is the last time . . .

Answers

Dialogue 1: Someone has sent an important document to someone else and is calling to say that it is in the post.
Dialogue 2: The man is asking the woman if he can borrow something.
Dialogue 3: The woman is inspecting a drawing that the man is doing for her.
Dialogue 4: Someone has arrived late for work and her boss is asking for an explanation.

Play the tape again and ask students to tick the responses they hear.

Answers

Yes, certainly. ✓
Sorry! ✓

146

Can you hear me now?
I'm sorry, but I'd rather you didn't. ✓
Of course I can.
Is that better? ✓

WB 28.4

7. Practise making requests by asking students to write down a list of five things which they have to do today. They should then write notes to various people asking for help to perform the tasks.
8. When students receive the written requests, they should write back agreeing to or refusing the request. As the students do this exercise make sure that they are giving suitable responses to the requests. If they refuse a request, they should say what they're doing instead and suggest another time to help.
9. Present offering to do things by asking students to match the responses with the pictures.

Answers

A I'm very thirsty.
3 I'll get you something to drink, shall I?

B It's so hot in here!
1 I'll open the window, shall I?

C I've got such a headache!
2 Shall I get you an aspirin?

D It's very dark in this room!
5 I'll turn on the light, shall I?

E I can't hear myself think!
4 Shall I turn the radio down?

F This bag is so heavy.
6 Shall I carry it?

10. Practise I'll . . ., (shall I?) and Shall I . . .? by asking students to write down some similar statements to the ones in 9. Then ask them to go round the class making the statements and offering to do things for other students. Make sure that everyone has understood how to respond to the offers.

WB 28.5, 28.6

11. Practise listening for general sense by playing the tape and asking students to tick the chart according to who does what. Explain that Koji is about to leave London at the end of his stay and that he is talking to Diana about all the things he has to do.

Tapescript

KOJI: Ah, Diana! There you are.
DIANA: Hello, Koji. Have you got everything packed yet?
KOJI: No, I haven't. I'm just going to do that now so I won't have to get up so early in

the morning. Diana, could you do me a favour?

DIANA: Certainly. What is it?

KOJI: Could you phone the airline to confirm my flight home. I really haven't got time.

DIANA: Yes, of course. Is there anything else I can do?

KOJI: Oh, that's very kind of you but . . . well, yes, there's one thing. Could you ask someone to type my report? That would be very helpful.

DIANA: Yes, of course.

KOJI: I want to pay my hotel bill this evening. If I do that, I'll be able to leave early for the airport tomorrow morning.

DIANA: That's a good idea. Have you booked the restaurant for this evening?

KOJI: Oh, no! Do we have to?

DIANA: Well, if we book it now, we'll be sure of getting a table by the window. It's such a nice view over the river.

KOJI: Could you do that for me, please?

DIANA: Yes, don't worry. I'll look after that.

KOJI: What else have I got to do? Oh, I must buy some presents as well.

DIANA: What about the taxi for tomorrow morning? Would you like me to phone and book one now?

KOJI: Oh, could you? Thank you very much. Oh, and I must phone my wife to tell her when to meet me at the airport.

DIANA: Is that everything?

KOJI: Yes, I think so . . .

Answers

	Koji	Diana
Confirm flight home		✓
Pack suitcases	✓	
Buy presents	✓	
Pay hotel bill	✓	
Type report		✓
Book restaurant		✓
Phone wife	✓	
Book taxi		✓

12 Revise talking about future plans by playing the tape again and asking students to note down what will happen if Koji packs his suitcases tonight, etc. Students then write full sentences describing what will happen.

Answers

If he packs his suitcases tonight, he won't have to get up so early in the morning.

If he pays his hotel bill this evening, he'll be able to leave early in the morning.
If she books the restaurant, they'll be sure of getting a table by the window.
If he phones his wife, she'll meet him at the airport.

13 Practise talking about the future by getting students to discuss their plans for the future. Ask them to do this exercise in pairs and then to go round the rest of the class talking about their plans.

WB 28.7, 28.8

14 Practise making suggestions by asking students to make plans for one of the situations shown in their books. They should work in groups of three or four and then decide who should do what. They should use all the structures they have learnt in this unit. When everyone is ready, they should present their ideas to the rest of the class.

LEARNING SKILLS

Ask students to note down as many places or situations in which they can hear or read English every day of their lives. Ask them to think about films, television, radio, books, magazines, newspapers and labels on various goods and equipment. Encourage them to share their knowledge about the opportunities which exist in your town to hear or read English.

PRONUNCIATION TAPESCRIPT

28.1 Listen and repeat.

/g/	/k/
glass	class
game	came
bag	back
good	could

Now listen and tick the words you hear.

game   back   class   good

28.2 Listen and write the words in the correct column.

big /g/, card /k/, cigar /g/, coat /k/, cold /k/, come /k/, got /g/, great /g/, grow /g/, lock /k/

28.3 Listen and mark the intonation with arrows: ⤴ for polite requests and ⤵ for commands.

a) Could you open the window.

b) Please open the door.

c) Will you turn the music down.

147

d) Would you please sit down.

e) Will you do the washing up.

f) Can you phone for a taxi.

STRUCTURE REVIEW TAPESCRIPT

28.1 Ask people to do things, like this:

You're in a restaurant and you want the waiter to bring you the bill.
Can you bring me the bill, please?

Now you.

a) You're in a restaurant and you want the waiter to bring you the bill.
Can you bring me the bill, please?
b) You're listening to some music and you want your friend to turn it down.
Can you turn it down, please?
c) You want to smoke a cigarette. Ask someone to give you a light.
Can you give me a light, please?
d) You're making a phone call and you want your friend to speak louder.
Can you speak louder, please?
e) You're in the classroom and you want the other students to be quiet.
Can you be quiet, please?
f) You're in a hotel and you want reception to send you up some champagne.
Can you send up some champagne, please?

28.2 Reply to people asking you to do things, like this:

Could you help me?
Yes, of course.

Will you lend me £50?
I'm sorry, I'd rather not.

Now you.

a) Could you help me?
Yes, of course.

b) Will you lend me £50?
I'm sorry, I'd rather not.
c) Could you lend me £5?
Yes, of course.
d) Will you lend me your pen?
I'm sorry, I'd rather not.
e) Can you call me a taxi?
Yes, of course.
f) Will you buy me dinner?
I'm sorry, I'd rather not.

28.3 Offer to do things for people, like this:

I need to do some shopping.
I'll take you to the shops.

Now you.

a) I need to do some shopping.
I'll take you to the shops.
b) It'll take a long time.
I'll wait in the car.
c) I've got a lot of shopping.
I'll put it in the back.
d) I'm hungry.
I'll buy you lunch.
e) I must leave now.
I'll ask for the bill.

28.4 Accept or refuse offers, like this:

Shall I water your plants?
Oh, thank you very much.

I'll tidy the flat, if you like.
No, it's all right.

Now you.

a) Shall I water your plants?
Oh, thank you very much.
b) I'll tidy the flat, if you like.
No, it's all right.
c) I'll feed the cat, shall I?
Oh, thank you very much.
d) Shall I collect your letters?
Oh, thank you very much.
e) I'll turn on the lights.
Oh, thank you very much.
f) I'll do some shopping, if you like.
No, it's all right.

29 | Saying what you think

UNIT SUMMARY

Functions

Talking about similarities and differences

Structures

Same

– and	so nor neither	does did is was has can	he. she.

Different

– but	he she	does. doesn't. did. didn't. is. isn't. was. wasn't. has. hasn't. can. can't.

Same

So Nor Neither	do did have am was can	I.

Different

But I	do. don't. did. didn't. have. haven't. am. 'm not. was. wasn't. can. can't.

Saying what you think

He thinks that . . . and so do I.
She doesn't think that . . ., but I think . . .

Functions

Making suggestions

Structures

Let's Shall we Why don't we I think we should	have	a party.(?)
What How	about having	

Agreeing and disagreeing

That's a good idea. Yes, all right.		

No,	let's . . . . I'd rather . . . .

Topics

Personal details, personal background

Lexical items

- ambition   career   education   family life   favourite   hobby   housing   include   leisure time   training   travel (n)
- bikini   gloves   scarf   videocassette

TEACHING GUIDE

This unit revises the language associated with expressing opinions and preferences, and practises structures for talking about similarities and differences. Encourage students to use vocabulary introduced in previous units; there is scope for wide-ranging lexical revision in this unit.

WARM-UP

Suggested warm-up activity: 13.

1   Practise listening for specific information by playing the tape and asking students to complete the chart. Remind them that they don't need to understand every word to be able to do the exercise.

Tapescript

Simon Groom's birthday is the twelfth of August, and he was born in Derby. He's tall – he's one metre eighty-five with fair hair and blue-grey eyes. In his spare time, he likes training Goldie, the *Blue Peter* dog, playing the drums, and doing up old cars.
Simon studied English at Birmingham University, and then went to teach in a comprehensive school. He's also worked as a disc jockey for eighteen months in Germany and London. His favourite food is breakfast, and his favourite colour is blue. Handel, Delius and

Wagner are his favourite classical composers, and his favourite pop bands are OMD, Dire Straits and The Who. He enjoys cricket and football, and he drives a Jaguar. His ambition is to drive a Formula 1 racing car. He really likes music programmes and cars. He *doesn't* like coconut – and ties!

Janet Ellis was born in Kent on the sixteenth of September. She's one metre fifty-five, and she's got dark brown hair and green eyes. She likes singing, going to the cinema, sewing and collecting small teddy bears. She went to seven different schools both in Britain and abroad because her father was in the Forces. She trained at the Central School of Speech and Drama, and she's done a lot of theatre and TV work, including *Dr Who* and *Jigsaw*. She loves seafood, and her favourite colour is pink. Her favourite classical music is Mendelssohn, Sibelius and Holst, and she also likes The Police, The Smiths and Wham! Her favourite sports are roller skating and tennis, and she drives a Ford Escort XR3. Her ambition is to make a pop record. She likes funfairs, cats and rainbows, and she hates broken telephones – and rudeness.

Peter Duncan was born on the third of May in London. He's one metre seventy-one, and he's got fair hair and blue eyes. His hobbies are singing, decorating, and thinking up dangerous stunts to do on *Blue Peter*! Peter went to secondary school, and has starred in many children's drama series on TV. He is also a successful film and theatre actor. His favourite food is fresh fruit, and his favourite colour is green. His favourite music is Bach and the Beatles, and he loves football. He has a BMW.

Peter would like to be a singer and he'd also like to travel in outer space. He loves the cinema and the country – and he dislikes people who are greedy – and boiled egg white!

Students check their answers in pairs. Make sure they ask colloquial questions, e.g. *Where was Peter born?* (Not *What was Peter's birthplace?*)

Answers

ABOUT THE BLUE PETER TEAM			
	SIMON	JANET	PETER
Birthday	12th August	16th September	3rd May
Birthplace	Derby	Kent	London
Height	1.85 m	1.55 m	1.71 m
Colour of hair	Fair	Dark brown	Fair
Colour of eyes	Blue/Grey	Green	Blue
Hobbies	Training Goldie, playing the drums, doing up old cars	Singing, cinema, sewing, collecting small teddy bears	Singing, decorating, thinking up stunts for *Blue Peter*
School, Training and Career	Studied English at Birmingham University, taught in Comprehensive School, 18 months as DJ in Germany and London	7 schools in UK and abroad because father in Forces, Central School of Speech and Drama, theatre and TV work including *Dr Who* and *Jigsaw*	Secondary school. star of many children's drama series on TV, also film and theatre actor
Favourite food	Breakfast	Seafood	Fresh fruit
Favourite colour	Blue	Pink	Green
Favourite music (Classical)	Handel, Delius and Wagner	Mendelssohn, Sibelius and Holst	Bach
Favourite music (Pop)	OMD, Dire Straits The Who	The Police, The Smiths, Wham!	The Beatles
Favourite sport	Cricket and football	Roller skating and tennis	Football
Cars	Jaguar	Ford Escort XR3	BMW
Ambition	To drive a Formula 1 racing car	To make a pop record	To be a singer and travel in outer space
Likes	Music programmes and cars	Funfairs, cats and rainbows	The cinema and the country
Dislikes	Coconut and ties	Broken telephones and rudeness	Greedy people and boiled egg white

Ask students to look at the photo of the *Blue Peter* presenters and decide who is who.

2   Present the language for talking about similarities and differences by finding similarities and differences between the three presenters. Give two or three model sentences, and then ask students to work in pairs and to find a few more similarities and differences.

3   Practise talking about similarities and differences by asking students to compare themselves with the people in the *Blue Peter* team. They should continue to work in pairs. Go round each pair and check that everyone is using the structures correctly.

4   Practise talking about similarities and differences by asking students to complete the chart with details about their partners and then to find three people in the class with whom they have things in common.

5   Practise talking about similarities and differences by asking students to find five more things which they all have in common.

6   Give further practice by asking students to report back to the rest of the class about their similarities. Then ask the students to form new groups in which people have very little or nothing in common.

7   Practise writing by asking students to write sentences about the things they have in common with other people in the class. Go round and correct each student's work individually. Make a note of any serious errors and point them out to the class as a whole.

WB   29.1, 29.2, 29.3

8   Practise saying what you think and using the future simple by asking students to make a few predictions about what life will be like in the future. You may need to give them some help with vocabulary at this stage; encourage them to be as inventive as they wish. Remind them that they have already learnt the language for saying what they think in Unit 19. Ask them to write their predictions down. Then get them to find students who have made predictions about the same topics as they have. Ask them to read out their predictions and to agree or disagree. Remind them that the structures for agreeing and disagreeing are the same as those for talking about similarities and differences.

Practise talking about the future by asking students to work in groups with students who have made different predictions to their own and to write a paragraph together describing what life will be like in the future.

9   Practise saying what you think by asking students to discuss what is happening in the pictures. Prompt them with questions, e.g. *What is the man*

on the left doing? Who are these people? What are they going to do – and why? Why is the dog there? When were these photos taken? Students will probably ask you for these words: *dig, hole, bury,* and *souvenir.*

10 Practise reading and understanding text organisation by asking students to put the sentences in the correct order. Explain that a box of souvenirs for the future like the *Blue Peter* box is called a time capsule, and encourage them to guess the meaning of other unfamiliar words from the pictures and the context.

Answers   E   C   G   A   F   D   B

▦ Then play the tape so that students can check their answers.

Tapescript

In 1971, the presenters of *Blue Peter* decided to bury a *Blue Peter* time capsule. They filled a waterproof box with souvenirs of the programme and they carefully screwed down the lid. They buried the box in a deep hole just outside BBC Television Centre. They also planted a beautiful tree near the box. In the year 2000, the tree will be very tall and people will be able to dig up the box and read all about the programme.

11 Practise reading skills by asking students to read what the *Blue Peter* box contains. Then ask them to note down five items which they would put in their own time capsule.

12 Practise listening for specific information by
▦ playing the tape and asking students to tick the items which the speakers are going to put in their time capsule. Remind students that they don't have to understand every word of the text; they need only recognise the items.

Tapescript

MAN:	Well, the first thing I'm going to put in is a copy of today's newspaper.
WOMAN:	Yes, that's a good idea. When they dig up the box in the future, they'll want to know what the news was.
MAN:	And then I think we should put a model car in the box.
WOMAN:	A model car? What do you mean?
MAN:	You know, a toy car. To show them the kind of transport we used.
WOMAN:	All right. Why don't we put in some food?
MAN:	Well, yes. But it will have to be a can of something . . .
WOMAN:	I know, a can of tomatoes.
MAN:	No – a bottle of Coca Cola!

WOMAN:	OK. Now what else? Oh, I know. How about a pair of trousers to show them what we wore?
MAN:	I'd rather put in something smaller. Let's put a scarf and gloves in.
WOMAN:	. . . and a bikini.
MAN:	Yes, all right. Shall we put in a photograph of a typical family, just to show them how we lived?
WOMAN:	All right. And I think we should put in a videocassette as well, with some television programmes on it.
MAN:	To show them how we spend our leisure time.
WOMAN:	And a football?
MAN:	Yes, all right. But how big is this time capsule going to be . . .?

Answers

Newspaper, toy car, bottle of Coca Cola, scarf, gloves, bikini, family photograph, videocassette, football.

13 Practise the language for making suggestions by asking students to work in groups of three or four and to choose ten items to include in their own time capsule. If your circumstances allow it, you may like actually to collect the items and to bury them in a suitable container. Encourage students to discuss their choice of items and to agree or disagree with the others in their group. Students should then explain their choice of items to other groups.
14 Practise writing, by asking students to write a paragraph explaining which objects they have chosen and why. When they have finished, they should correct each others' versions.

WB 29.4

LEARNING SKILLS

Give students the transcript of four or five lines of a listening passage from the book with the stressed words blanked out. Ask them to listen and fill in the missing words.

Example (Tapescript 19.7)

WOMAN:	Oh . . ., you . . . look very . . . . What's the . . .?
MAN:	It's my . . . . I feel . . . .
WOMAN:	Oh, I . . . sorry. Would you like me to . . . the . . .?
MAN:	. . ., I'd like some . . . . I've got a . . . as . . . .
WOMAN:	Why don't you . . . . . .?
MAN:	. . ., that's a . . . .

This activity will give students training in listening for the stressed words, which carry the main ideas in English.

PRONUNCIATION TAPESCRIPT

29.1 Listen and repeat.

/eɪ/	/aɪ/
bay	buy
may	my
wait	white
late	light

Now listen and tick the words you hear.

may   wait   light   bay

29.2 Listen and write the words in the correct column.

line /aɪ/, island /aɪ/, way /eɪ/, tie /aɪ/, stay /eɪ/, why /aɪ/, day /eɪ/, play /eɪ/

29.3 Listen and mark the stressed words.

a) He can swim, but I can't.
b) She doesn't like football, and nor do I.
c) He's got two sisters, and so have I.
d) She hasn't got a camera, but he has.
e) I like cheese, but you don't.
f) He likes flying, and so do I.

STRUCTURE REVIEW TAPESCRIPT

29.1 Say whether it's the same or different for other people, like this:

Phil can ski.
Can he? Pete can't.

Jill doesn't smoke.
Nor does Wayne.

Now you.

a) Phil can ski.
   Can he? Pete can't.
b) Jill doesn't smoke.
   Nor does Wayne.
c) Henry's a teacher.
   So is Terry.
d) Julie was tired.
   So was Jim.
e) Fran liked the film.
   Did she? Tom didn't.
f) Luigi can't speak English.
   Nor can Antonio.

Note:
Students need to know whether these are masculine or feminine names in order to do the exercise.

153

29.2 Say whether it's the same or different for yourself. Answer the questions, like this:

I liked school.
Did you? I didn't. or *So did I.*

I've never smoked.
Haven't you? I have. or *Nor have I.*

Now you.

a) I liked school.
....

b) I've never smoked.
....

c) I don't want to live abroad.
....

d) I'm going to work hard.
....

e) I have a large family.
....

f) I can speak fluent English.
....

29.3 Make suggestions, like this:

I've stayed in all weekend.
Let's go to the theatre.

Now you.

a) I've stayed in all weekend.
Let's go to the theatre.

b) I'm bored.
Let's watch TV.

c) I haven't seen the news.
Let's buy a newspaper.

d) We haven't seen Gerry for weeks.
Let's invite him for dinner.

e) It's too far to walk.
Let's take a taxi.

f) Oh dear, the car won't start.
Let's call a garage mechanic.

30 | Checking what you know

SUMMARY

Functions

In Units 25 to 29, students learnt how to:

Ask and say what people have done
Ask and say how long people have done things
Talk about personal experience
Make suggestions
Accept and refuse suggestions
Ask and say what people have or haven't done yet
Ask and say what has just happened
Ask and say what the weather will be like
Ask and say what will happen

Talk about plans for the future
Make requests
Agree to and refuse requests
Offer to do things
Accept and refuse offers
Talk about similarities and differences
Ask and say what people like
Say what they think
Agree and disagree

Topics

The topic areas covered have been:

Sightseeing, town facilities, leisure activities, routine activities, news items, the weather, seasons, banking, numbers, personal details, personal background

TEACHING GUIDE

WARM-UP

Suggested warm-up activities: Choose any one or a number of activities for general revision.

WB

Students should be able to do the *Workbook* exercises at any stage of this revision unit.

1 Revise talking about plans for the future by asking students to predict what Carla, Richard, Diana, Koji, Nancy and Bob plan to do in the future.
2 Practise listening for specific information by playing the tape and asking students to check their answers.

Tapescript

CARLA:	Well, I don't know about the future, really. I think we'll leave Hong Kong fairly soon, though.
RICHARD:	Yes – I'm looking for a new job – but you'll be able to keep yours, won't you?
CARLA:	Yes, that's the good thing about working for a big newspaper – I can work almost anywhere in the world. But you know, I'd really like to have another child . . .

RICHARD:	Well, I hadn't thought about that . . .! If we have another child, we'll have to find a larger flat . . .
DIANA:	What I'd really like is to buy a house in the country – not too far from London. I'm fairly sure that I'll leave London soon – I really don't like living here. And apart from that . . . well, who knows?
KOJI:	Maybe you'll get married, Diana!
DIANA:	Yes – maybe I will . . . and what about you, Koji? What are your plans?
KOJI:	Well, it's difficult, but I'd like to spend more time with my family. In my job, I travel a lot, and I don't see much of my wife . . . and my children.
DIANA:	Are you going to look for another job?
KOJI:	No, I think I'll retire early – if we can afford it.
NANCY:	You? Married!
BOB:	Yes, why not? I'd like to get married one day – if I meet the right girl. Wouldn't you?
NANCY:	Oh, I guess so – if I meet the right man. But not yet. I think I'll work abroad for a year. Maybe I'll come and see you in London, Bob!
BOB:	If you don't, I'll come back to the States to see you!

155

Answers

Carla and Richard: leave Hong Kong, change jobs, have another child.
Diana: buy a house in the country, leave London, get married.
Koji: retire early, spend more time with his family.
Bob: get married, come back to the States.
Nancy: work abroad for a year, go to London.

3   Practise listening for specific information and revise talking about plans for the future by playing the tape again and asking the students to note down any conditions to their plans.

Answers

Carla and Richard will have to find a larger flat if they have another child.
Diana will buy a house in the country if she leaves London.
Koji will retire early if he can afford it.
Bob will get married if he meets the right girl.
Nancy will get married if she meets the right man.

Practise writing, by asking students to write a short account of the plans of two or three of the characters. You can ask students to correct each other's versions. Check that everyone is using the construction *If* + present simple/future simple.

4   Revise all tense forms and talking about similarities and differences by asking students to work in groups of three and to solve the puzzle. Make sure they do not look at each other's passages.
This kind of jigsaw reading activity creates a genuine information gap and encourages students to share their information with each other in a realistic way.

Answers

A: Jane
B: Dave
C: Peter
D: Jill
E: Tony
F: Jackie
G: Tom
H: Fred
I: Diana

5   Revise all the structures and functions in *BBC Beginners' English* by asking students to prepare the board game TAKING OFF – AROUND THE WORLD. Have a few spare sheets of paper available for the students' question cards. During the course of the game, students should cover many of the language points which they have learnt; you may wish to stop the game every ten or fifteen minutes to do some simple revision work.

LEARNING SKILLS

Ask students to form groups of four or five. Having played TAKING OFF – AROUND THE WORLD, they should be aware of how much English they have already learnt. Ask them to look back over *BBC Beginners' English*, Stage 1, and to decide which language areas are most useful to them. What would they like to learn next? One last question: ask them if they're going to carry on learning English!